IMAGES
of America

WATERFORD

On the Cover: These were the early years of the Barge Canal, Waterford Lock 2E. When the Barge Canal opened, most boatmen were not prepared to use it, and World War I was demanding much of the country's resources. The canal was built to accommodate larger cargo boats moved by tugboats—the mule was gone. Problem was, no larger boats were built and would not be until 1921. The *Columbia*, on the right, was a steam-powered canal boat that carried cargo and towed three other traditional mule-era boats. This was not what the state had in mind. After 1921, the situation righted itself, and the canal was then utilized as intended. (Author's collection.)

IMAGES
of America

WATERFORD

Richard F. Herzog

ARCADIA
PUBLISHING

ISBN 978-1-4671-3459-0

Published by Arcadia Publishing
Charleston, South Carolina

Printed in the United States of America

Library of Congress Control Number: 2015939879

For all general information, please contact Arcadia Publishing:
Telephone 843-853-2070
Fax 843-853-0044
E-mail sales@arcadiapublishing.com
For customer service and orders:
Toll-Free 1-888-313-2665

Visit us on the Internet at www.arcadiapublishing.com

*This book is being dedicated to memories of yesteryear.
No matter what age group or generation you are from,
you will always retain thoughts of your youth.*

Contents

ACKNOWLEDGMENTS

Many thanks to Helen Grochmal Anderson, Fran Santspree Cullett, Merle Doud, Talia Futia, Tracy McGarry Herzog Geel, Richard F. Herzog, J. Bert Mahoney, Michael D. Marchese, Frank McClement, Bill Paquette, Russ Van Dervoort, Patricia Wilcox, Donald Bowles, Ellen and Neil Breslin, Donald E. Child (grandson of Sydney Hammersley), Mike Cicchinelli, Donald P. Currier and Edward Wilson, F.B. Peck Hose Co., J.W. Ford Hose Co. No. 2, Jeff Diviney, Cheryl Sober Folkman, Charles Girard, J. Henry Glavin IV, Mike Judge, Kayla Keeler, Key Bank, Alan LaBrecque, Anna Marie Wilkes Lamos, Jean Lavigne, James T. Lefebvre P.C., Kavanaugh Hook and Ladder Co., Knickerbocker Steamer Co. No. 1, Ceil VanValkenburgh Maloney, Elaine Neveu McAllister, Carol Ann Michon (granddaughter of George Michon), Mary Michon, Teri VanWagenen Patton, Ward Patton, Gwen E. Terry Piacente, Dennis Rivage, Monroe VanValkenburgh, Rob VanBramer WPD, the families of the late James Michon and Hugh Holton, J. David Mahoney, Town of Waterford Capital Resource Corporation, Don and Paul's Coffee Shop, Nathaniel Bartlett Sylvester (*History of Saratoga County 1609–1878*), George N. Michon and the Michon Collection, Col. Sydney Ernest Hammersley (*The History of Waterford, New York*), Saratoga County Historian's Office, and the Waterford Historical Museum and Cultural Center (WHMCC) and its members Paul Archambault (former director), Patricia Burke, Tracy Murray, and Nancy Fontaine Spretty.

Unless otherwise noted, all images are courtesy of the author's collection.

Introduction

Waterford is located at the junction of the Hudson and Mohawk Rivers. It is a small territory, about seven square miles, of which nine-tenths of a square mile, or about 12 percent, is water. An almost perpendicular range of slate bluffs run along the Mohawk River, and a range of clay hills border the valley of the Hudson River. These hills, along with the fertile lands running north from the village, so valued by early settlers, are all evidence of its glacial days and the mile-thick ice mass that once covered most of New York State. Glacial events created the two terraces of Prospect Hill (the upper terrace) and Broad Street (the lower terrace). Formed during this period, the Cohoes Falls are the result of Mohawk River water obstructed by and pouring against the Hudson's melting glacier. The overflow reached as far north as Ballston and broke through locally at Crescent. The 70-foot Cohoes Falls powered early industry and allowed early settlements to expand into a prominent town.

The first occupants of Waterford were the Mahican Indians (Algonquin race). The Mahicans were enemies of the Mohawk Indians, who lived to the west. After the Indian wars, the Mahicans joined the Scaticooks. The first settlers in the area were the Holland Dutch, as early as 1623. Although there is little information recorded through to the American Revolution, merchants and businessmen came to Waterford early on, attracted by the confluence of the Mohawk and Hudson Rivers. They realized the area was a perfect location for commercial business. These hopes would be further realized with the opening of the Erie and Champlain Canal systems. The projects, constructed simultaneously, were completed in 1825. The project was considered more daring than the construction of the Pacific Coast Railway, but early settlers were determined to complete one of the most important lines of communication on the continent as canals, which were the main mode of transportation before the rise of the railroad industry. Many industries and businesses flourished with the building of the canal system. But the single greatest contribution to industrial development in Waterford was the King's Water Power Canal. Built in 1828, the project powered dozens of industries, from paper to textiles to flour.

One of the major industries to develop from the King's Canal was the historic Button Fire Engine Company. The company improved the design of steam engines, and the business grew rapidly. The machines were of such high quality that they were found in every state, Canada, South America, and Europe. Another prominent name in Waterford to come out of this era of industrial development was Eddy. Isaac Eddy obtained the first patent for pulverizing printer's ink in 1824 and established the Franklin Ink Works in 1831. His son Thomas went on to invent colored printing ink. His other son George founded the Mohawk and Hudson Iron Foundry and Machine Shop. He made such things as iron castings and steam car wheels, of which none were ever found to be defective. George Eddy was awarded a medal at the Columbian Exposition of 1893 for inventing the taper seat valve and was known throughout the world for his Mohawk fire hydrant.

Early Dutch settlers were Calvinists and believed every person should be capable of reading. James Dugan taught at the first recorded Waterford school in 1788. Through 1838, there were six private schools in Waterford. Two of these schools were for young children. The third, conducted by a Miss Shaw in 1831, was a successor to Emma Willard's institution, which would become one of the first and most prominent schools for young women at this time. Another famous school was the Waterford Academy. The reputation of the academy was so well established that many out-of-town students studied here.

Known as the mother church, the Dutch Reformed Church has the distinction of being Waterford's first house of worship, and its building was used by every other church in the village. It was built long before the American Revolution and survived until 1876. The first Waterford Methodist Church was formed in 1802. In 1811, Warden Vibbard bought the Methodist church. Episcopalians then used it for worship until 1841, when it was burned in the great fire. It was then remodeled and furnished with a new organ. It would be demolished in 1894. The first Presbyterian church was formed in 1804, uniting with the Presbyterians of Lansingburgh. The unprecedented floods in the spring of 1913 partly surrounded the church and caused part of the building to collapse. It was then ordered torn down and later rebuilt in 1915 with new modern construction methods, which provided a more stable structure. The first Roman Catholic church was built in 1843 and is presently still serving the community. A new Catholic church was erected in 1911. The Baptist church was constructed in 1867 after the great fire destroyed the original building

Waterford currently has four volunteer fire departments. They have served the community since 1794, when they would arm themselves with fire buckets. In 1833, following a $50,000 fire on King's Canal that destroyed several shops, a meeting was called to organize for fires. In 1834, Waterford modernized the service again with the Village Fire Company of Waterford. Continuing through the years, village and town fire departments are also responsible for handling Waterford floods as well as fires.

The Village of Waterford was incorporated on March 25, 1794, and has the distinction of being the oldest continuously incorporated village in the United States. The Town of Waterford was incorporated on April 17, 1816, and will be celebrating its 200th anniversary, remembering persons and places past and present.

Since the first settlers of 1623, Waterford has encountered devastating floods and the disastrous fire of 1841. Yet it has survived and over the years prospered. Now years later, it is your turn to leave your memories of the community.

As you visit your old neighborhood, the first thing you are aware of is how the area has changed. Some of the old buildings are gone, businesses have changed, and you do not recognize anyone and most do not know or recognize you. As you begin your trip around town, you walk down the main street and notice all the old hangouts are gone. You pass where the old school was and still think it could have been saved. You walk past the corner lot that used to be the football field and now houses a business. You can see the old black bridge that used to serve as your diving board, and the Champlain Canal was your swimming pool. Everywhere you walk, thoughts turn to the classmates, friends, and family who were lost during your youth, knowing 40, 50, even 60 years later they are still remembered, either in thought or in conversation with others. The expression "Gone but not forgotten" is so very true. As you get farther into the old neighborhood, you stop in front of your childhood home, where you probably spent 15 to 20 years of your life. The memories begin to come flooding back of family and relatives and all the good times. As you stand there, you realize all your relatives and parents have since departed. You are the oldest surviving member of your family and begin to understand it is soon going to be your turn. Your thoughts turn to your children and grandchildren, knowing you are going to live on in them. As you get ready to depart the old neighborhood, you turn for a final look and ask yourself, what if?

One

Business, Industry, and Prominent People

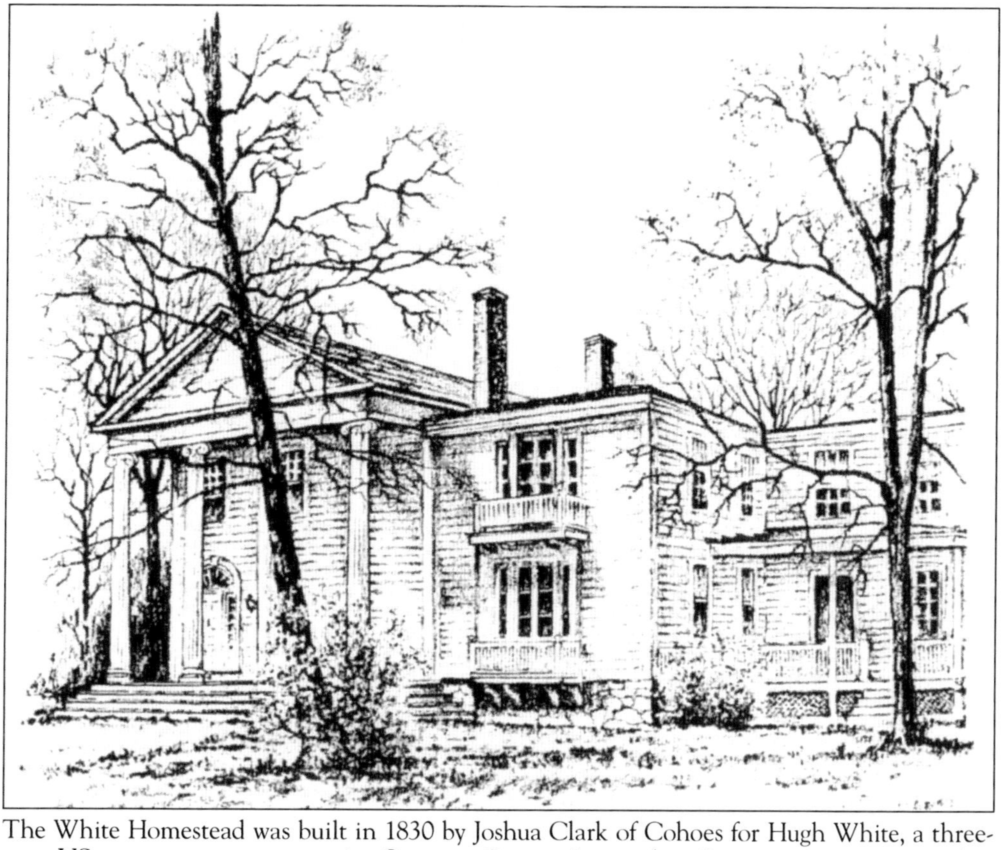

The White Homestead was built in 1830 by Joshua Clark of Cohoes for Hugh White, a three-term US congressman, representing Saratoga County. Located on Saratoga Avenue, ownership stayed in the family until 1948, when White's great-granddaughter Roma Niles sold it to Rosalie Ketchem, who eventually sold it to the Grand Union. In 1964, the house was scheduled to be demolished, and a group of concerned residents fought to preserve the grand old house. They succeeded, and the home was moved to its current location on Museum Lane and is now the Waterford Historical Museum and Cultural Center. However, the entire home could not be moved. Improvements to the back of the home were believed to have been added every time a child was born. As the additions were not built on a foundation, that section was deemed unsafe to move and destroyed.

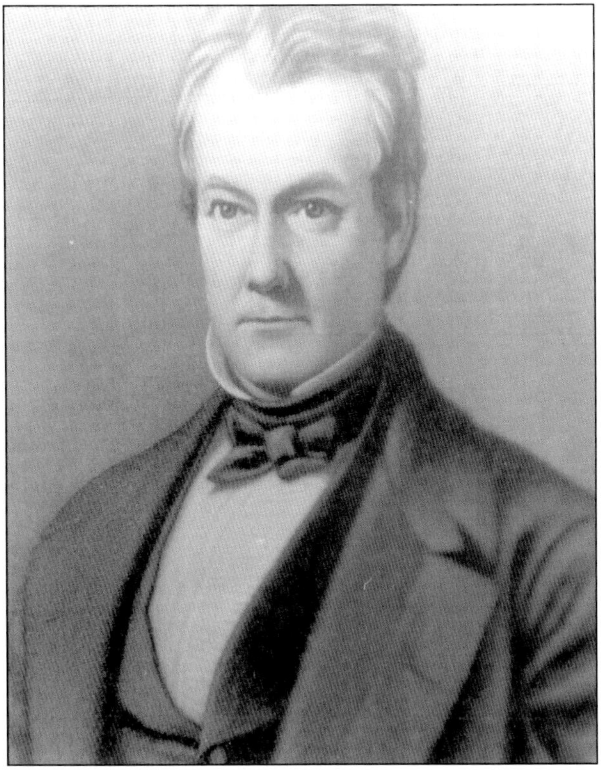

The Honorable Hugh White was elected to the House of Representatives (1844–1851), and he also held several positions at the Saratoga County National Bank of Waterford. There he was a director of the bank as well as vice president and in 1870 was elected president of the bank. White was instrumental in the invention and manufacture of hydraulic cement.

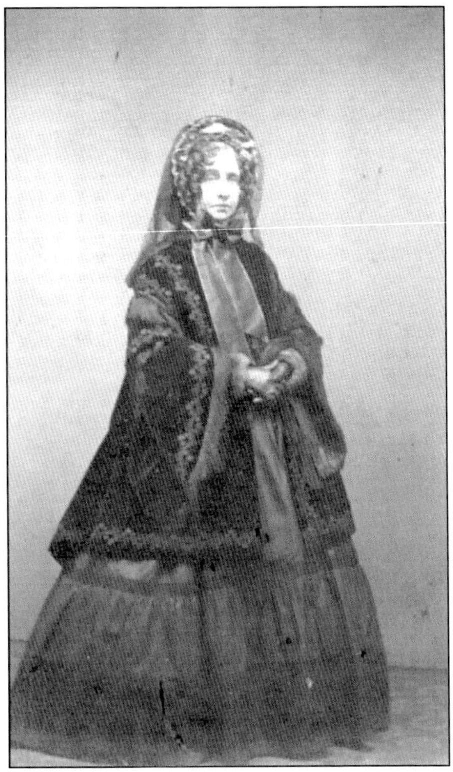

On April 10, 1828, before coming to Waterford, Hugh White married Marie Mills Mansfield, daughter of William Penderson Mansfield. Together they had seven children, with only three surviving into adulthood. When White and his wife moved to Waterford in 1830, so did William P. Mansfield, building homes across from one another. (Courtesy of WHMCC.)

As John Cramer became older, he chose a profession in law. In 1822, Cramer opened a law office in Waterford, where he resided for the remainder of his life. He became very successful as an attorney. Cramer was an active politician and held office in the state assembly, state senate, and the House of Representatives.

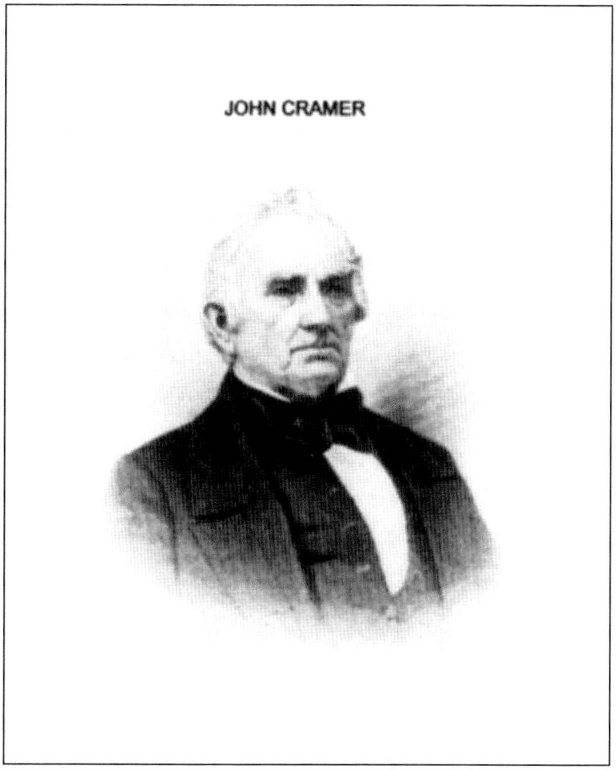

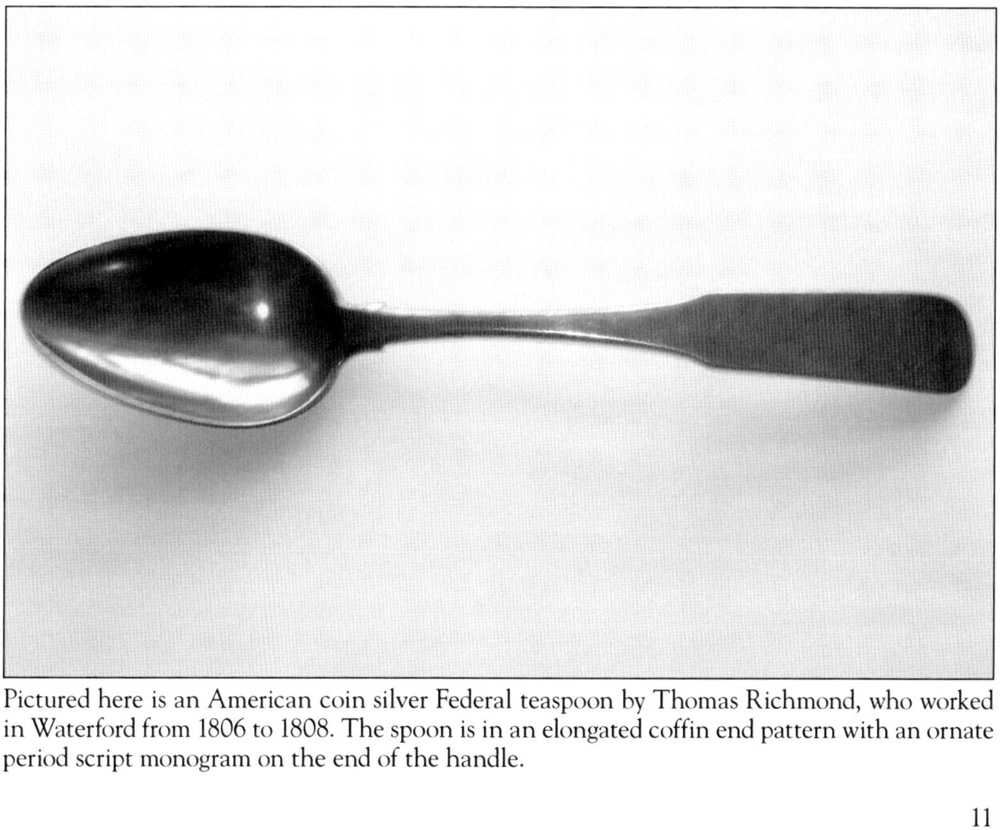

Pictured here is an American coin silver Federal teaspoon by Thomas Richmond, who worked in Waterford from 1806 to 1808. The spoon is in an elongated coffin end pattern with an ornate period script monogram on the end of the handle.

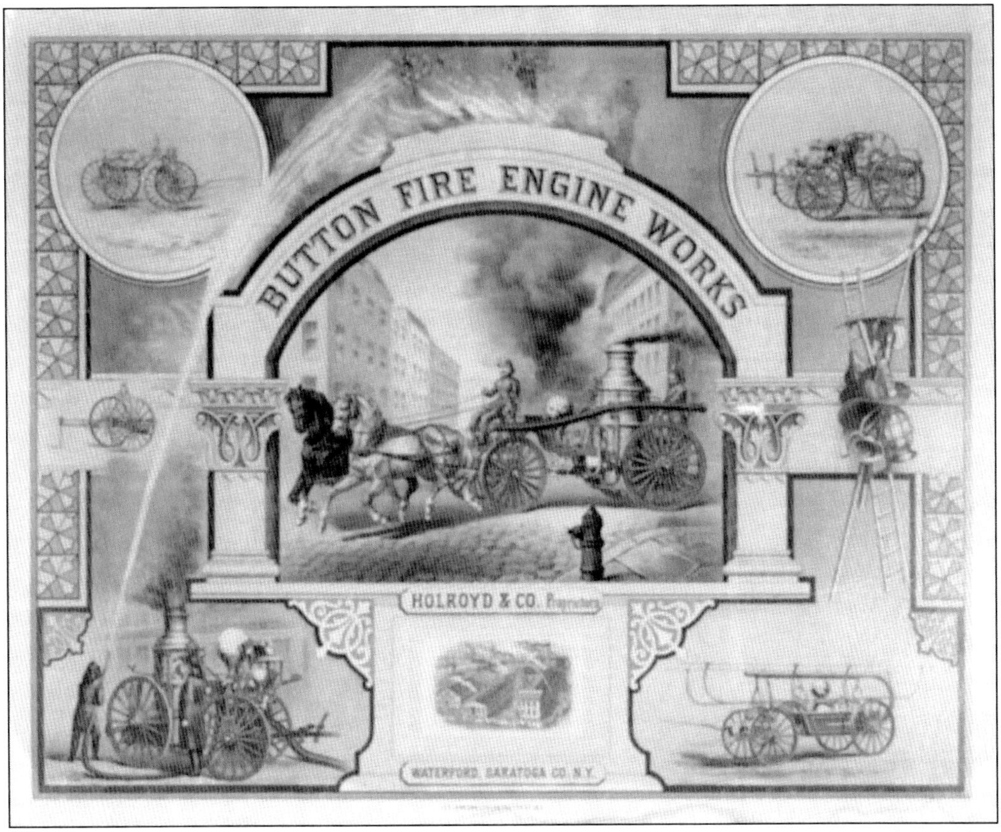

This is an advertisement for the Button Fire Engine Works, originally owned by William Platt and Judge Nicholas Doe Lysander. Button became a foreman in the company and eventually became the sole owner, changing the name to L. Button & Son. After more than 40 years of making some of the finest fire equipment, Button sold the company to Holroyd & Company in 1882. (Courtesy of the Saratoga County Historians Office.)

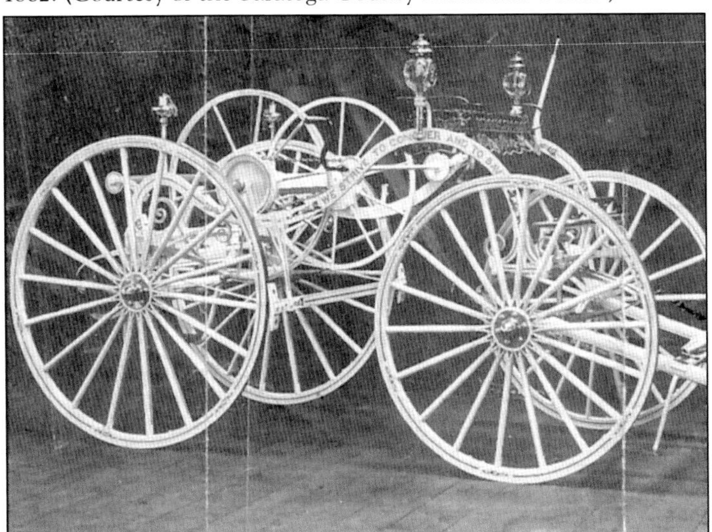

This ornate hose carriage is one of many built by the Button company. Most were built with the single purpose of transporting hose to a fire scene, while others were made for parade use as well. Ornate hose carriages were usually ordered by larger cities aided by a local philanthropist. Button personified the inscription on this carriage: "We Strive to Conquer and to Save." (Courtesy of Hugh Holton.)

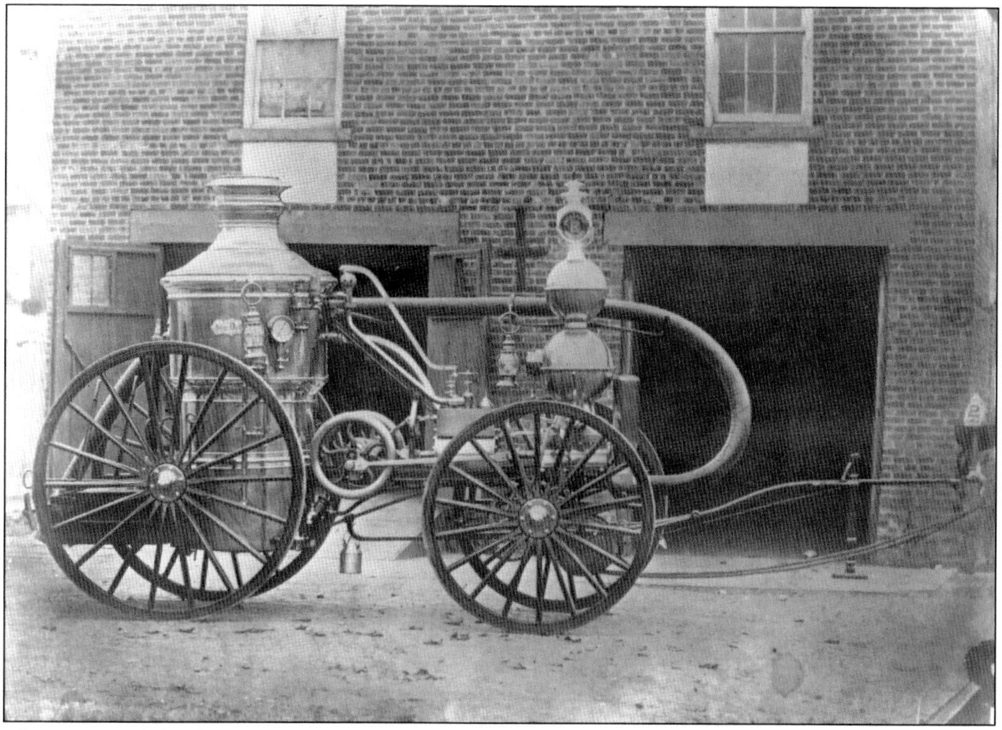

This is one of the first steam fire engines built by L. Button & Son. In 1876, the Button Steamer, as it was known, won the Centennial Award at the Philadelphia International Exhibit. It was considered a strong and reliable engine. Many of the Button fire engines still exist around the world today and are still in working condition. (Courtesy of Dennis Rivage.)

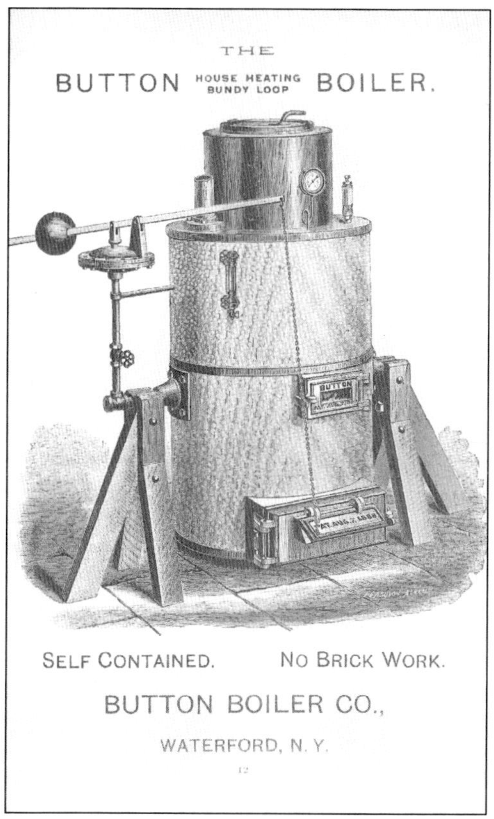

Not only was Theodore E. Button, son of Lysander Button, involved in the building of fire engines, but he also had his own business. He owned the Button Boiler Company, with his first patent date of August 7, 1888, and catalog in 1889. Boilers were priced $200 to $500 each. (Courtesy of Merle Doud.)

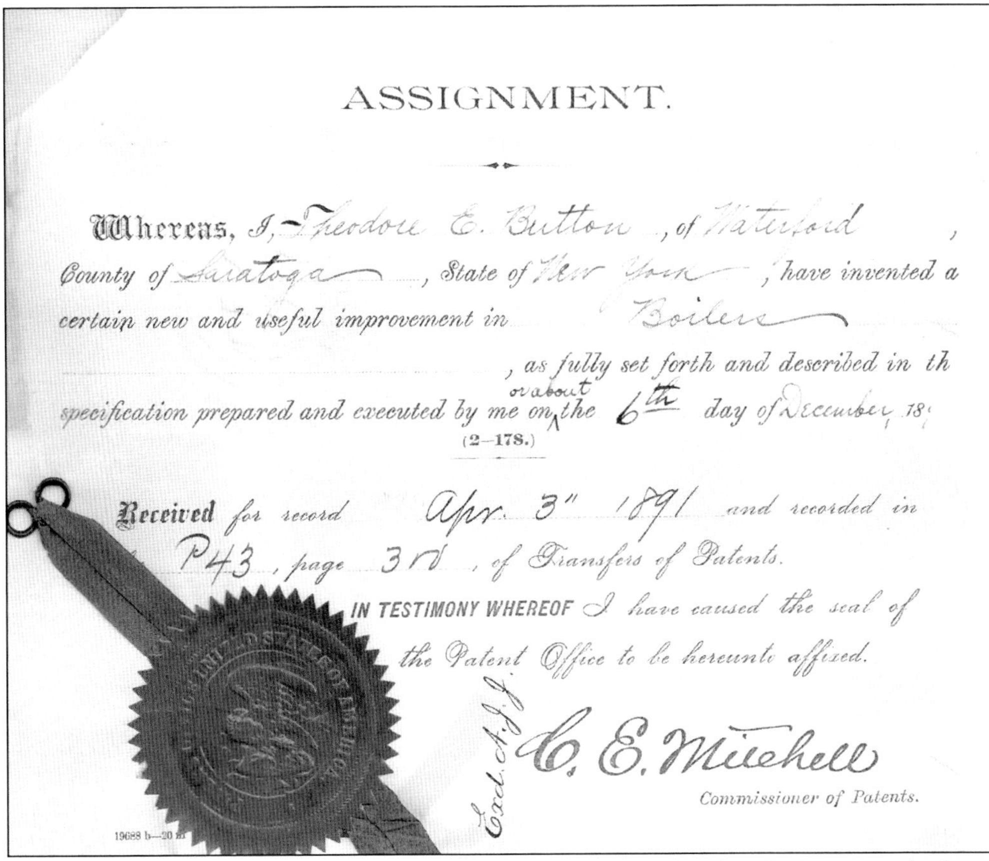

ASSIGNMENT.

Whereas, I, Theodore E. Button, of Waterford, County of Saratoga, State of New York, have invented a certain new and useful improvement in Boilers, as fully set forth and described in th specification prepared and executed by me on or about the 6th day of December 18

(2—178.)

Received for record Apr. 3" 1891 and recorded in P43, page 310, of Transfers of Patents.

IN TESTIMONY WHEREOF I have caused the seal of the Patent Office to be hereunto affixed.

C. E. Mitchell
Commissioner of Patents.

19688 b—20 m

On December 6, 1890, Theodore E. Button applied for a patent with a new and useful improvement for one of his boilers. The patent was approved by the US Patent and Trademark Office on April 3, 1891.

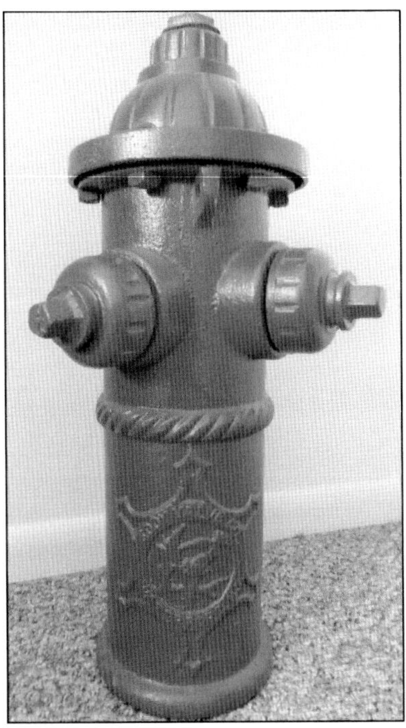

George Washington Eddy establishing the Eddy Valve Company around 1847. Pictured here is an Eddy fire hydrant with a patent date of November 5, 1889, and a manufacturing date in the early 1900s. The Eddy Valve Company was distributing fire hydrants not only locally, but nationally as well. The company was in business well into the 1940s, when it was sold to James Clow and Company. (Courtesy of Patricia Wilcox.)

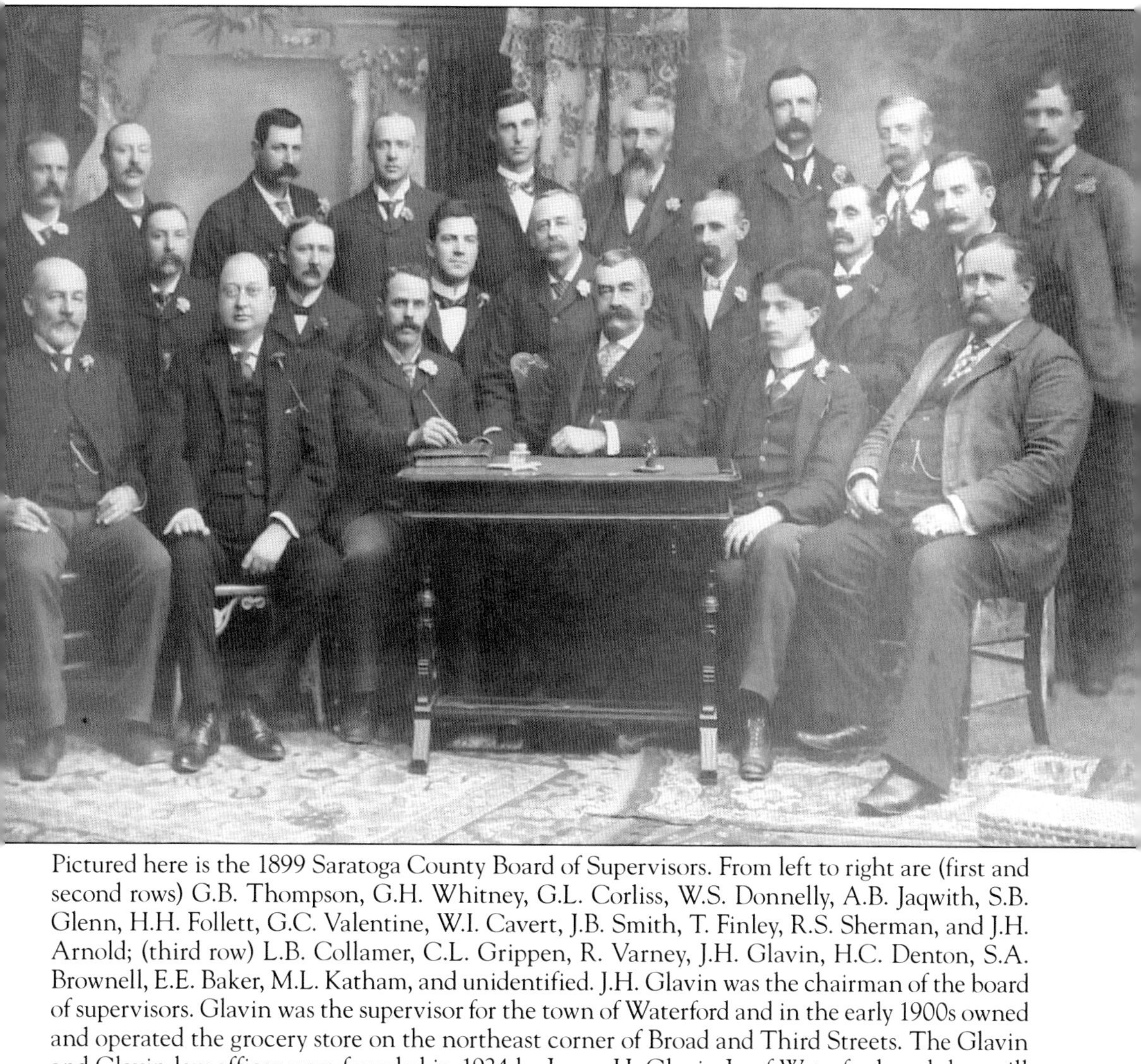

Pictured here is the 1899 Saratoga County Board of Supervisors. From left to right are (first and second rows) G.B. Thompson, G.H. Whitney, G.L. Corliss, W.S. Donnelly, A.B. Jaqwith, S.B. Glenn, H.H. Follett, G.C. Valentine, W.I. Cavert, J.B. Smith, T. Finley, R.S. Sherman, and J.H. Arnold; (third row) L.B. Collamer, C.L. Grippen, R. Varney, J.H. Glavin, H.C. Denton, S.A. Brownell, E.E. Baker, M.L. Katham, and unidentified. J.H. Glavin was the chairman of the board of supervisors. Glavin was the supervisor for the town of Waterford and in the early 1900s owned and operated the grocery store on the northeast corner of Broad and Third Streets. The Glavin and Glavin law offices were founded in 1924 by James H. Glavin Jr. of Waterford, and they still have a practicing law firm today. (Courtesy of J. Henry Glavin IV.)

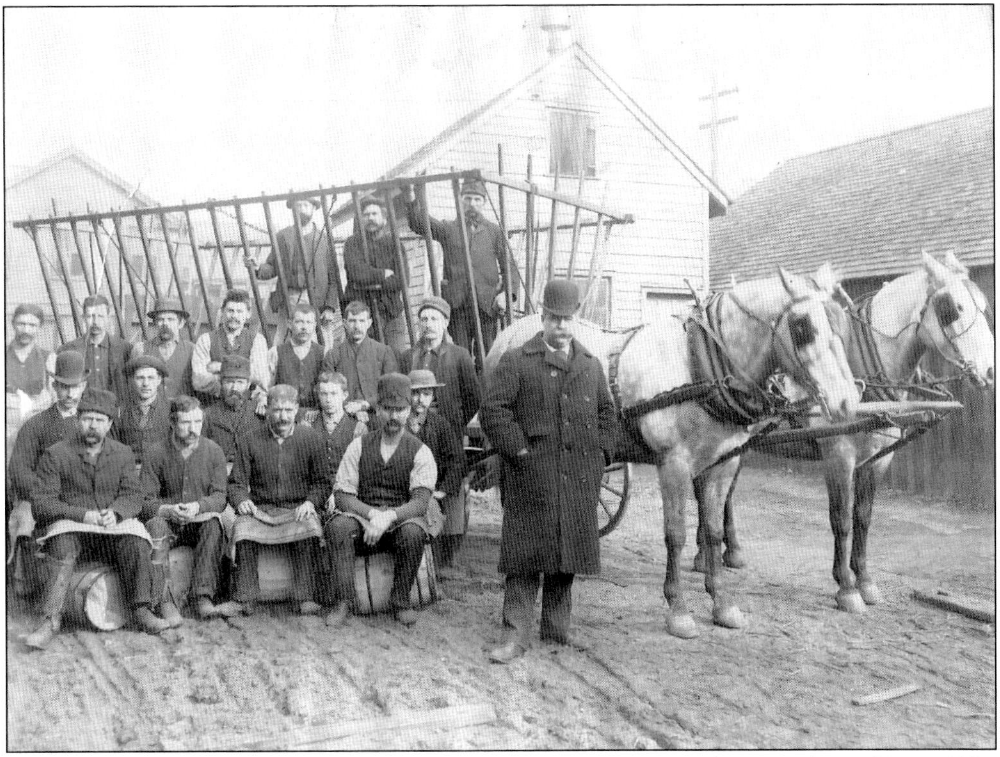

The Friedrichson Cooperage Company on Saratoga Avenue was in business from 1791 to 1991. Originally established by Joseph Fixture and purchased by John Friedrichson around 1818, the plant made barrels through five wars, turning out 1,000 new and old barrels a day in 1941. The workers are sitting on their finished product in front of the wagon used to transport the barrels. The gentleman in the coat and hat is John Friedrichson. (Courtesy of WHMCC.)

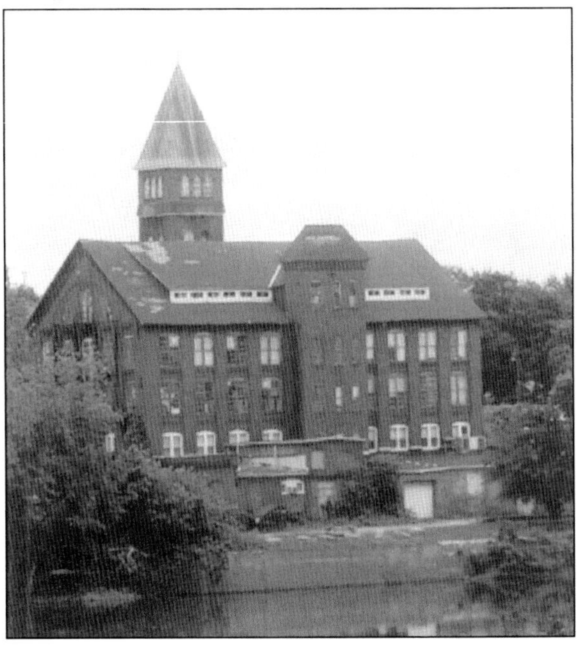

Laughlin Textile Mill, built in 1894, is now home to Ursula of Switzerland. The business started in 1972, and in 1992, Ursula Garreau-Rickenbacher became sole owner and president. In 1988, the company won the DEBI Award for Distinguished Excellence in the Bridal Industry. Up until 13 years ago, the dresses were made in Waterford; now they are sewn in Manhattan and then returned to the warehouse for shipping around the country and the world. (Courtesy of Talia Futia.)

After having been admitted to the bar in 1852, Nathaniel Bartlett Sylvester went on to write his book *History of Saratoga County 1609–1878*, which included a chapter on Waterford. Because of the 1841 fire in Waterford that destroyed all written records, without Sylvester's account of Waterford's early beginning, its industry, and its leaders, it is likely the information may have been lost to the public forever.

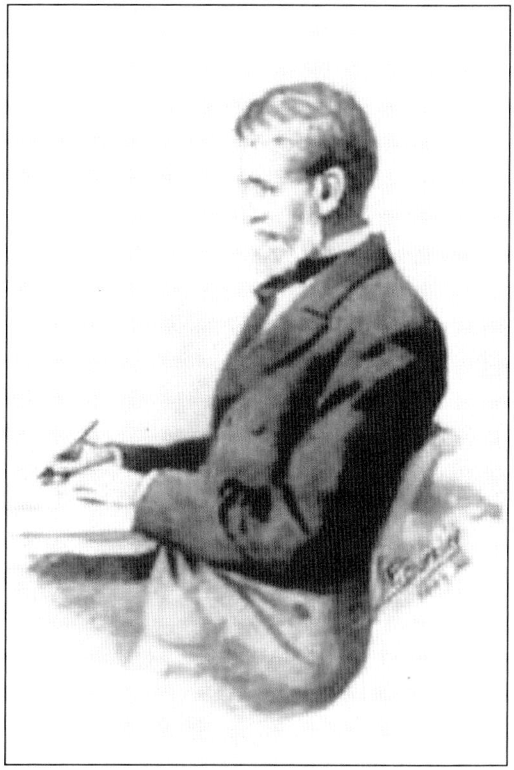

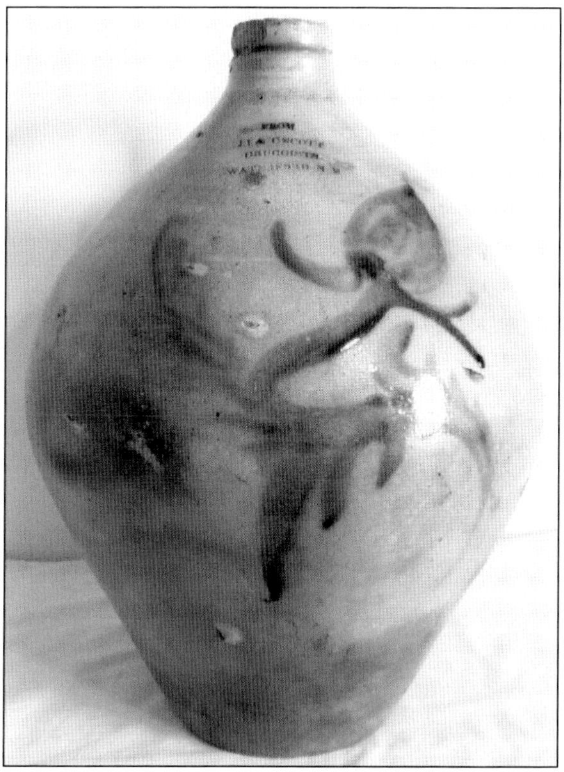

At left is an earthenware jug from the drugstore of J.I. & C. Scott Druggists. The jug may date back as early as 1835, when James and Charles Scott owned a drugstore on the corner of Broad and Third Streets. The jug has a floral design on the front and has what appears to be burn marks on the sides and back. It is possibly a survivor of the 1841 fire.

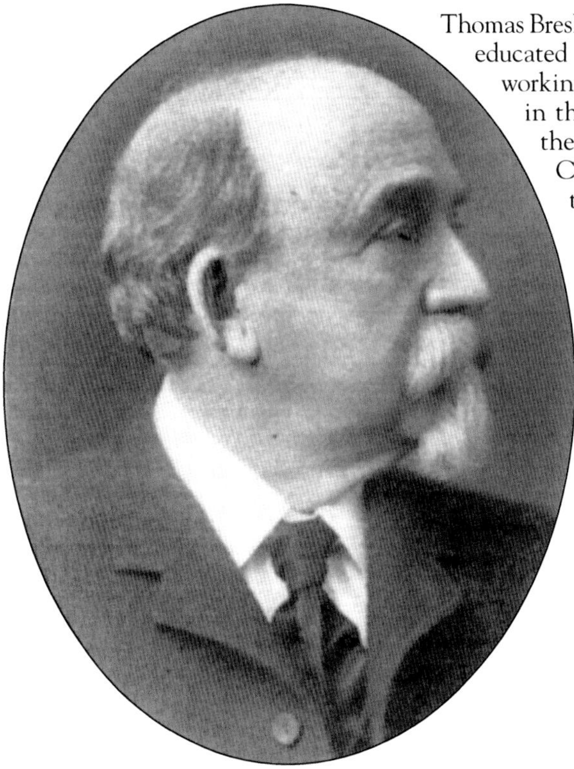

Thomas Breslin was born in Ushers, New York, in 1836, educated in Waterford, and by the age of 14 began working for J.M. King & Company. He engaged in the manufacture of knit underwear with the company known as Waterford Knitting Company. He later became president of that company. Breslin was a member of Ormsby Textile Company, vice president of Cohoes National Bank, and active in several other financial institutions. (Courtesy of Ellen and Neil Breslin.)

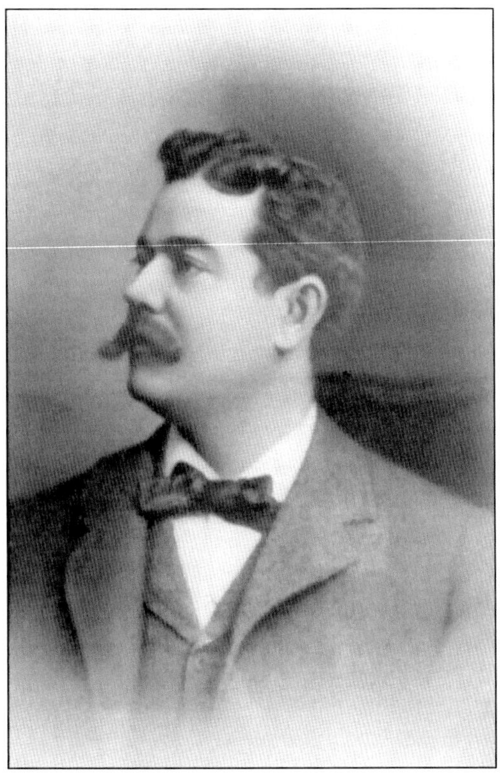

Charles H. Kavanaugh was a very prominent citizen of Waterford. He was president of the family's knitting mill and founded and served as president of the Bank of Waterford. Kavanaugh Hook & Ladder Company was named in his honor. Kavanaugh donated a set of chimes to the Grace Episcopal Church, erected a monument for Soldiers and Sailors Memorial Park, and funded a scholarship to Rensselaer Polytechnic Institute for a Waterford High School graduate. (Courtesy of Patricia Wilcox.)

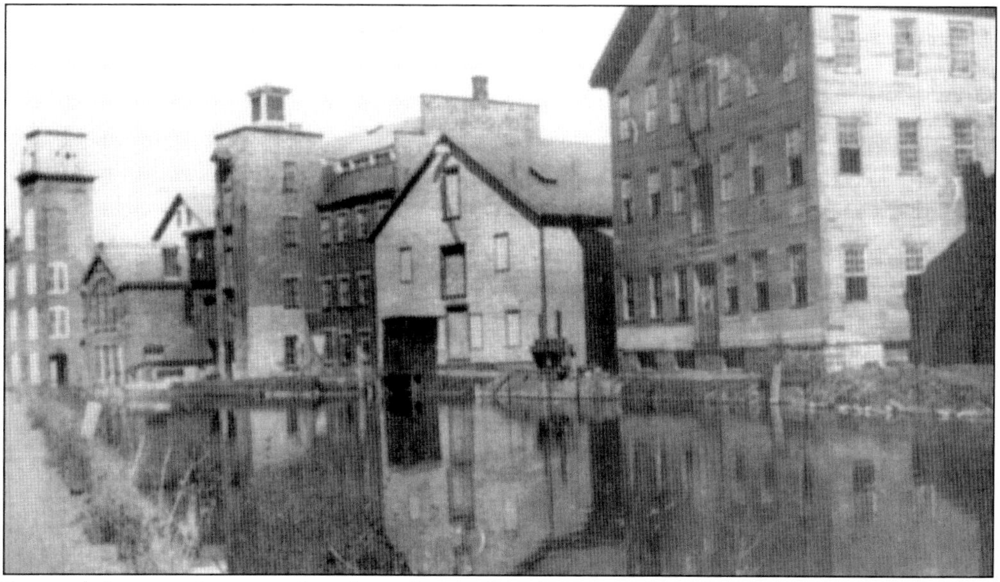

Pictured above is what was referred to as King's Canal in Waterford. It opened in 1828 and was one of the most important contributions to the growth of industry in Waterford. The raw waterpower turned waterwheels that produced the energy necessary to run the dozens of mills that sprang up along the manmade source of power. (Courtesy of Anna Marie Wilkes Lamos.)

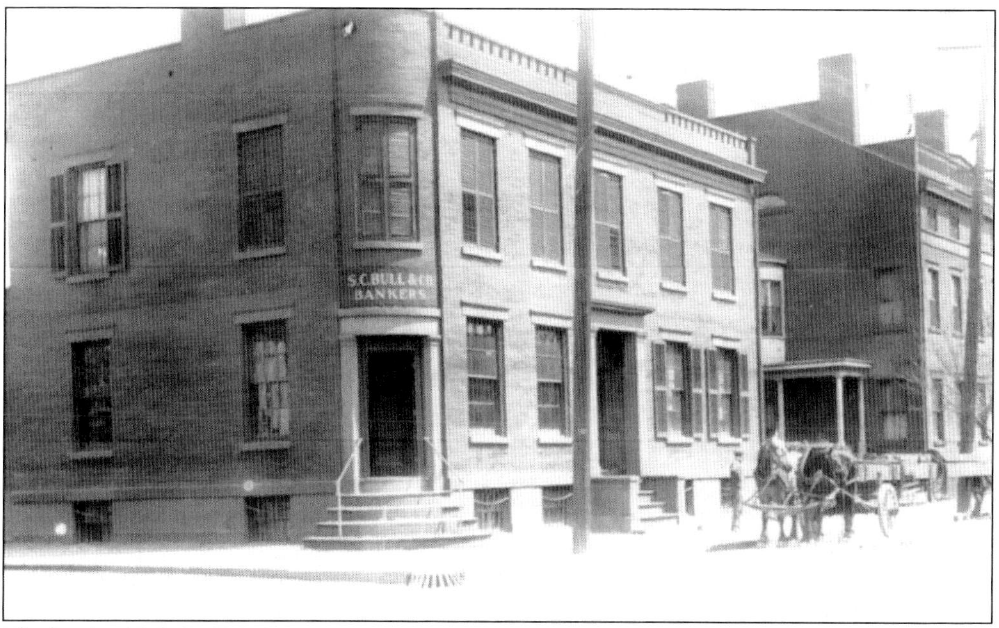

The bank of S.C. Bull & Company at 23 Broad Street, which was originally the Saratoga County Bank, organized in 1830. The bank is most remembered for being robbed of over $500,000 and jewelry. All the robbers were eventually caught and tried, but ironically, all were acquitted. S.C. Bull & Company succeeded it in 1885 and lasted until about 1909. Eventually, in the 1950s, it became Quandt's Mortuary. (Courtesy of the Saratoga County Historian's Office.)

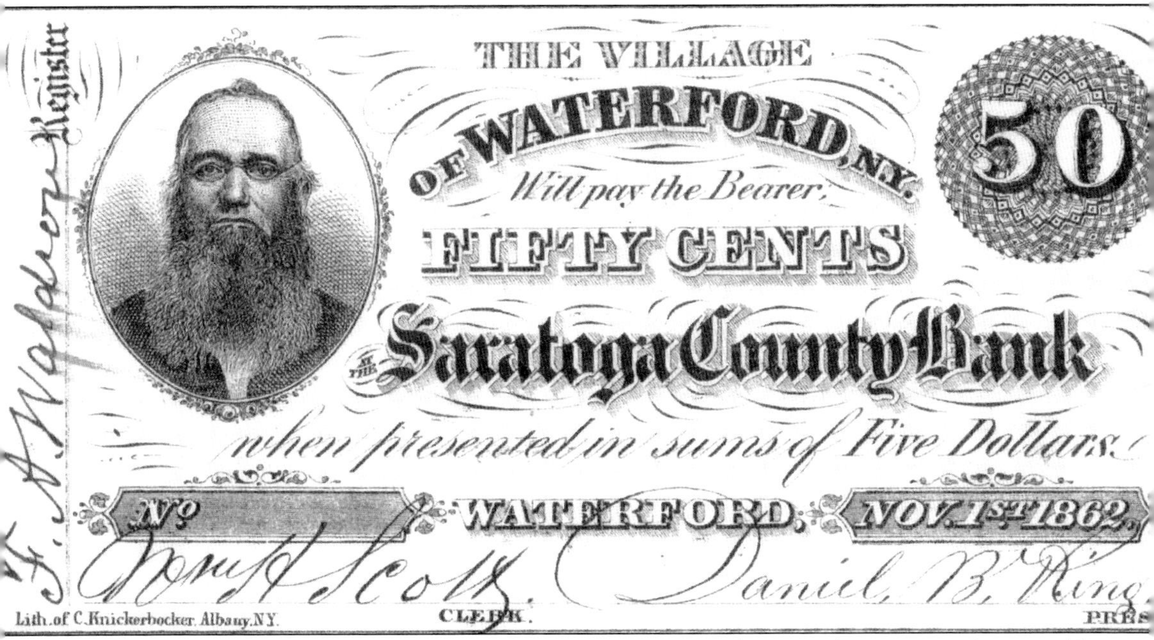

A banknote (often known as a bill, paper money, or simply a note) is a type of negotiable instrument known as a promissory note, made by a bank, payable to the bearer on demand. Banknotes were originally issued by commercial banks, which were legally required to redeem the notes for legal tender (usually gold or silver coin) when presented to the chief cashier of the originating bank. These commercial banknotes only traded at face value in the market served by the issuing bank. National banknotes are legal tender, meaning that medium of payment is allowed by law or recognized by a legal system to be valid for meeting a financial obligation. Historically, banks sought to ensure that they could always pay customers in coins when they presented banknotes for payment. Above is shown a 50¢ banknote issued by the Saratoga County Bank of Waterford in 1862. The bank also issued two other denominations—10¢ and 25¢.

Pictured here around 1898 is a team of horses pulling a Hemstead barrel wagon. The cooperage was in operation as early as 1845. The company made barrels for many products to be shipped through the old Champlain Canal and then to all parts of the world, including beef sent to the US Army during the Mexican War in the 1840s. (Courtesy of Tracy Geel.)

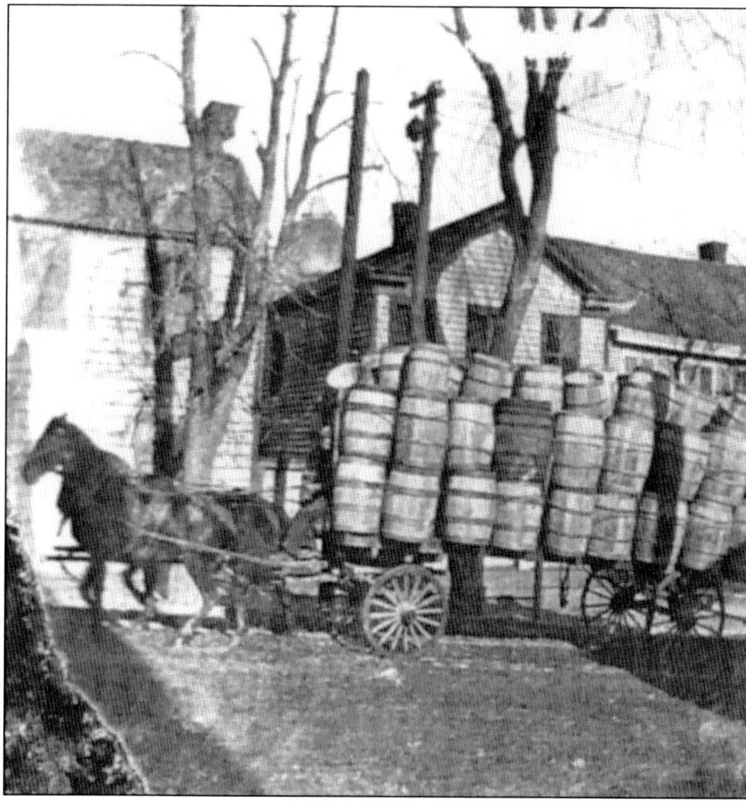

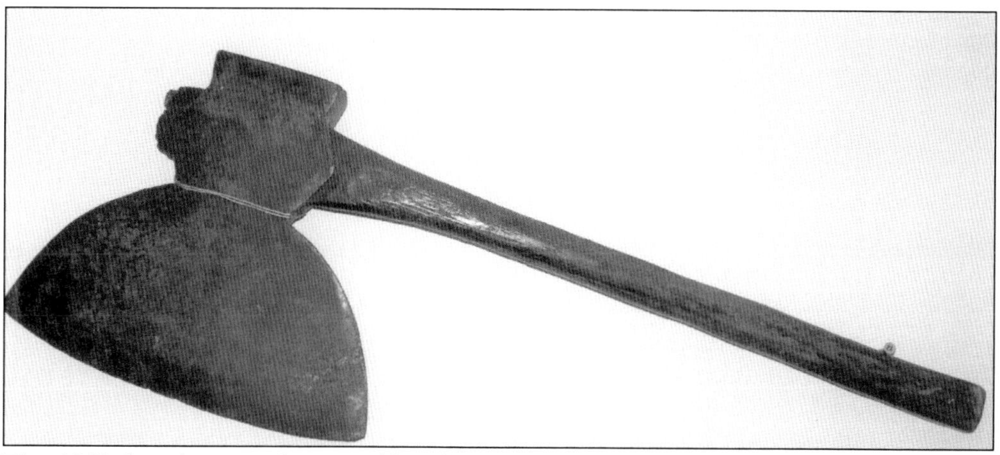

This 1860s broad axe, with original handle, is inscribed "C.P. Perkins & Co. Waterford, NY, Warrented Cast Steel." A broad axe is a large-headed axe used for hewing logs. The blade is flat on one side, and the other is beveled. The handle is curved away from the flat side. The flat blade is used to make the log surface flat. It can be used in only one direction and was made for left- or right-handed people. Broad axes were popular up until the late 1800s.

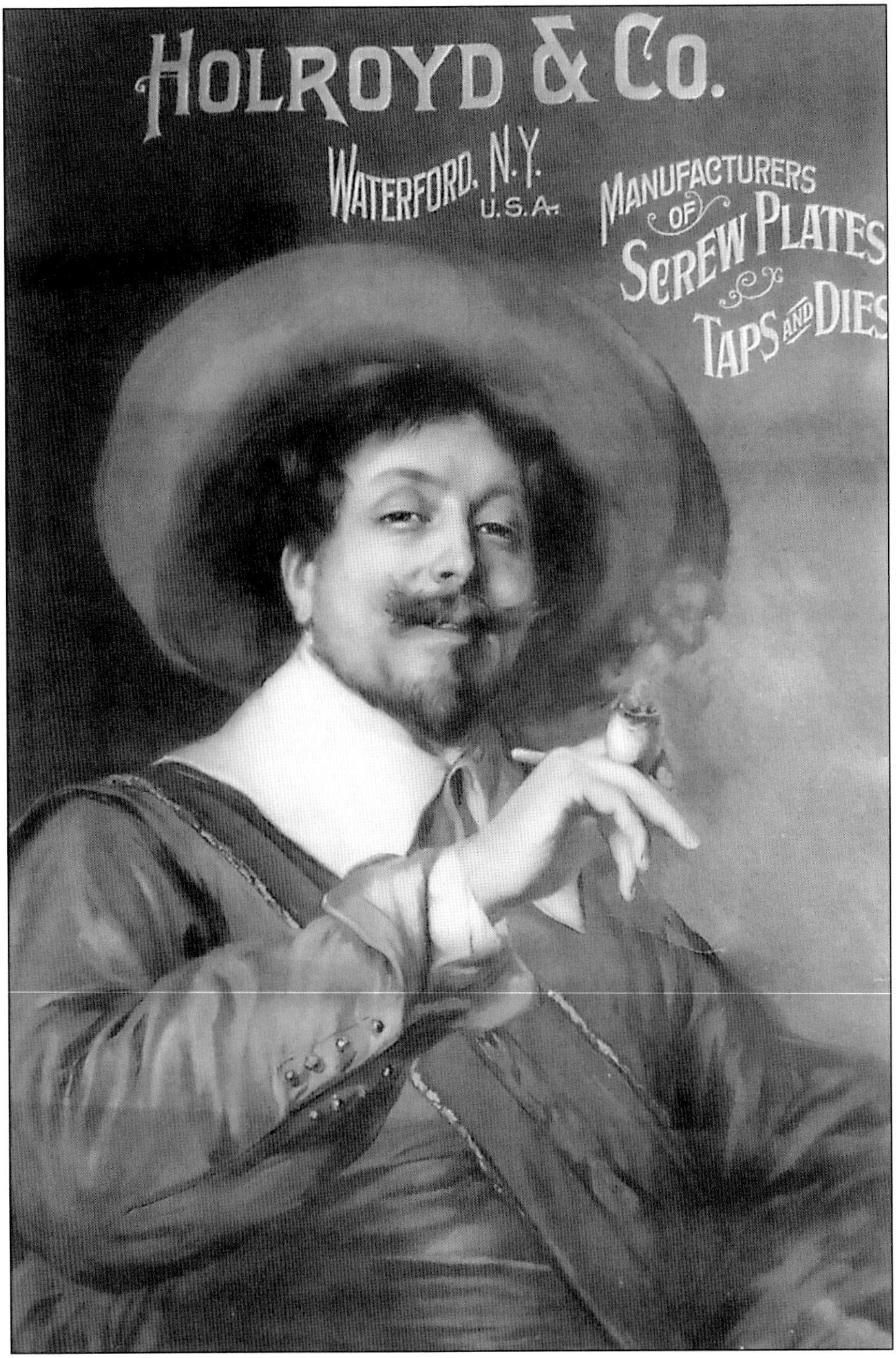

Pictured is a lithograph advertising Holroyd & Company. The company was established in 1847 by James Holroyd and manufactured screw plates, taps, and dies for blacksmiths' and machinists' use and also for gas or steam fittings. Located on King's Canal, the original buildings were demolished in 1864, and new, more efficient structures were erected on the same site. The company provided employment for 40 to 50 men and had an estimated annual income of $60,000 to $70,000.

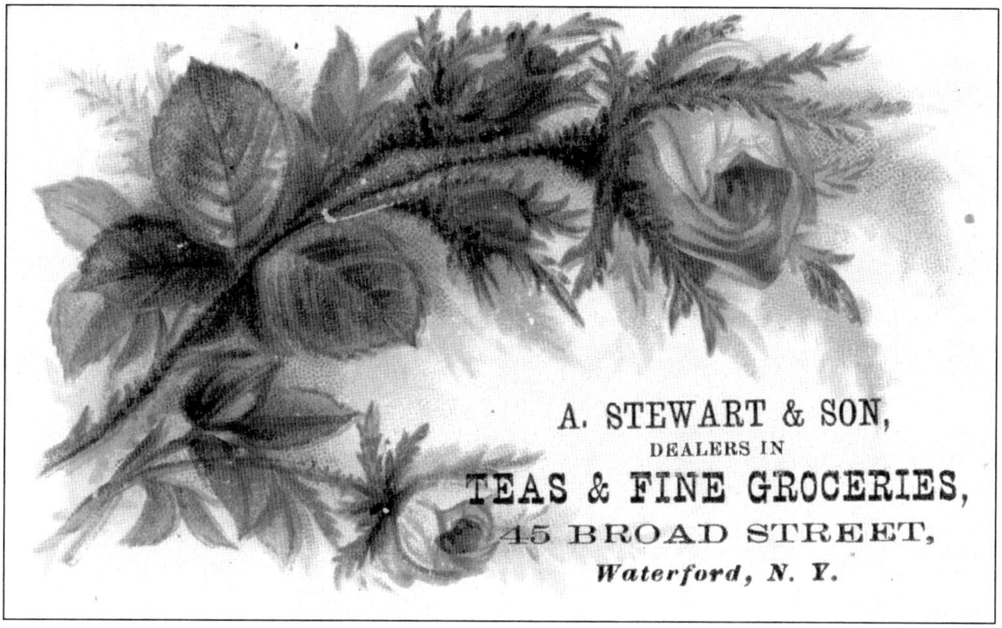

Without the modern conveniences of radio, television, or the Internet, trade cards, which originated at the beginning of the 1600s, were used as a means for merchants to advertise their trade or line of business or services. Usually there was an image on one side and space on the other side for the business to add its own information. The trade card was the forerunner of the modern-day business card. A. Stewart & Son, Grocery, located at 15 Broad Street, and the Weigh-Lock Grocery were both from the early 1800s. The Weigh-Lock Grocery was located on the western shore of the Champlain Canal, north of Division Street. This store not only relied on local traffic, but also the canals for their business. (Both, courtesy of Merle Doud.)

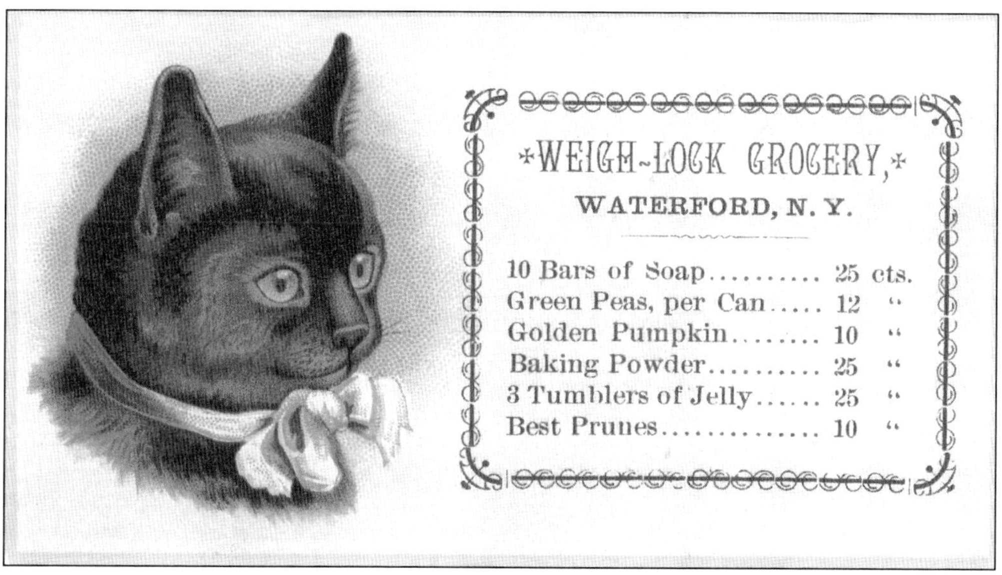

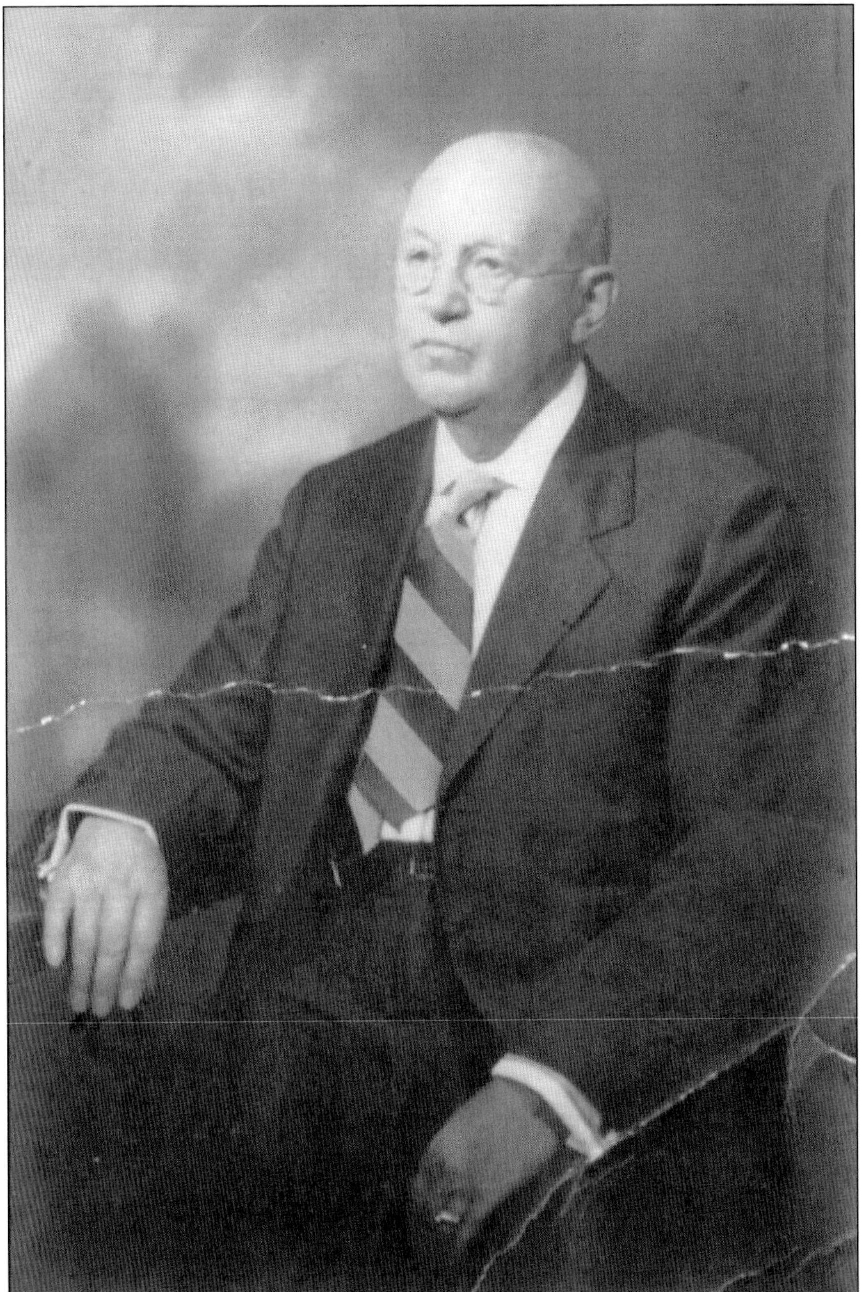

George N. Michon was born in Lansingburgh, New York, in 1869, and moved to Waterford at a very early age. He eventually married Rose Doherty. Spending most of his life in Waterford, Michon became interested in photography, taking shots of Waterford from the late 1800s into the 1940s. Michon's photographs, many of them postcards, became so numerous and sought after, it is now referred to as the Michon Collection. Michon also ran a newsstand/variety store in Waterford for almost 30 years. Michon died on December 7, 1946, at the Leonard Hospital in Troy. His wife, Rose, ran the variety store until her death in 1951, and their son Warren took over until his death in 1964. (Courtesy of Carol Ann Michon.)

Col. Sydney Ernest Hammersley spent several years of dedicated research in writing *The History of Waterford, New York*. Colonel Hammersley has a detailed account of what life was like in a small town, from the early days—beginning in the 1600s with the fur traders, trappers, and Native Americans—through to the publication of his book in 1957. (Courtesy of Donald E. Child.)

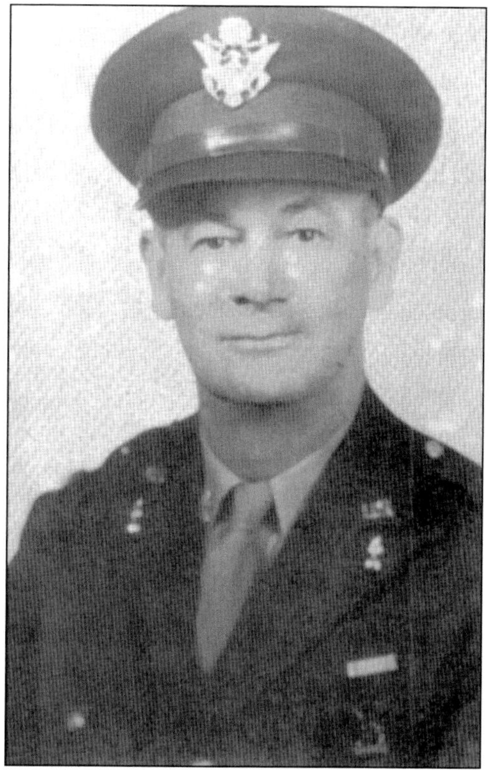

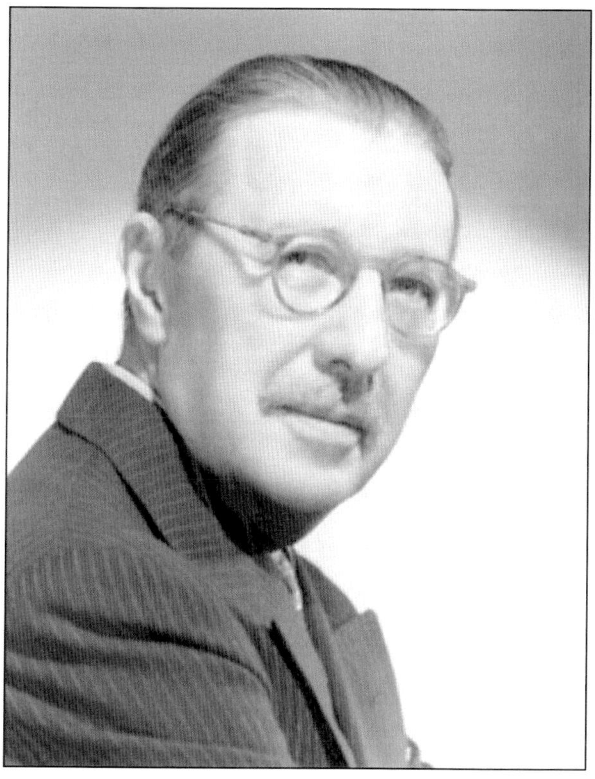

Howard Lindsay, a very well-known playwright and actor, was born Herman Siegmond Nelke in Waterford on March 29, 1889. Lindsay was most known for the play *Life with Father*. Not only did he write it, he also played the father on Broadway. In 1960, he was given the Antoinette Perry Award for writing *The Sound of Music*, used as a basis for the play starring Mary Martin. (Courtesy of Patricia Wilcox.)

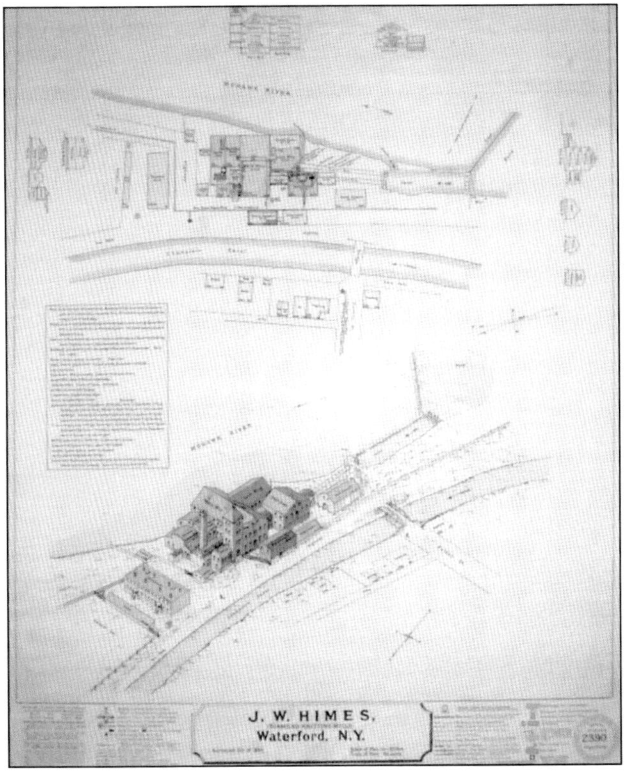

In 1871, Jehiel W. Himes was involved in knitting mill operations in the city of Cohoes as well as an investor in a planned railway operation between Waterford and Cohoes. By 1890, he was the owner of Himes Underwear Company, operating on the King's Canal in Waterford. It was one of many underwear producers, and its specialty was flat woolen underwear for men, ladies, and children. They employed over 200 hands.

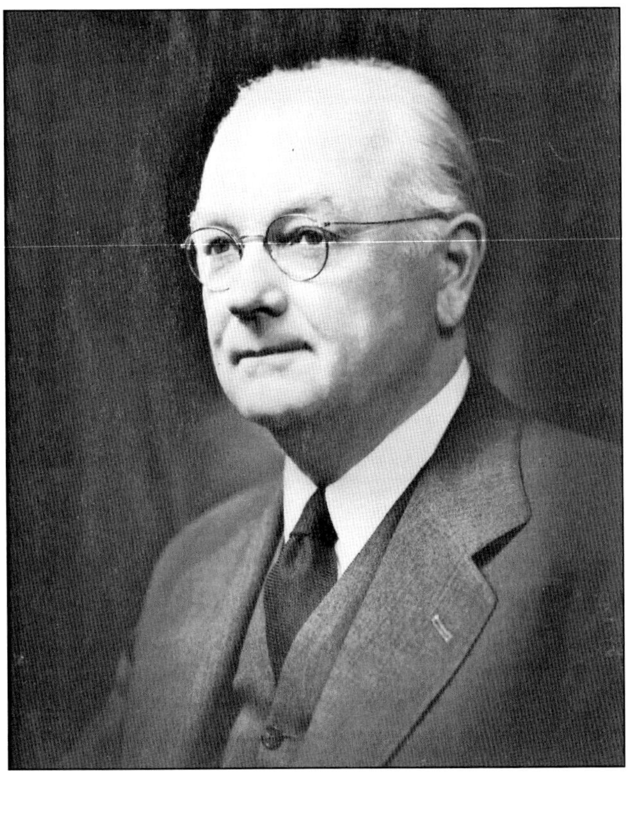

The grandson of Irish immigrants, George E. O'Connor was born in Waterford. O'Connor was a prominent lawyer in Waterford, graduating from Yale University and Columbia University. He married Annabella Maria Gallagher, and they had three children. In 1931, O'Connor purchased Mohawk Papermakers, Inc. The company is owned today by his grandson Thomas O'Connor Jr. (Courtesy of WHMCC.)

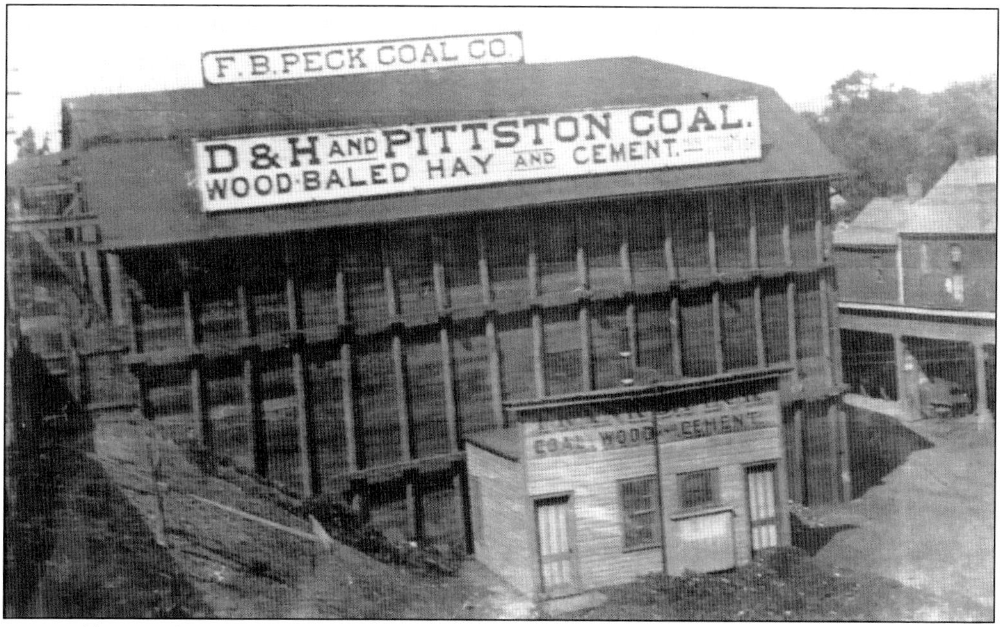

Pictured here is the F.B. Peck Coal Company, located on the Champlain Canal Towpath on street level in the village. Not only was the coal needed for homes and businesses, it was also utilized by the "canallers" for the same purpose on their canal boats. Such was the demand for coal that Johnny Evers operated Ever's Coal Dock on the other side of canal. (Courtesy of the Saratoga County Historian's Office.)

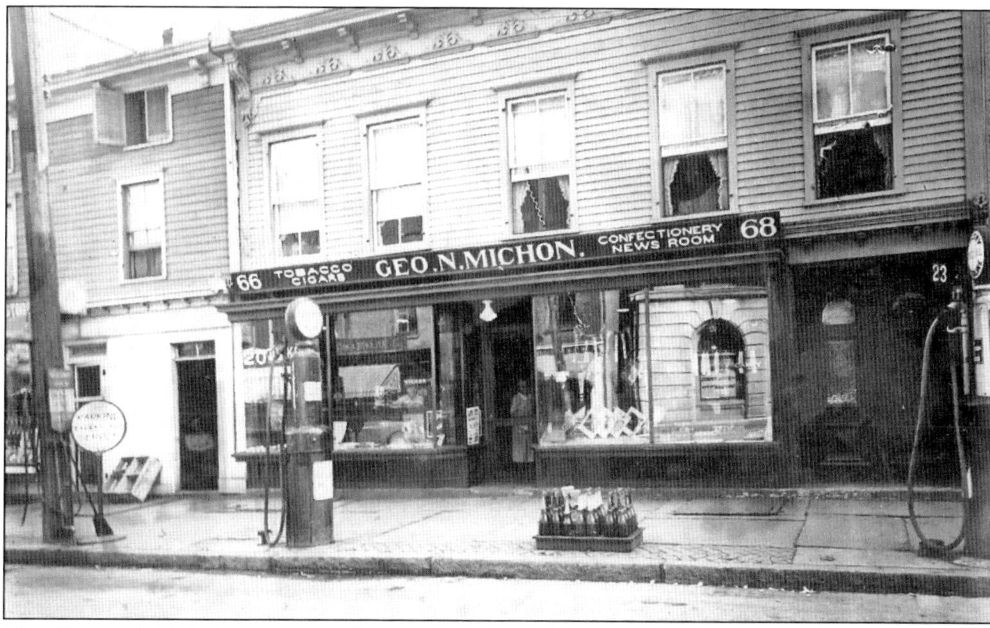

The George N. Michon store and newsroom opened at 66–68 Broad Street around 1907 and featured tobacco, cigars, confectionaries, and newspapers. The sign next to the utility pole reads "No Parking Except for Service." The gas pumps offered Socony Special Gasoline, and Socony oil was also for sale. The lady standing in the doorway is thought to be Rose Michon. (Courtesy of Mary Michon.)

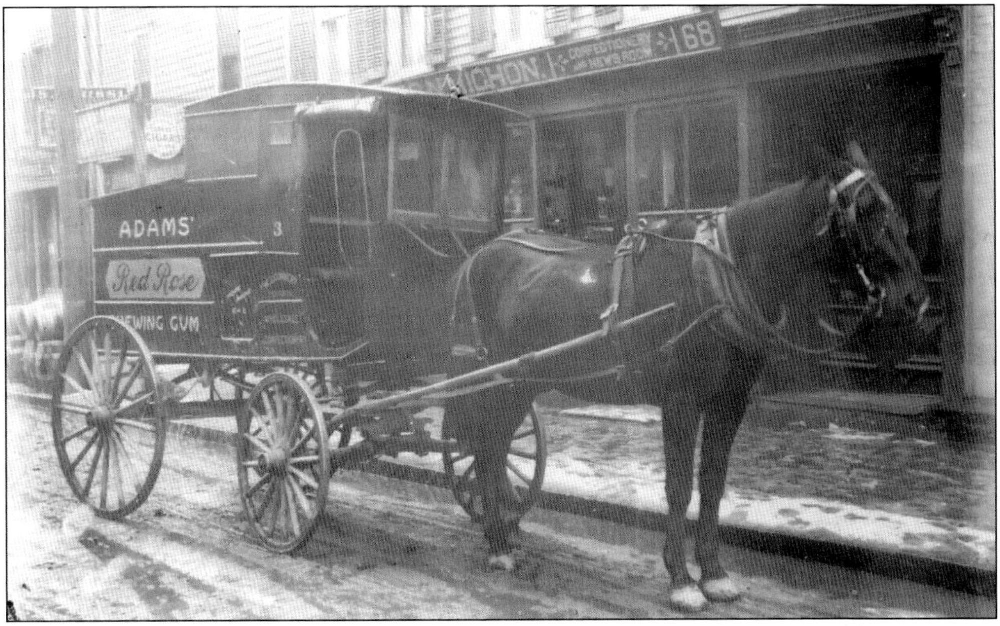

There are still Waterfordians about today who remember the horse-and-wagon delivery system. Some of the local dairies still utilized this method into the 1950s, as did the Freihofer Bread Company until 1962. What many do not have an appreciation of is that everything on land was transported by the horse and wagon or, in wintertime, often by horse and sleigh. (Courtesy of Donald Bowles.)

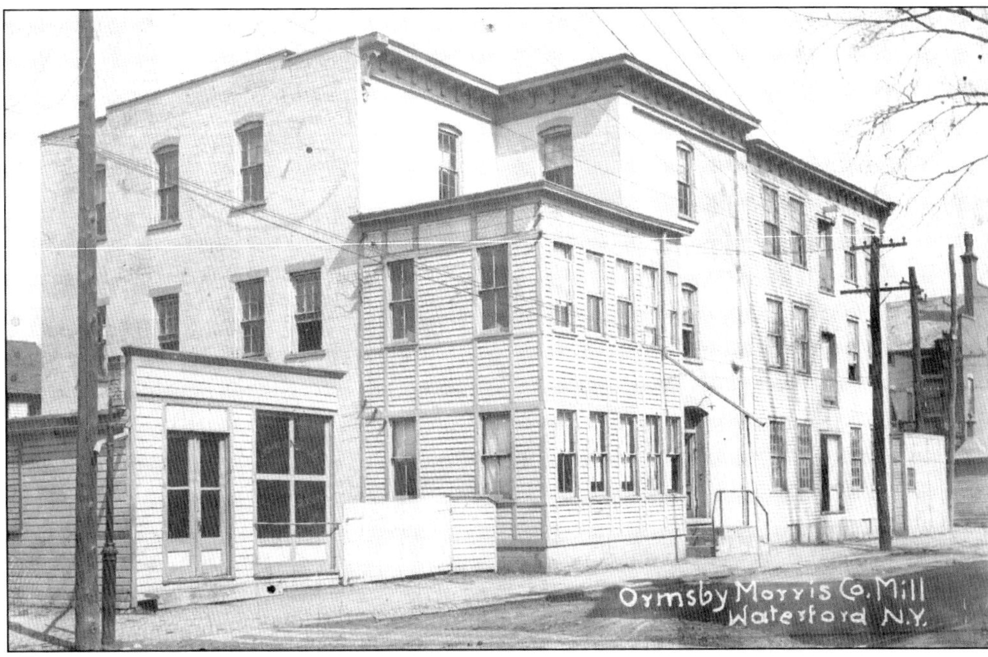

The Ormsby-Morris Company mill was located on the corner of Fourth and Division Streets. The company specialized in the manufacture of knit gloves. In 1909, the company's capital assets were $10,000. C.C. Ormsby was president and Thomas F. Morris secretary. (Courtesy of Michael D Marchese.)

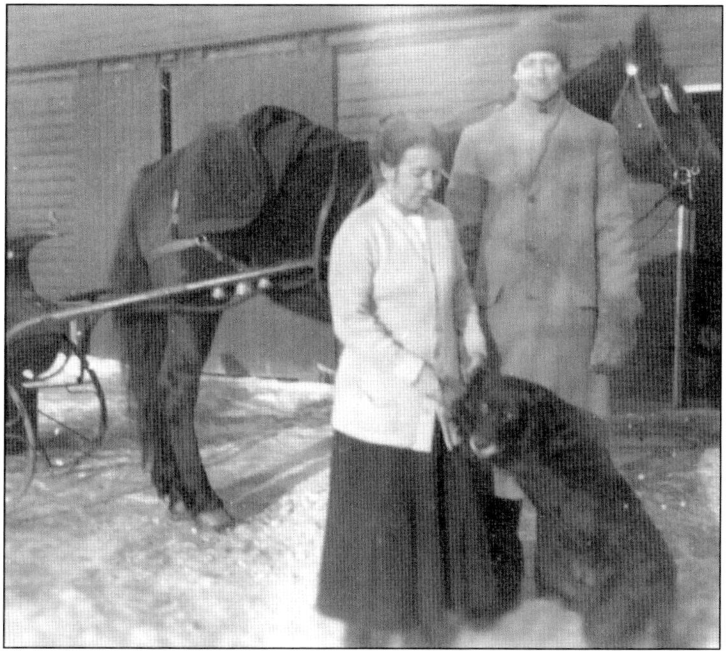

Pictured here are James G. Anderson and his wife, Bess, around 1916, standing with their dog Jack in front of their barn. James Anderson was the proprietor of the Waterford Dairy. The dairy farm was located outside of the village on Fonda Road, and the bottling and distribution plant stood behind their home on upper Third Street. James G. Anderson died on August 22, 1930, of appendicitis at the age of 45. (Courtesy of Helen Grochmal Anderson.)

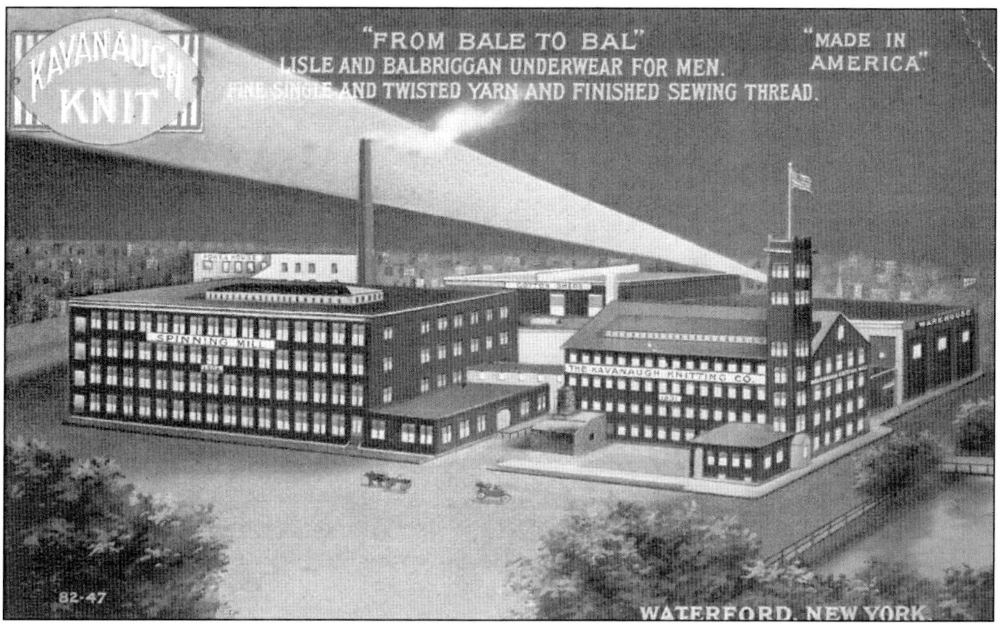

Flour milling was an early industry in Waterford, and when that began to vanish, many of the existing structures were converted to knitting mills. This transition occurred around 1911, and by 1912, the town's principal product was underwear. The Kavanaugh Knitting Company was one such mill. The Kavanaughs were pioneers in this industry and saw the textile trade as an important commercial venture. (Courtesy of Bill Paquette.)

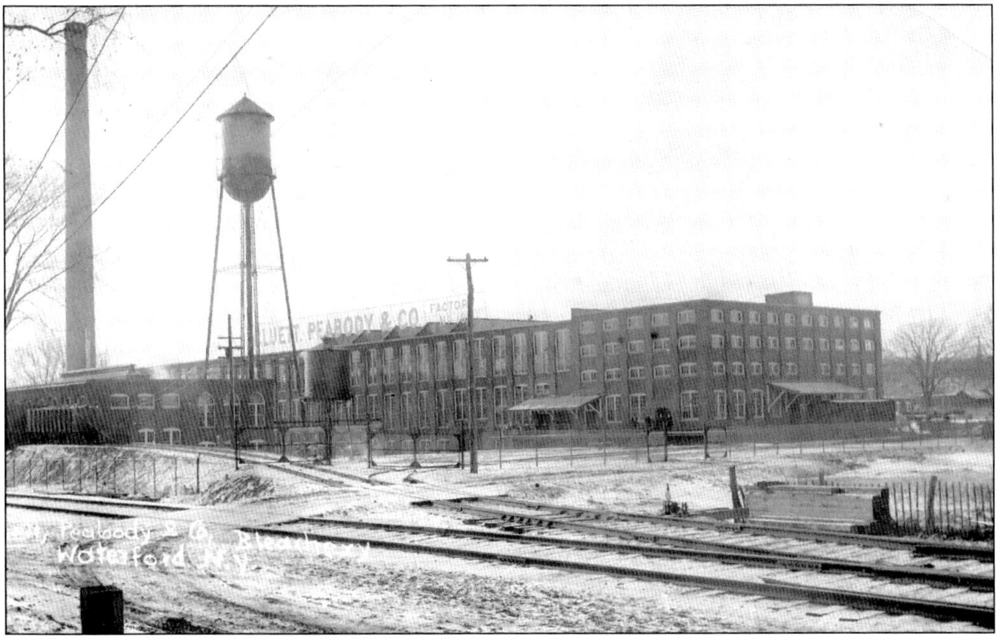

Cluett Peabody began in 1910 as a manufacturer of men's detachable collars. The bleachery processed miles of cloth and would run endless rolls of cloth through fire to remove minute imperfections and then wash, bleach, and Sanforize (trade name) the material to insure it against shrinkage. The water resource on Peebles Island was the main attraction for building there. (Courtesy of Hugh Holton.)

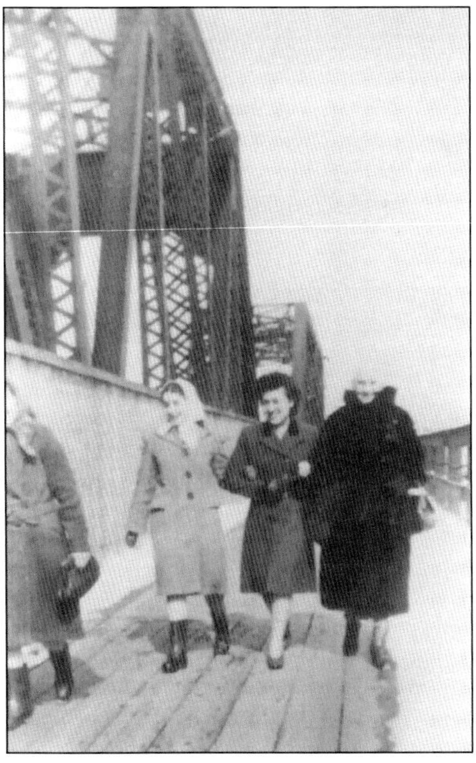

For many years, this bridge served as an important pedestrian link between Waterford and points south. The ladies pictured here around 1940, were on their way to work at the Cluett Peabody & Company, located on Peebles Island. Cluett Peabody was renowned for making shirts, detachable collars, and cuffs. (Courtesy of Tracy Geel.)

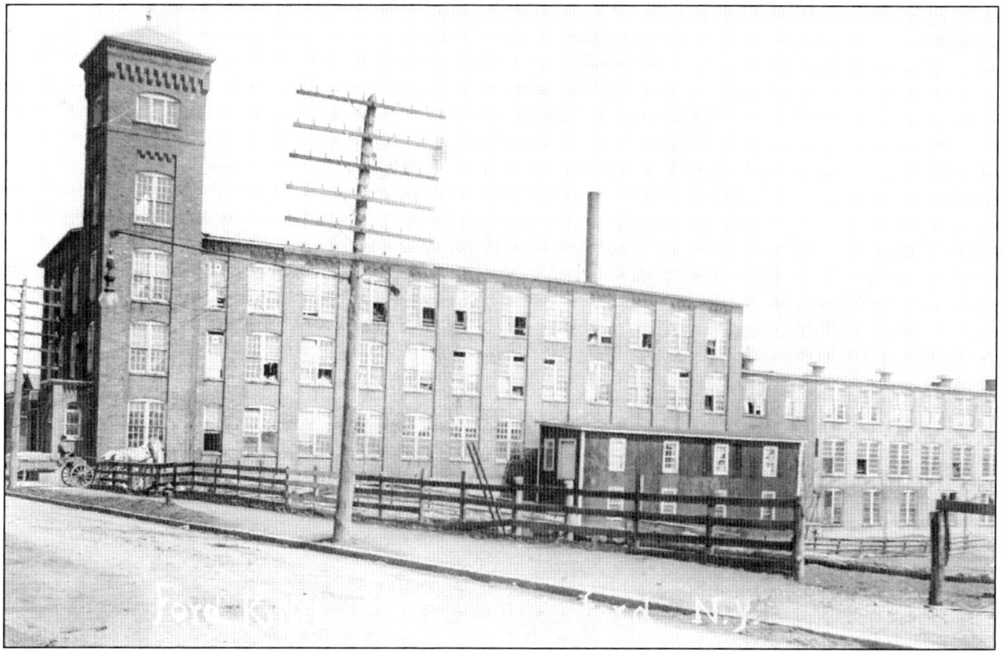

When the original Ford Manufacturing Company was destroyed by fire, John Ford purchased land at 123 North Second Street and constructed a new building. In 1897, construction was completed, and in 1919, the company was purchased by Robert Reis, who did not change the name of the company. In the 1960s, it employed 400 people. As sales dropped in the 1970s, the company went bankrupt. It was the longest-running mill of its kind within Waterford. (Courtesy of Frank McClement.)

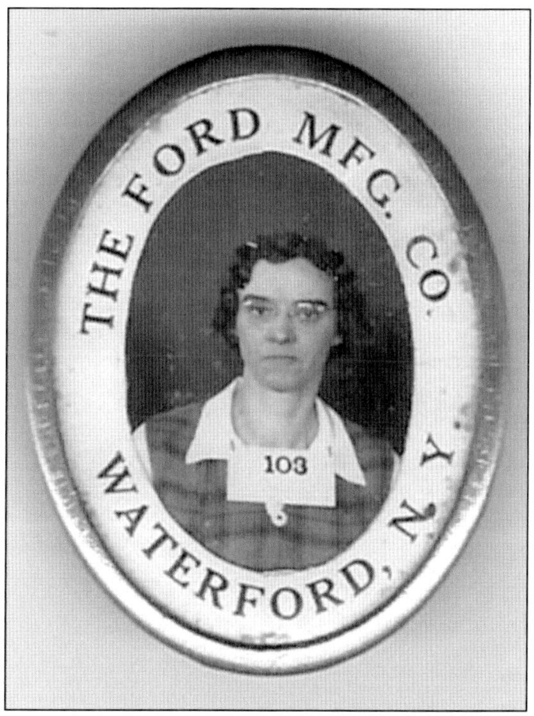

This was an identification tag worn by all employees of the Ford Manufacturing Company, owned by John Wheeler Ford. The mill was one of several underwear factories and employed mostly female labor. The women performed piece work, which meant that they were paid for each piece that they produced. Later known as Reis's Mill, it was also referred to as Reis's Academy, when many students eager to enter the workforce would leave school for quick employment at the mill. (Courtesy of Talia Futia.)

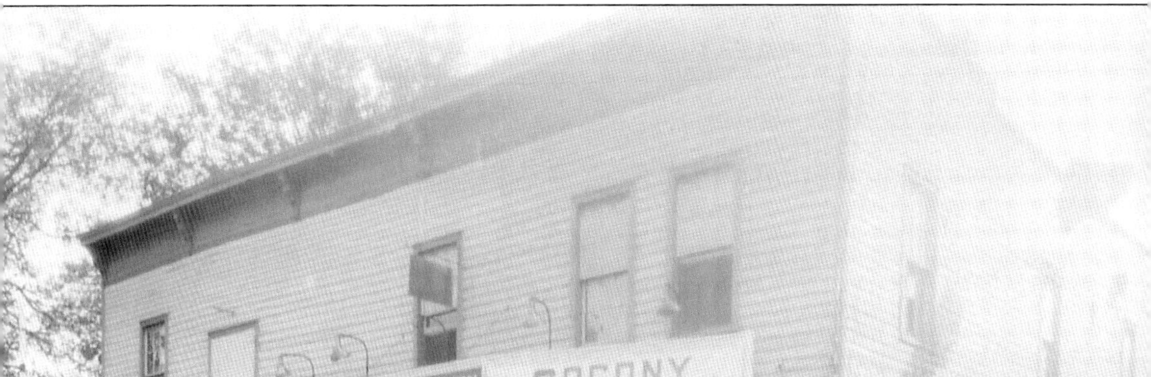

Dunn Tire & Battery Service was located on Fourth Street across from Burgess Printing and Kavanaugh Hook & Ladder Firehouse. The Tierney Mansion is to the left. The Dunn family was prominent in Waterford during the late 1800s through the mid-1900s. They operated a wide variety of business types on both Broad Street and Fourth Street. There was Dunn's Liquor Store, a paint store, and the Dunn Building, which was home to many other operations, such as Sarge's Pool Hall. The last known use for this building was a Dairylea Barn. The current use of this property is a mini mart with self-service gasoline. (Courtesy of Russ Van Dervoort.)

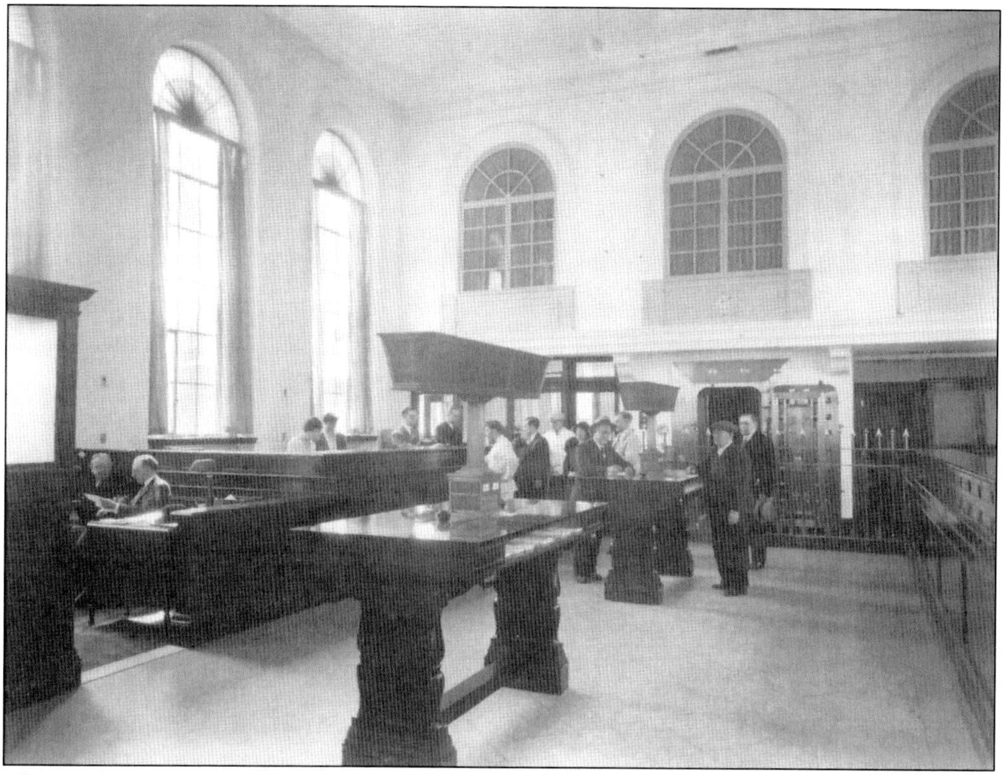

The Bank of Waterford, also known as Key Bank and National Commercial Bank and Trust Co., pictured here around 1935, demonstrates the serious businesslike manner of a traditional, well-established, old-time bank. They could do business without electricity. Key Bank, commonly referred to as "The Bank," was the successor to National Commercial Bank and Trust Co., but it was always known as "The Bank" in Waterford. Owner and Waterford resident Wellington Bishop was known for his signature no-collateral loans. It was truly a hometown bank under his stewardship. (Courtesy of Key Bank.)

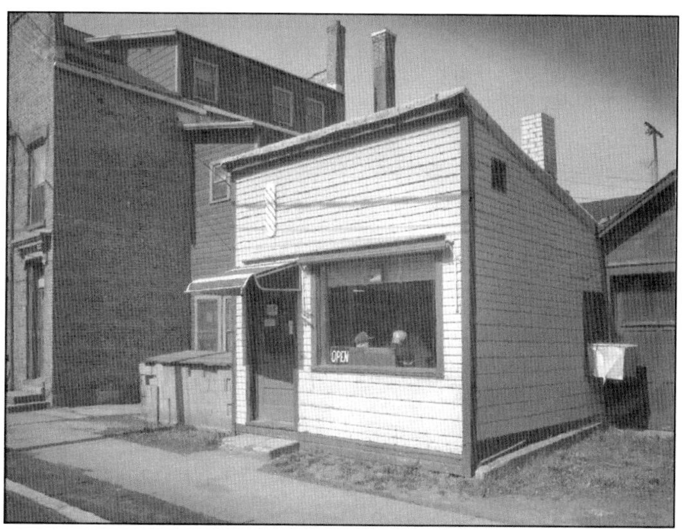

Swasey's Barber Shop was owned and operated by Harold Swasey. An iconic men's barbershop from the 1940s through the 1960s, at one time this small building housed three barbers. It was a typical shop with magazines, straight razors, warmed shaving cream, aproned barbers, men's calendars, and the news of the day—all for 75¢. Today, Chuck Girard, a barber and Swasey's successor, is a few doors north. (Courtesy of Charles Girard.)

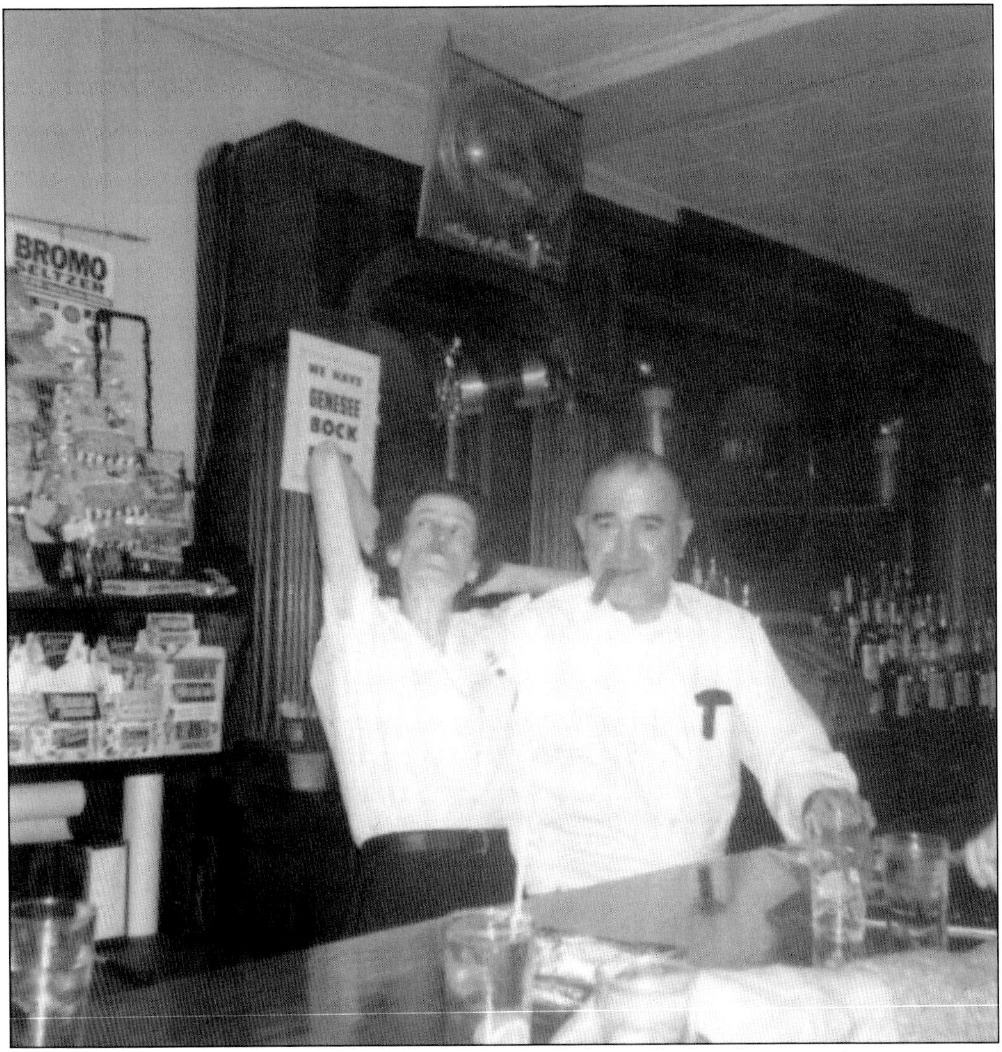

Camp's Grill, Restaurant, and Bowling Alley was previously located on the northwest corner of Broad Street and Fourth Street. John and Ric Bachiocci ran Camp's Grill after the Campolis, who were preceded by the McGrieveys. It was without question one of the most popular places in Waterford, from the World War II era through 1977, when the Bachioccis sold the business. (Courtesy of WHMCC.)

Two

STREET SCENES, NEIGHBORHOODS, AND RESIDENTS

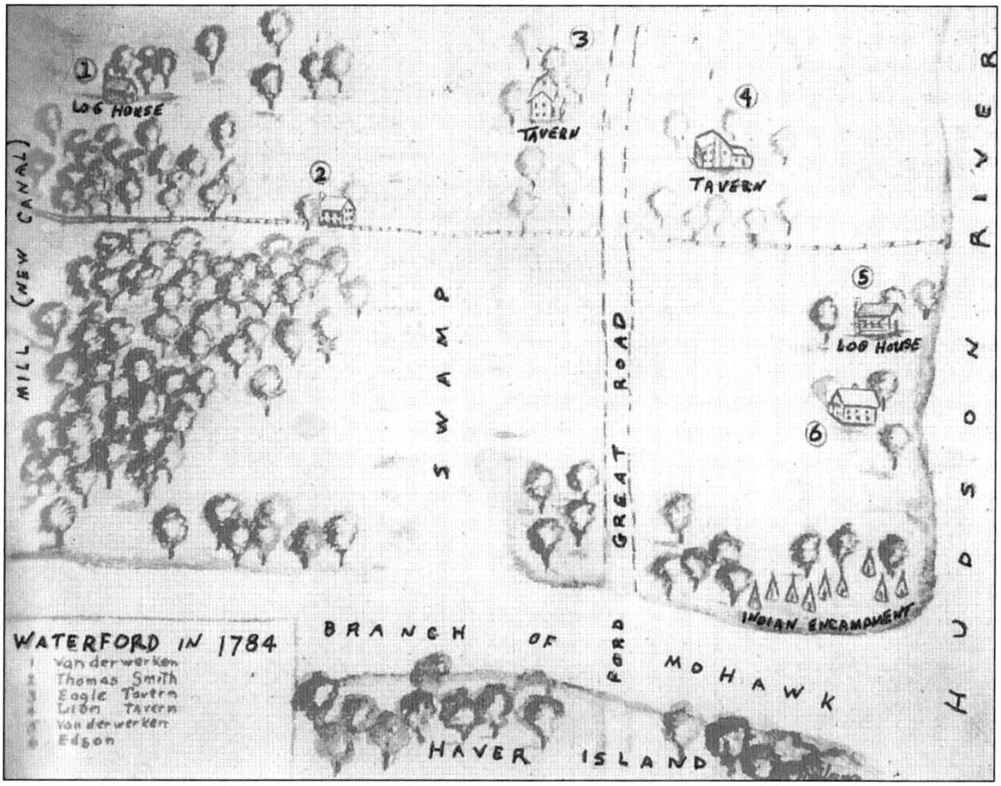

"In 1676, Annetie Lievers disposed of two tracts of land to Roelof Garretse (Vanderwerken) under the date of February 4, 1686–1687. These tracts of land contained 1124 acres." The Vanderwerkens lived in two of the six dwellings (log homes), Nos. 1 and 5. Also noted is an account of the 1686–1687 Cohoes Company's dam (where the mill/new canal is indicated) to the west of log home No. 1. House No. 2 was the home of Thomas Smith. No. 3 is the Eagle tavern, which during the American Revolution was the haven for so-called rebels, and No. 4 was the Lion Tavern, frequented by the then hated Tories. House No. 6 may have been the home of Adam Edson, who was reported to be an innkeeper. Note there is an Indian encampment at the junction of the Hudson and Mohawk Rivers, which was referred to by the Mahigan Indians as Naditenach. Also pictured here is Haver Island, which will come to be called Peebles Island.

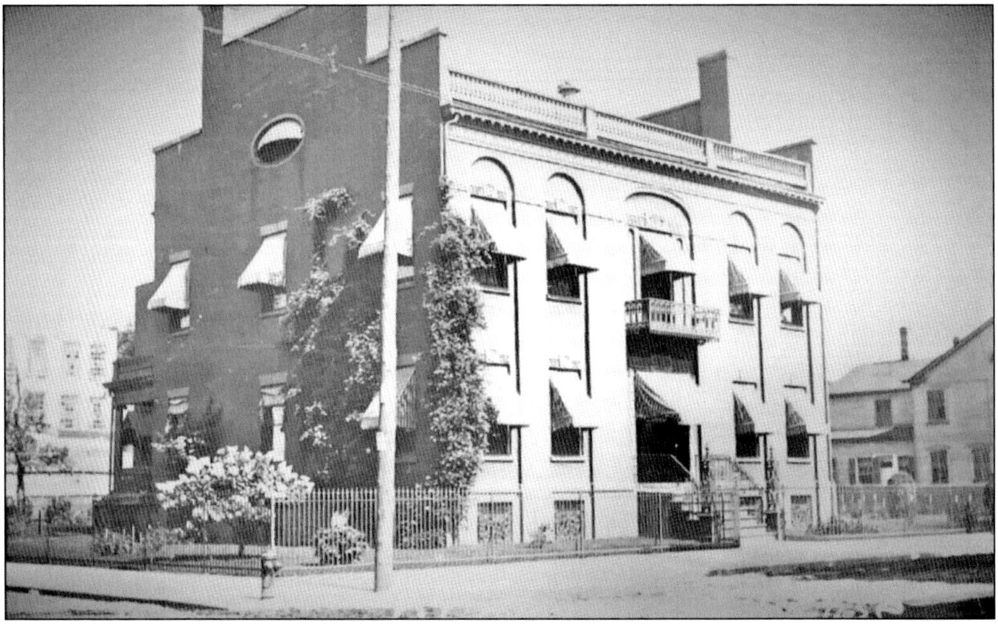

This house was built in 1812 and occupied over the years by many families, including the Van Alstynes, the Amsdens, the Mandevilles, the Pruynes, the Porters, and the O'Connors. The house was constructed of Holland brick and located at the northwest corner of Third and Division Streets. The house was demolished around 1935. (Courtesy of Jim Michon.)

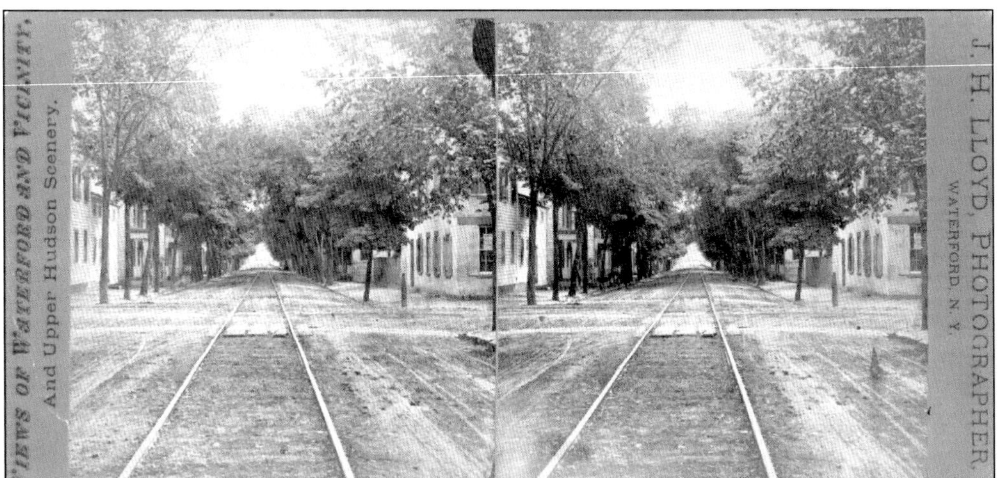

This is a stereoscopy, which was introduced in the 1830s and appeared drawn. By the 1850s, it was possible to have them appear as photographic images, creating a three-dimensional effect. Above is the intersection of Broad and Second Streets looking north. On the northeast corner is the Saratoga County Bank.

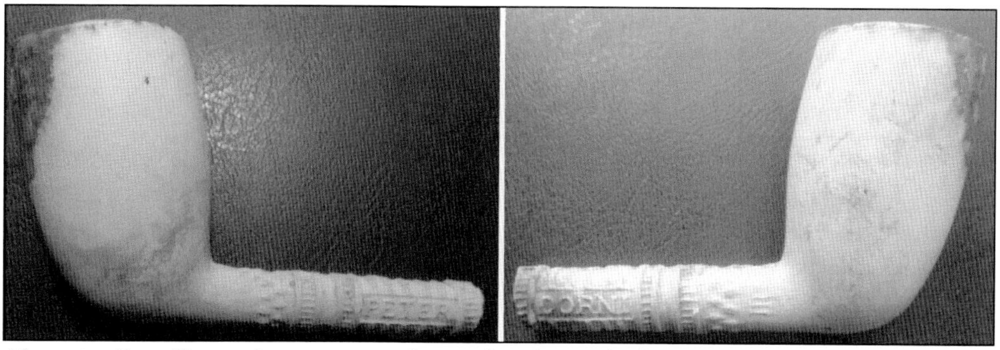

Above is a Peter Dorni clay pipe, manufactured in the Netherlands between 1835 and 1898. The pipe was found while digging the dumps along the Champlain Canal in Waterford. The dumps ran north from the Black Bridge along the eastern edge of the towpath hillside for about a mile. The open-air dumps were utilized from the 1880s through the 1950s.

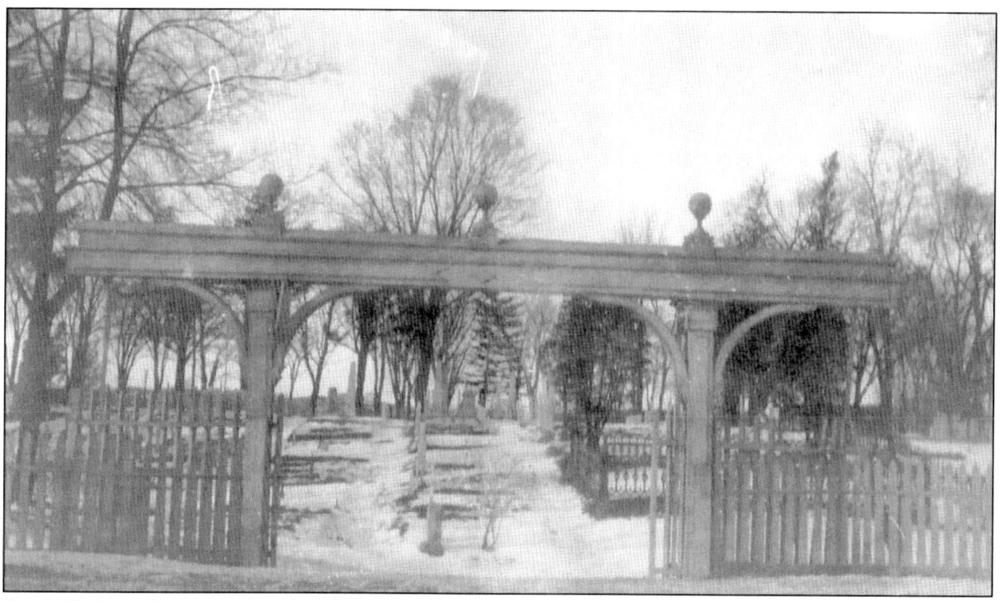

In 1845, the village trustees decided that the small cemetery located in the village at the southwest corner of Fourth and Division Streets was full, and more space was required. They purchased three acres of land from Guert Van Schoonhoven to open a new cemetery, which became known as the Waterford Rural Cemetery. The oldest burial record is that of Agnes Visscher, who died on December 4, 1774. This is the original entrance gate to the Waterford Rural Cemetery. (Courtesy of Teri VanWagenen Patton.)

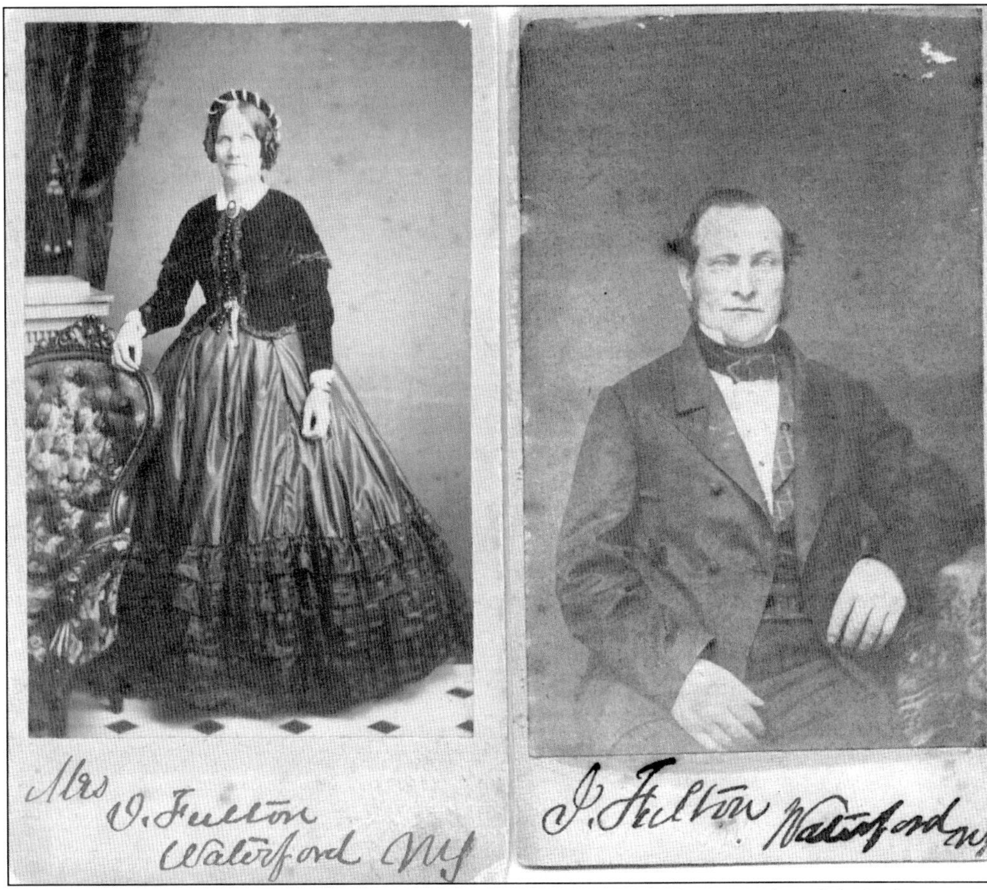

Pictured here around 1856 are Mrs. D. Fulton and J. Fulton. The photographs of the Fultons were able to be paired and later mentioned in a diary entry written by Castella "Cassie" E. Eddy on January 7, 1856. In her diary, she wrote, "Mr. Fulton came home and brought some peanuts we ate them and had a chat and then I retired for the night."

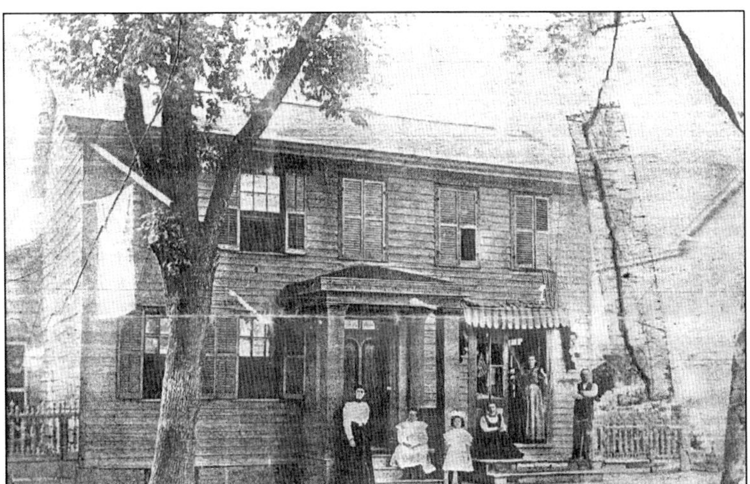

This is an early photograph, possibly from the 1870s, of the residence of Thomas Ranney, at 52 Fourth Street. The entranceway on the right appears to be a small storefront. Note there is not any electricity going into the house. (Courtesy of Jean Lavigne.)

This map from 1867 depicts the area known as Northside. From 1867 to 1878, it was known as Dodgeville, named after J. Dodge. It extends from the Waterford Rural Cemetery southward to the Mohawk River. Northside was a self-contained community with its own school, churches, and fire protection. Many French Canadians settled in this community, and French was spoken in school and at St. Ann's Church. (Courtesy of Bill Paquette.)

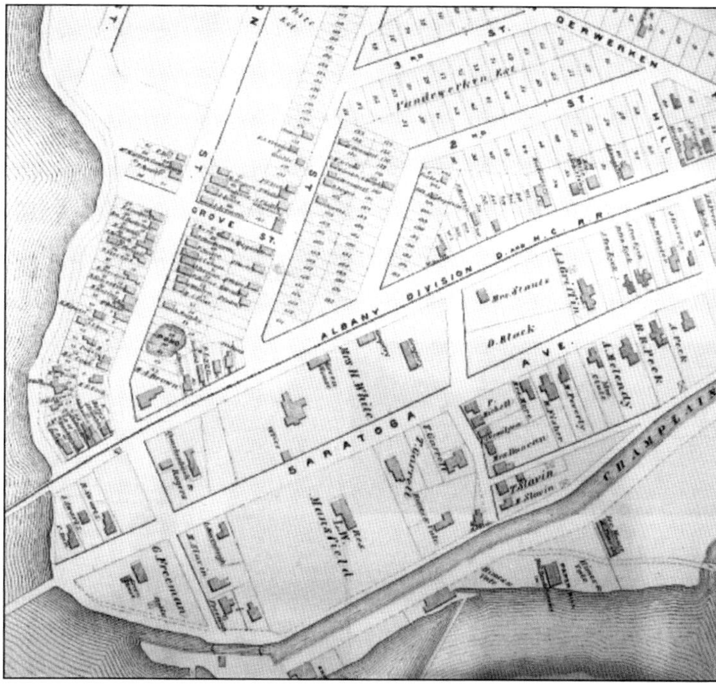

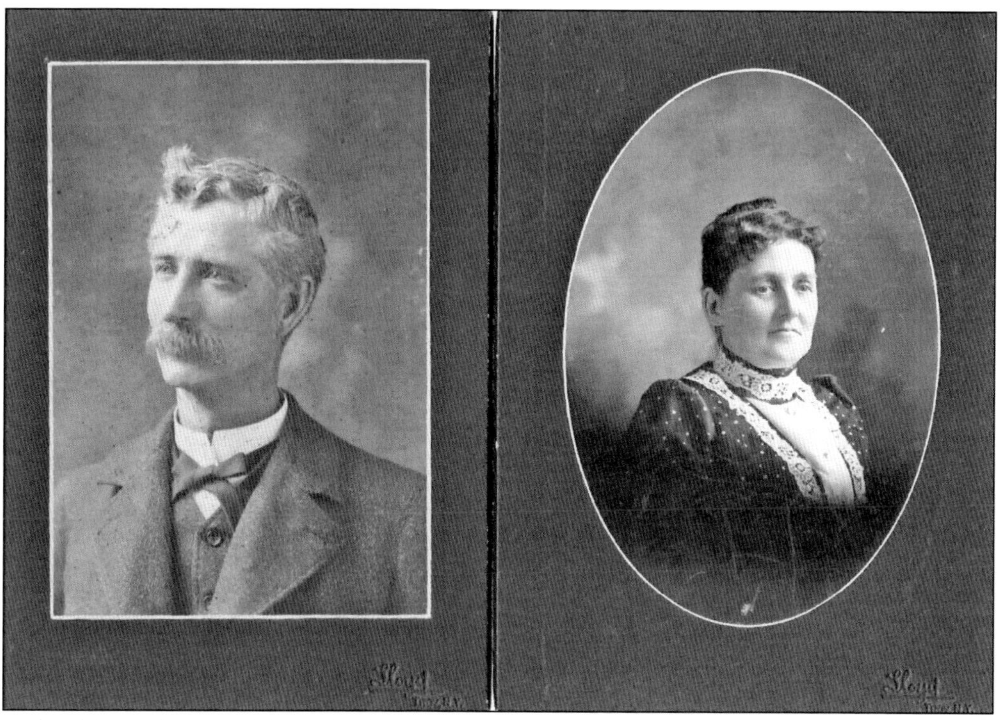

Richard K. Anderson and Sarah Hill wed on June 8, 1882, at home on 68 Second Street. Anderson was a member of the board of education from 1887 to 1889 and was instrumental in rebuilding the Presbyterian church after the 1913 flood. Sarah Anderson was educated at the Old Hudsondale Institute in Lansingburgh and then taught there for many years. She was very active in the Presbyterian church's missionary circles. (Courtesy of Helen Grochmal Anderson.)

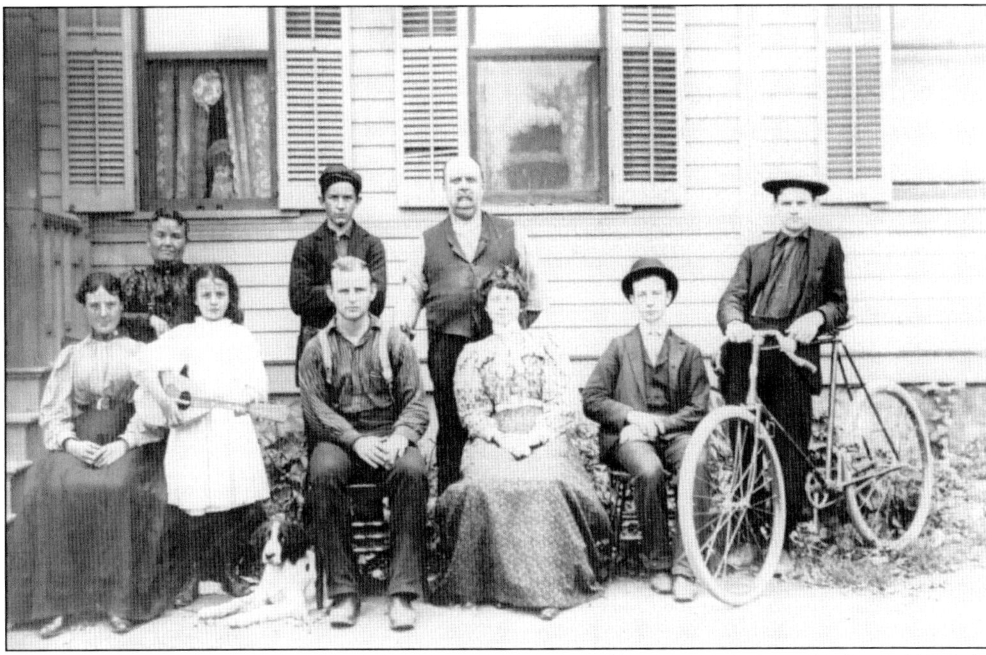

The Currier family is gathered at their residence at 14 Fifth Street in Waterford in 1890. Like many families, they migrated from Canada to Waterford to take advantage of the employment opportunities that the canal offered. Standing third from left is the patriarch of the family, William Currier. Note the doll in the window. It almost appears as if she is posing with the rest of family. (Courtesy of Daniel P. Currier and Edward Wilson.)

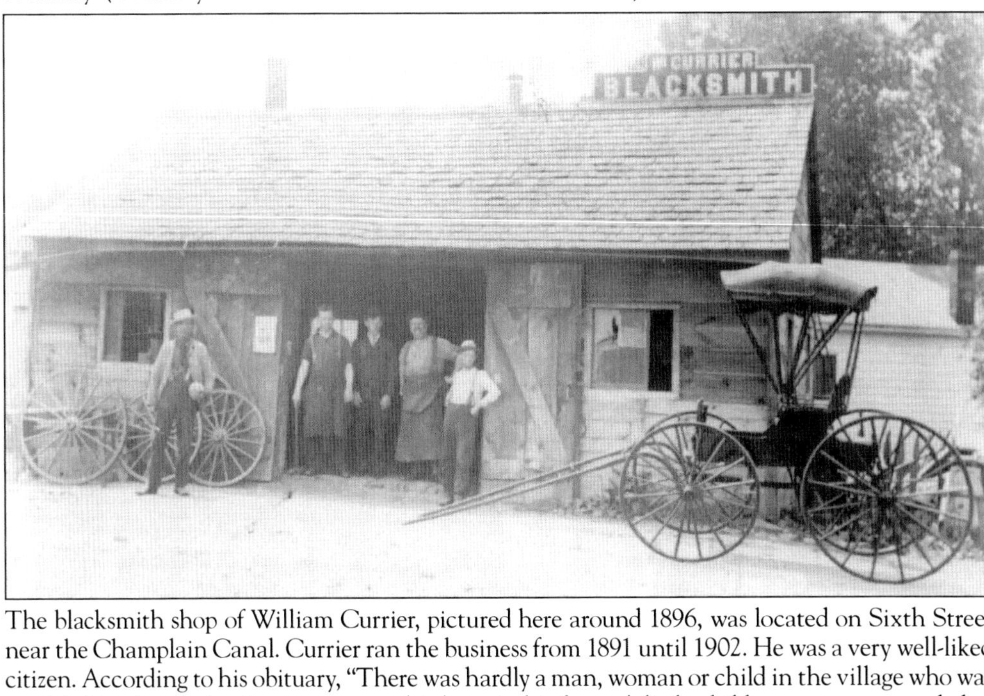

The blacksmith shop of William Currier, pictured here around 1896, was located on Sixth Street near the Champlain Canal. Currier ran the business from 1891 until 1902. He was a very well-liked citizen. According to his obituary, "There was hardly a man, woman or child in the village who was not his friend and who does not mourn his loss. At his funeral, little children came unattended to take a last look at his kindly face." (Courtesy of Daniel P. Currier and Edward Wilson.)

Pictured here is a stable and horseshoeing operation, next to the Kavanaugh Hook & Ladder Fire Company. The name L.B. Carleton is inscribed on the hanging horseshoe, and the name C.H. Kavanaugh is on the archway over the door of the fire company. Note the standard-bred harness horse in a racing sulky outside the stable. Horse racing was so popular it became necessary to write local laws prohibiting it on the village streets. (Courtesy of Charles Girard.)

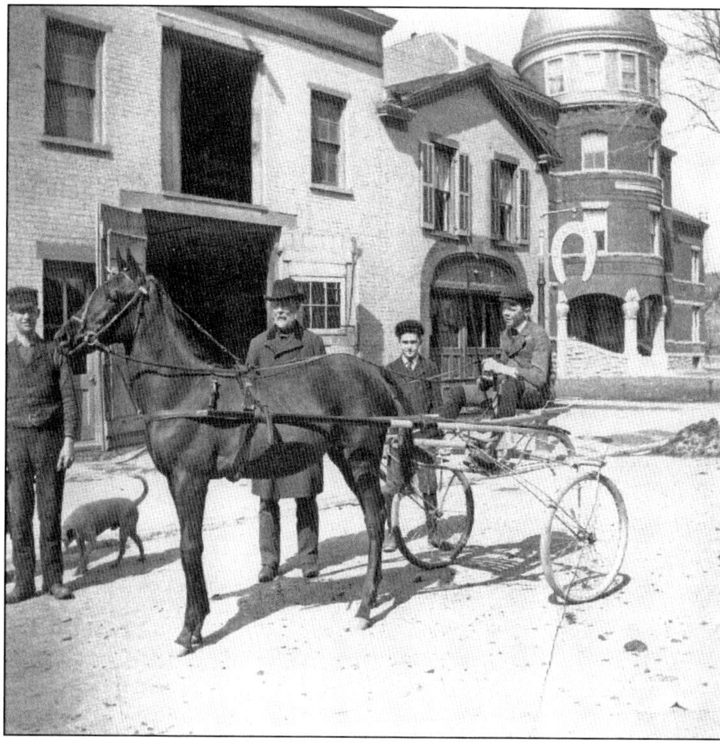

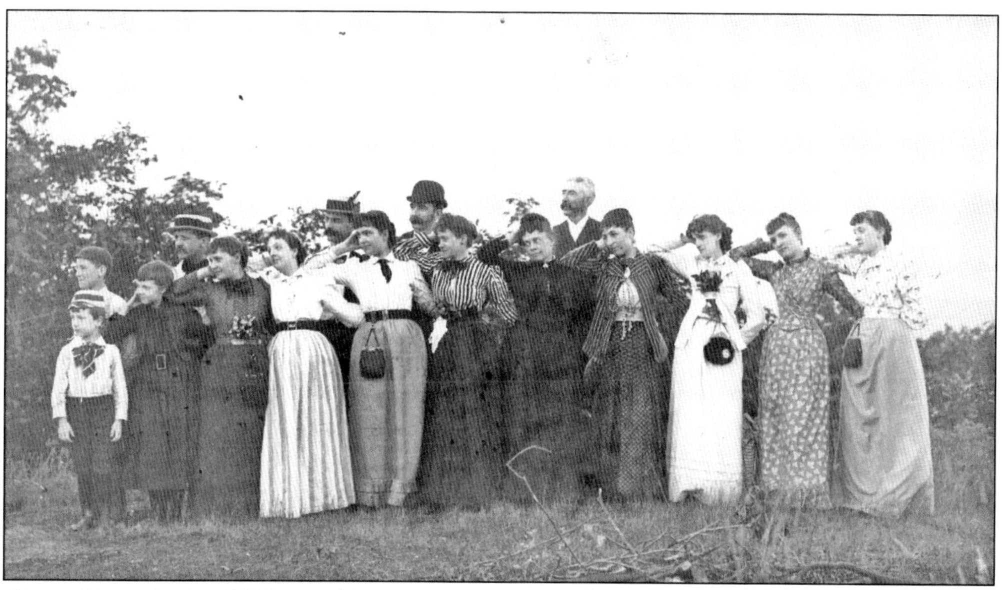

Pictured here in the 1890s are (first row, in no particular order) George Bell Jr., Mrs. Arthur Johnson, Abbie Relyea, Louise Button, Mary Scofield, Mrs. Frank Bell, Mrs. Professor Thompson, Eva Stone, Anna Page Foxwell, and two unidentified; (second row, from left to right) Bert Platt, Professor Thompson, Charles Button, Arthur Johnson, and J.C. Platt. Note the women carry purses from a belt on the waist. (Courtesy of WHMCC.)

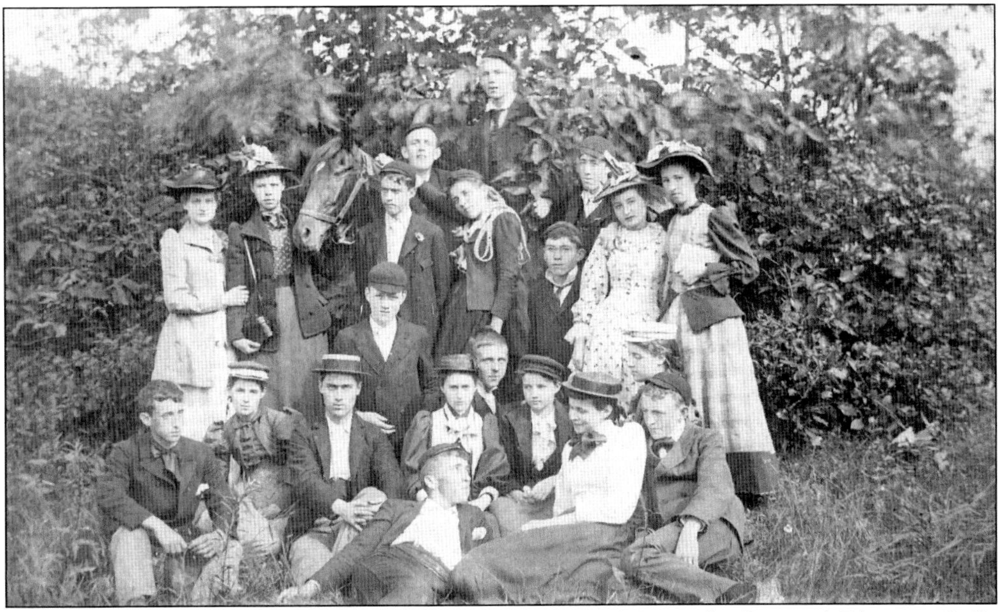

Pictured here celebrating the Fourth of July in 1892 are, from left to right (first row) Ed Young, Bella Kelly, Richard Kelly, Will Palmer, Sara Gibson, and Rob Dickson; (second row) Will Laughlin, Lillian Young, Charlie Knudson, Grace Sutherland, and Mary Kelly; (third row) Margaret ?, Edith Blake, Ed Laughlin, Grace Laughlin, Harry Tracy, Helen Smith, and Sara Chase; (fourth row) Kyle Laughlin, Fred Waldron, and L.G. Gleason. (Courtesy of WHMCC.)

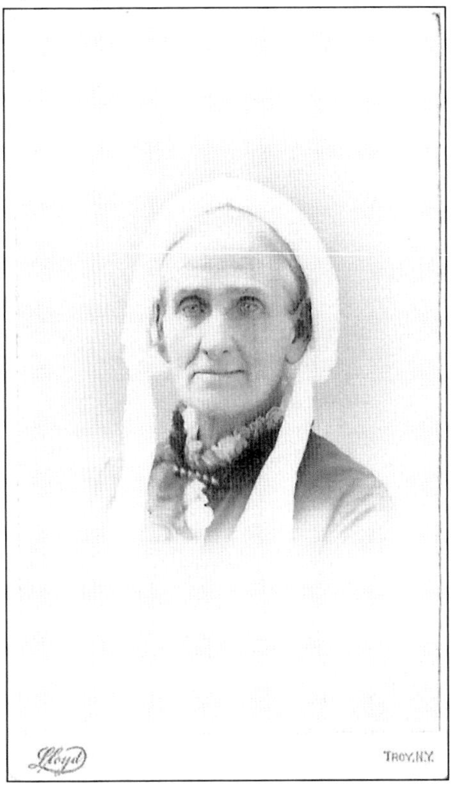

Arabella Anderson (pictured here) and her husband, James, came to Waterford from Belfast, Ireland, in 1848 to settle on a farm west of town. Their children were Richard K. (dairyman), Mary (Anderson) Kelly (storeowner), and Arabella Noyes and Sarah Jean Brown (missionaries). Arabella Anderson is the grandmother of James G. and Molly Anderson Haley and great-grandmother of Richard F. All four generations of Anderson men owned and operated Waterford dairies. (Courtesy of Helen Grochmal Anderson.)

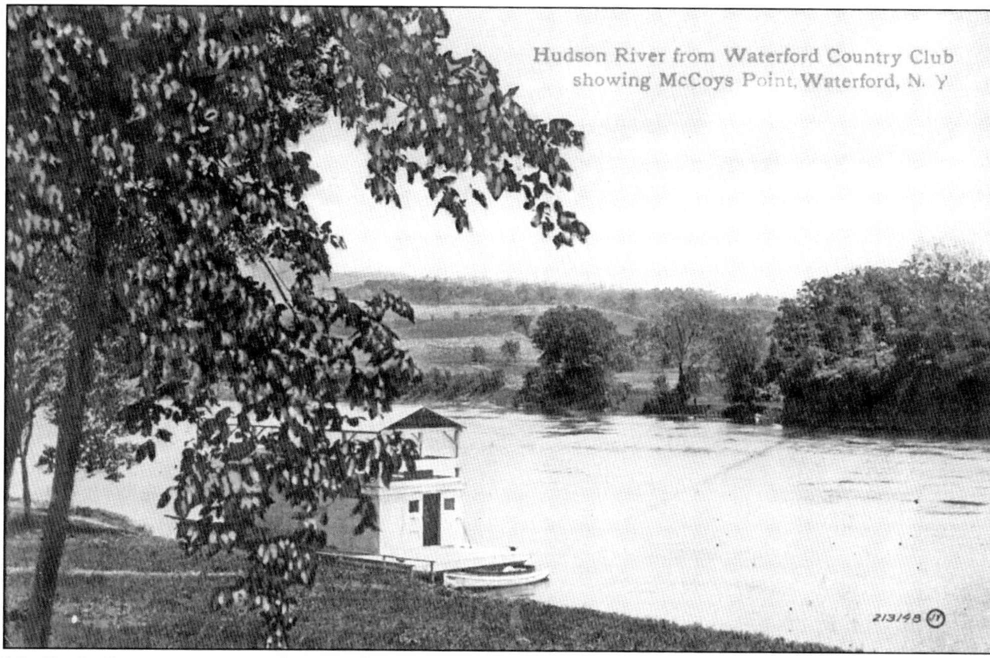

McCoy's Point was one of many locations along the Hudson River between Waterford and Mechanicville. There were many points and groves that usually were named after the land owner along that stretch of the river. Across the Hudson, the rolling hills of Rensselaer County can be seen. Route 32 and the Delaware & Hudson (D&H) Railroad tracks ran parallel to the river to the west. (Courtesy of Patricia Wilcox.)

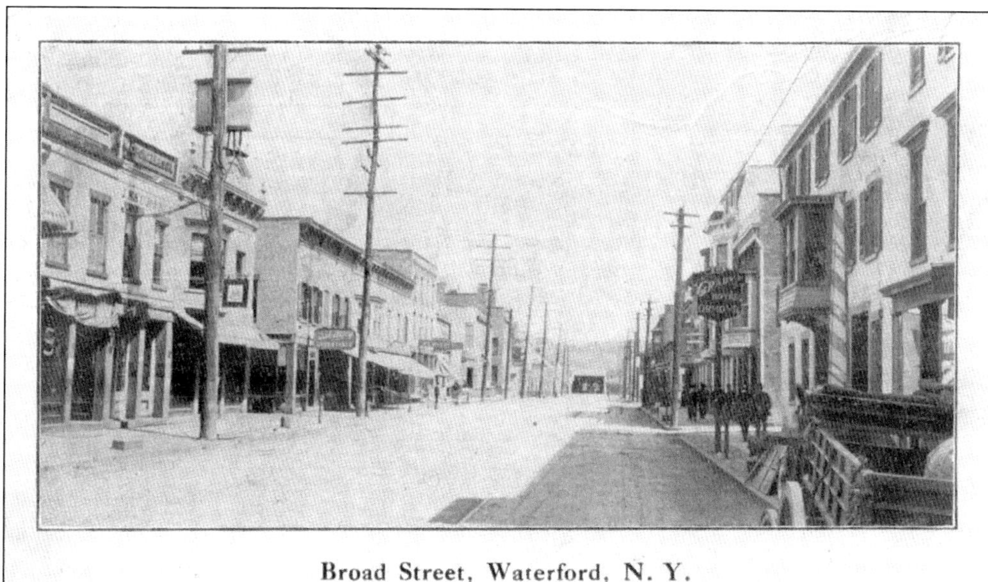

Broad Street was the main thoroughfare through the center of the village. It runs from the Union Bridge at the east end to the Ninth Street Bridge, where it turns into Ninth Street and then into Saratoga Avenue. The major businesses in the village lined both sides of this thoroughfare. Trolleys and cars provided transportation of the day, and pedestrians hustled along Broad Street to shop and purchase their daily needs. (Courtesy of Mike Marchese.)

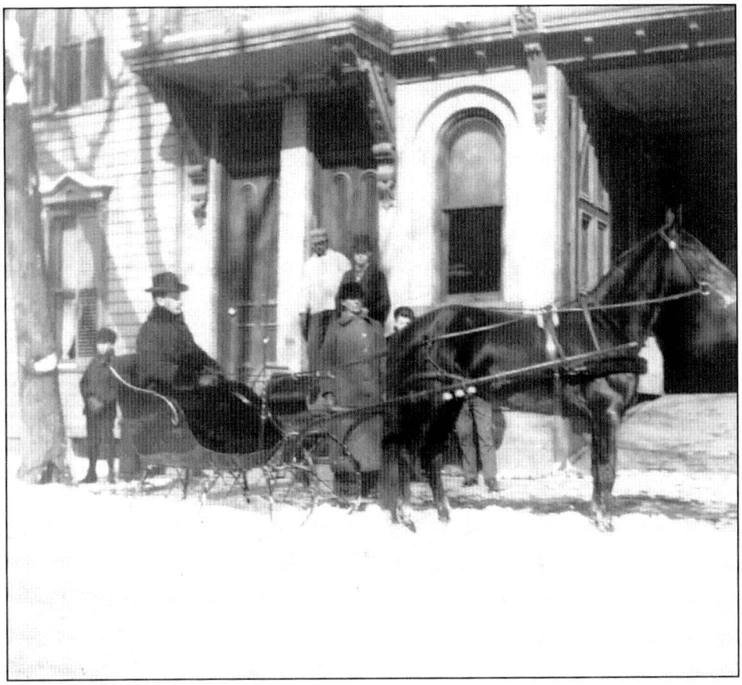

In the sleigh is Frederick William Kavanaugh, founder of the Kavanaugh Knitting Company. He was also town supervisor in 1903, sheriff of Saratoga County from 1904 to 1906, and a state senator from 1921 to 1924. Kavanaugh always had an interest in politics. He was quoted saying to his friends, "There is nothing substantial in politics for me, but I like the game. And I intend to play it as long as I live." (Courtesy of WHMCC.)

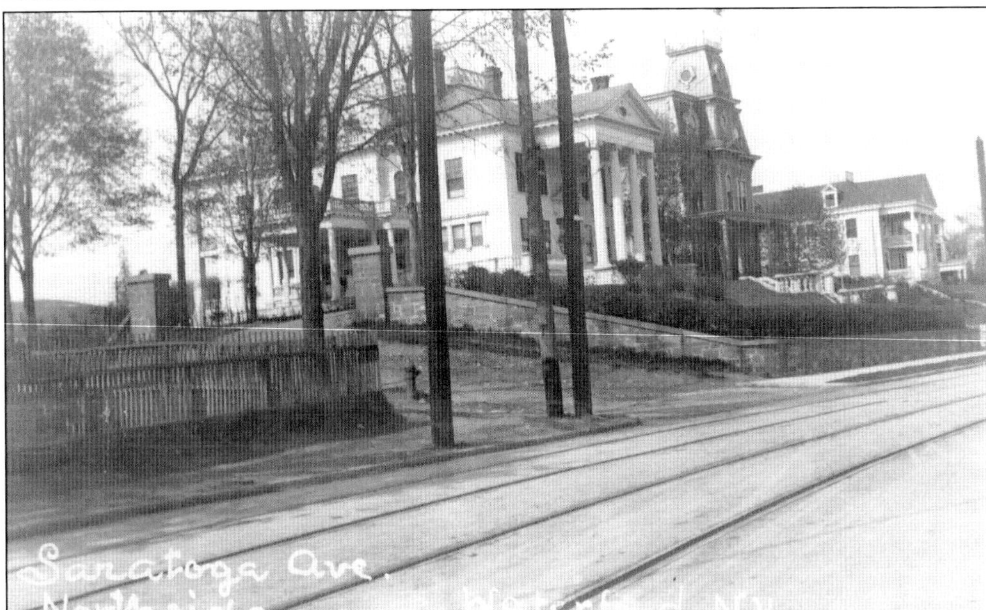

In the late 1800s and early 1900s, Waterford and Cohoes flourished, with many mills and factories. Pictured here is a prime example of a mansion along Saratoga Avenue. Prosperous mill owners from Waterford and Cohoes made their homes on Saratoga Avenue, which ran through the Northside community. In 1912, this Federal Colonial mansion at 112 Saratoga Avenue was owned by mill owner Matthew Davidson, and it is one of the few mansions left. It has four fireplaces, crown molding, wood beams, several bedrooms, and pocket doors. The trolley tracks also made it convenient for the homeowners, carrying passengers from Cohoes, through Waterford, to North Troy (Lansingburgh). (Courtesy of Frank McClement.)

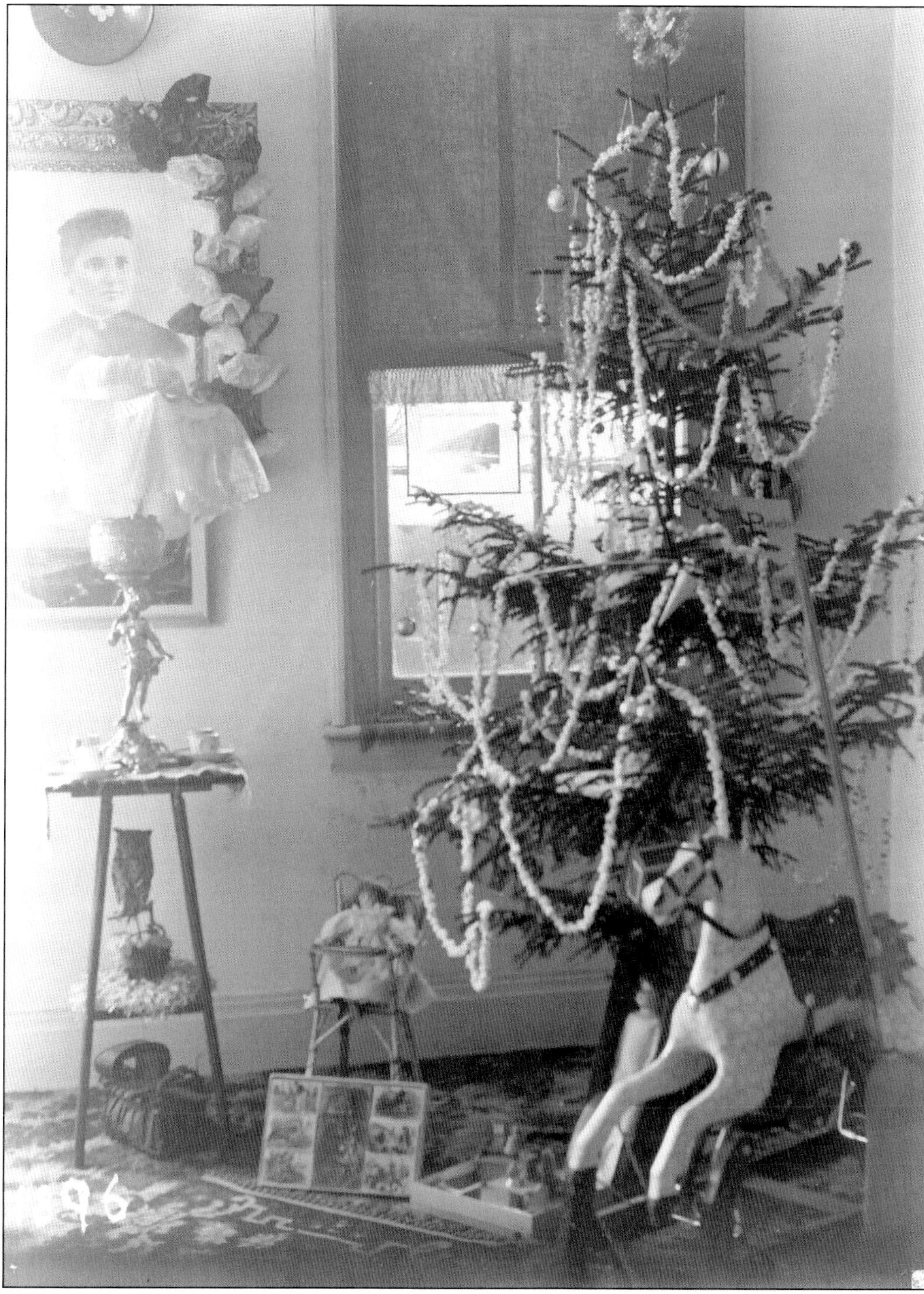

Pictured here is Christmas morning 1896. A lot of information can be gathered from this photograph. There may be three children in this family. Santa Claus appears to have left a rocking horse for a young boy, a doll in a highchair for a young girl, and an infant basket under the table. There is an absence of any type of lighting on the tree. What is the broom for—a gift for mom, or to sweep up the pine needles? (Courtesy of WHMCC.)

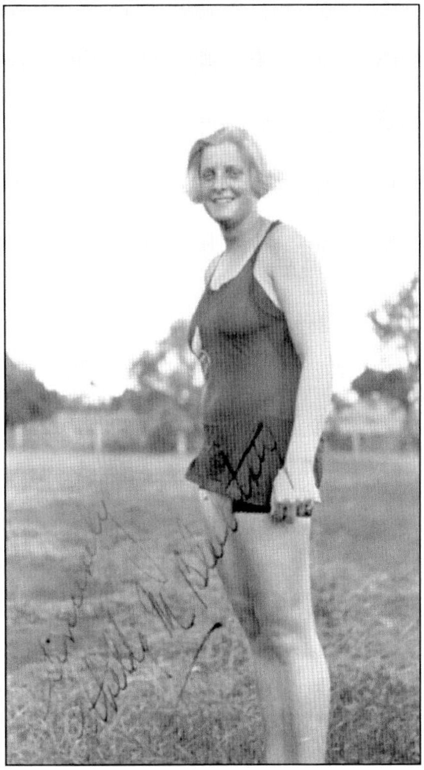

Pictured here is Ethelda Marguerite Bleibtrey (1902–1978). Born in Waterford, Bleibtrey began swimming to overcome the effects of polio. Competing in the 1920 Olympics, she was the first female to ever win three gold medals in all women's swimming events; the events included the 100-meter, 300-meter, and 4-by-100 freestyle race. Bleibtrey was never defeated during her amateur career. (Courtesy of J. Bert Mahoney.)

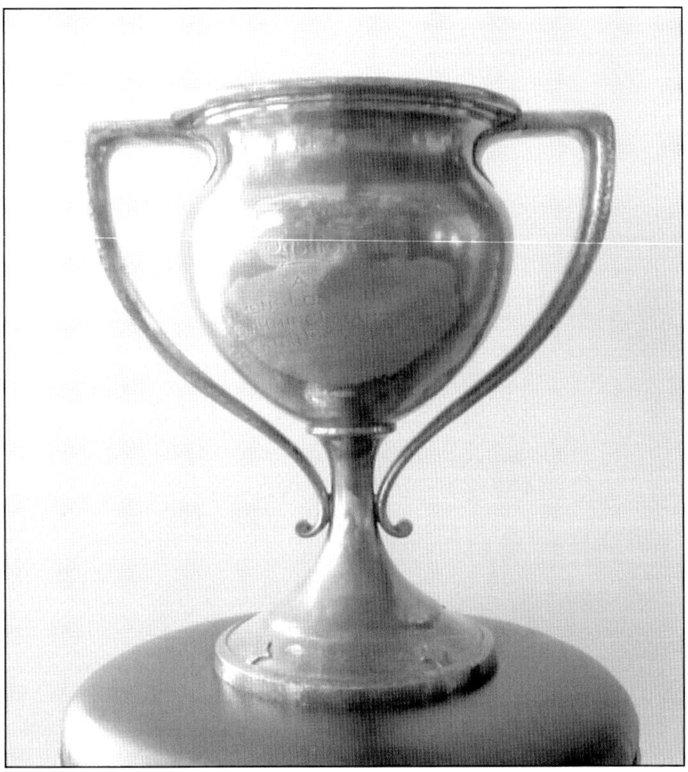

Ethelda Bleibtrey dominated women's swimming between 1920 and 1922; she won every national championship from 50 yards to one mile, held world records in freestyle and backstroke, and turned professional in 1922 after an undefeated amateur career. This is one of many trophies won throughout her career. It reads, "Presented by Fashionette -A-A-U- Womens Long Distance-Swimming Championship-Brighton Beach Baths-August 29, 1921." (Courtesy of J. Bert Mahoney.)

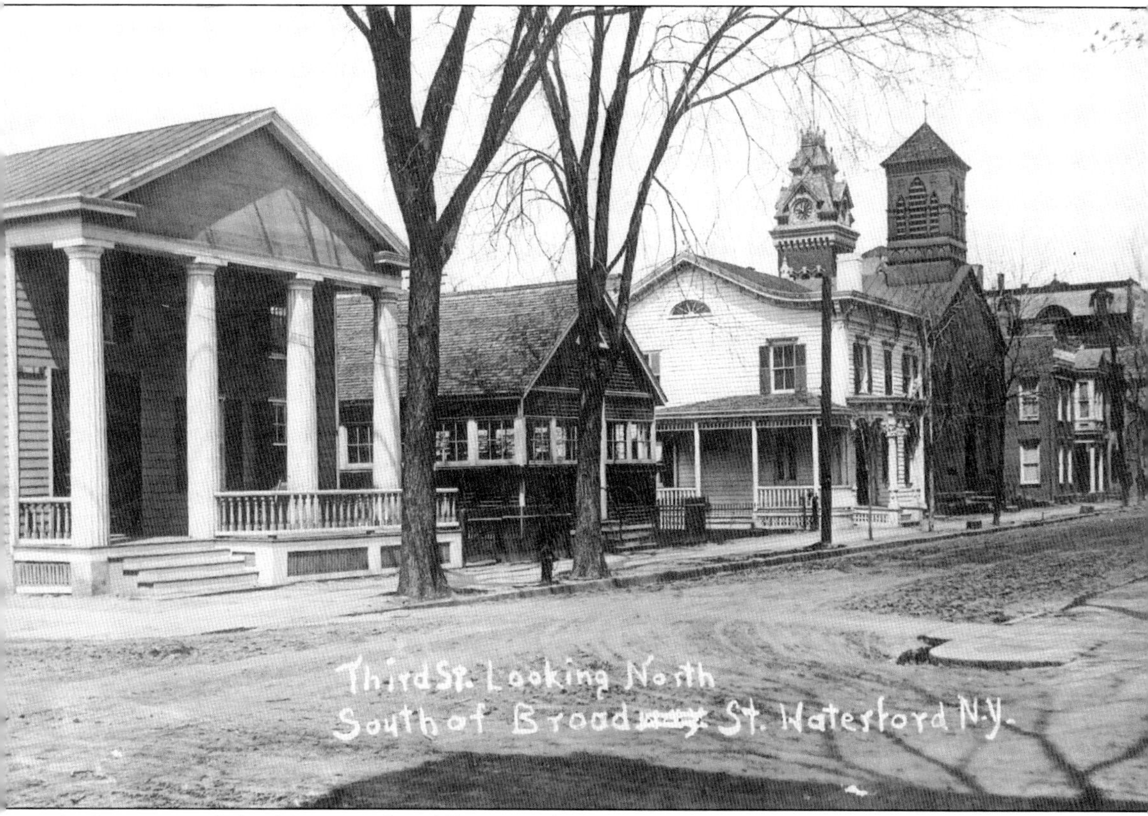

At the corner of Third Street and Middle Street, looking north, is a typical scene of the residences of the village during the 1890s. Streets had yet to be paved, houses were mostly made of wood or brick, and sidewalks were still dirt or constructed with pieces of slate. The fourth building is the Episcopal church and can be seen with its bell tower. The town hall can also be seen in the background. Third Street, north of Broad Street, had become the major route to Mechanicville and points north by this time, following the western shore of the Hudson River. This photograph is unique in the fact that the great fire of 1841 started behind the Episcopal church, destroying the surrounding dwellings, including the town hall. (Courtesy of Fran Santspree Cullett.)

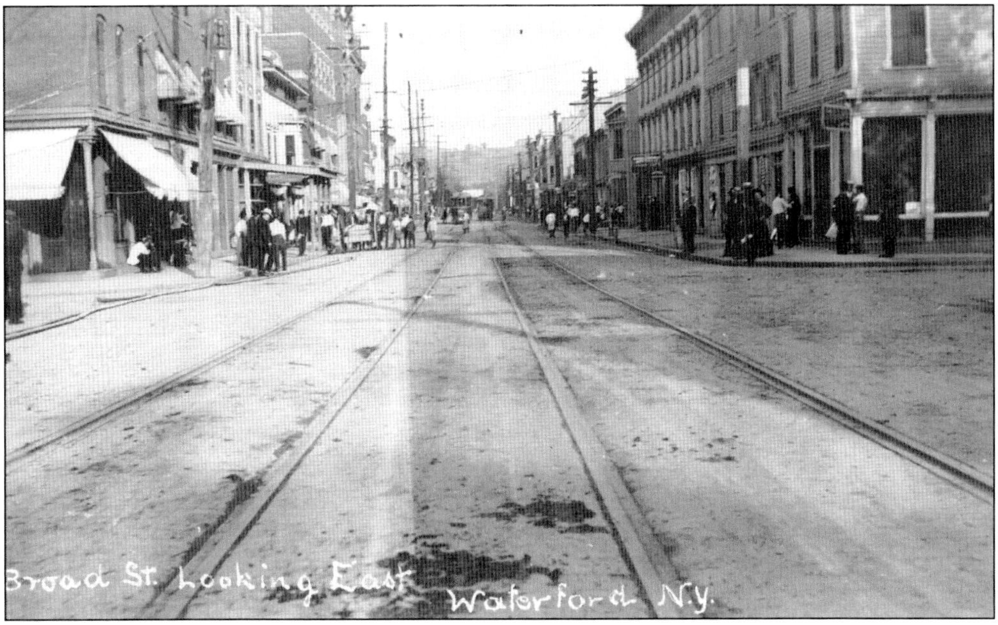

This is Broad Street at Fourth Street, looking east. The Union Bridge can be seen spanning the Hudson River. The trolley tracks were used into the 1930s. Note the number of people on the streets; Waterford village offered a variety of stores, banks, and restaurants. In addition to the residents of Waterford who frequented all the establishments were the canallers, who would leave their boats to gather supplies, food, and drink. (Courtesy of Merle Doud.)

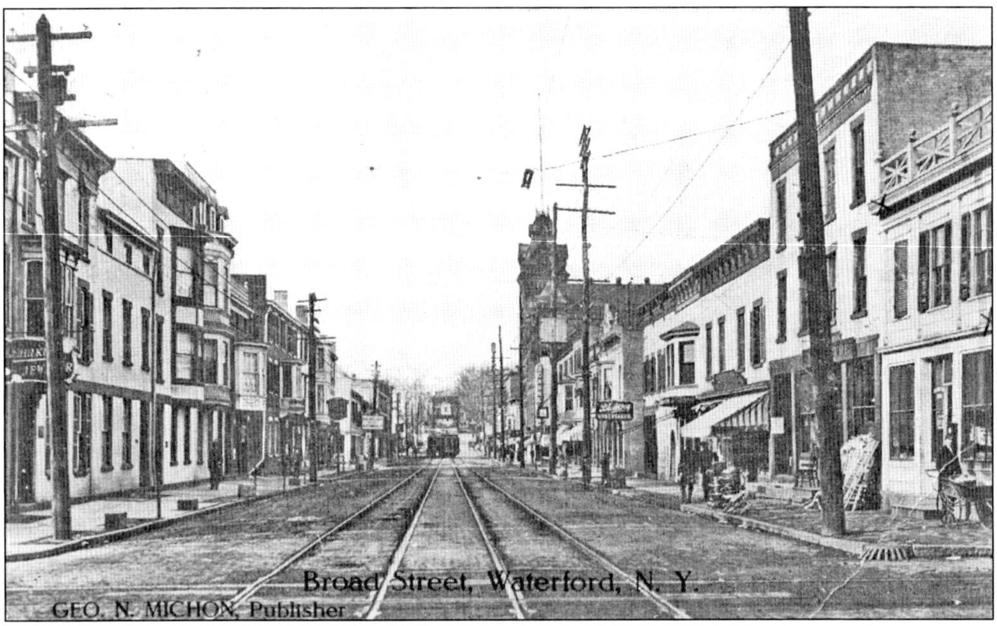

This photograph taken in 1908 predates the 1914 town hall fire. The view is showing the corner of Broad and Second Streets, heading west. Two of the businesses pictured are Bleibtrey Undertaker and Scannell's Drug Store. Looking up Broad Street, one can see the lift bridge over the Champlain Canal, which appears to be in the down, or road, position. The dual trolley tracks demonstrate the use of public transportation. (Courtesy of Tracy Geel.)

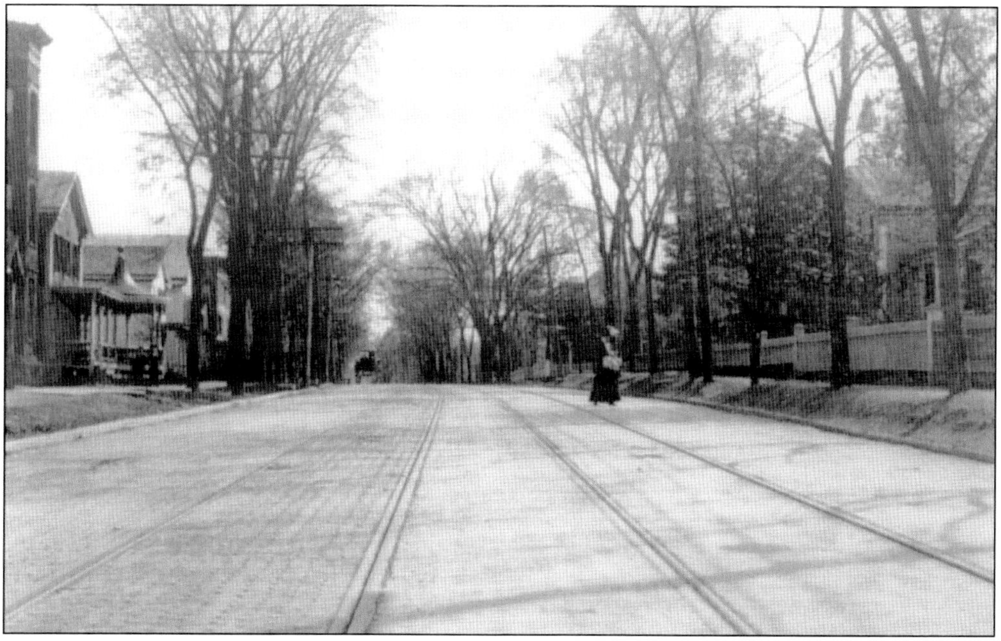

Looking south from Hill Street onto Saratoga Avenue, it is possible that the horse and buggy on the left was the Freihofer delivery team. Perhaps the woman crossing the street has just purchased some baked goods from the buggy. In 1913, delicious fresh-baked breads were distributed to the doorsteps of eager residents by means of transport—the horse and buggy. All of the homes visible in this photograph still stand today. (Courtesy of WHMCC.)

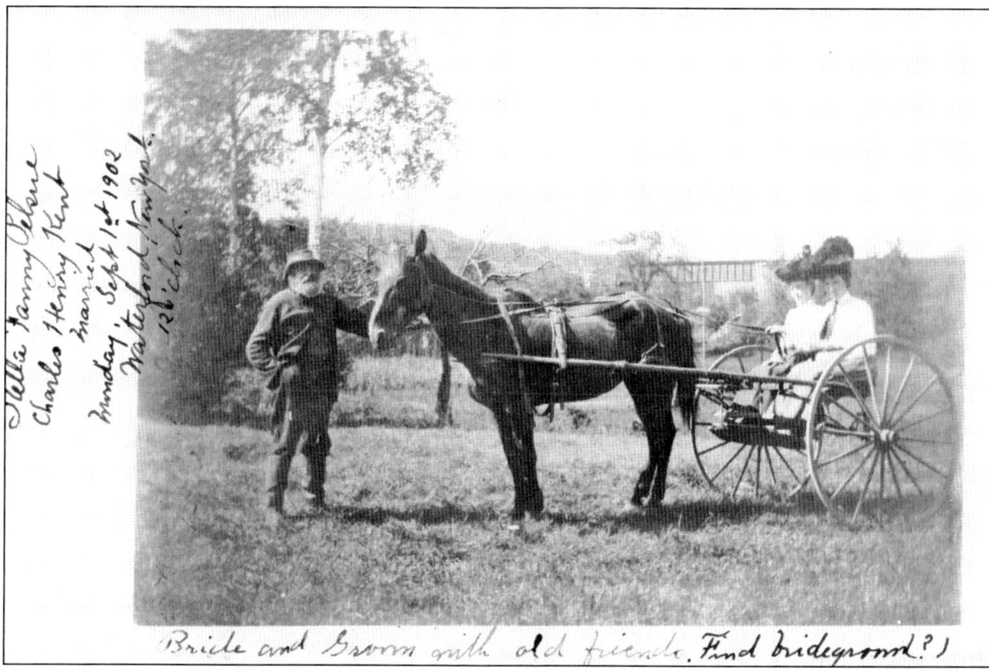

Pictured here in 1902 with an "old friend" are Stella Fanny Pelsue and Charles Henry Kent, who were married on September 1 of that year. The back of the card reads, "Tom I didn't take your old scrapbook, say I did and we will scrap."

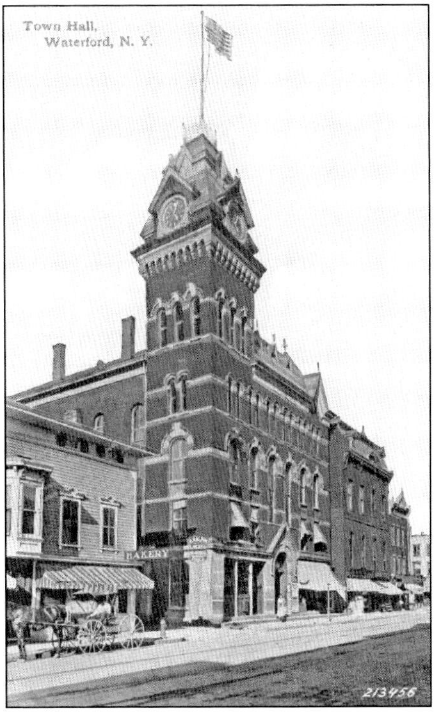

Pictured here is the second town hall. It was built in 1873 and destroyed by fire in January 1914. This image was taken from a postcard dated 1903. The first town hall was destroyed by fire in 1841, and between the two fires, all of the official records and items of historical interest were lost. The bell tower from this building serves the present town hall. (Courtesy of Alan LaBrecque.)

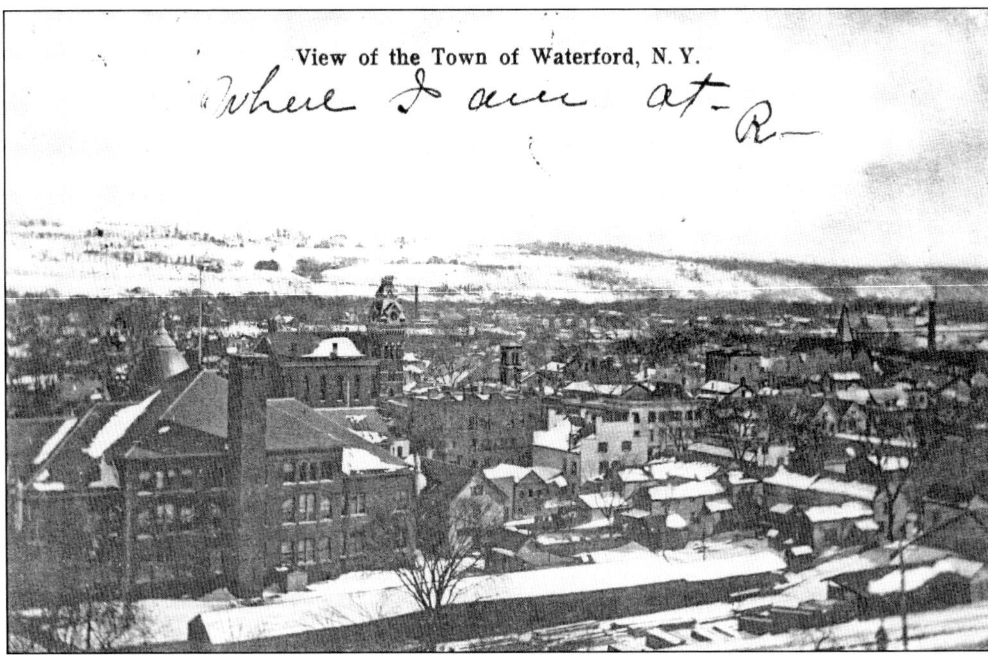

This is a different view of the town hall, taken in 1906. The same view can be seen today by standing on the towpath of the old canal, stopping at the Division Street Bridge, and turning toward Pleasantdale. Gone is the old school, the largest building seen here. The school was replaced by the building of the Waterford Rescue Squad, which occupies that location today. The town hall can be easily spotted and was the second one in use before the fire of 1914. (Courtesy of Fran Santspree Cullett.)

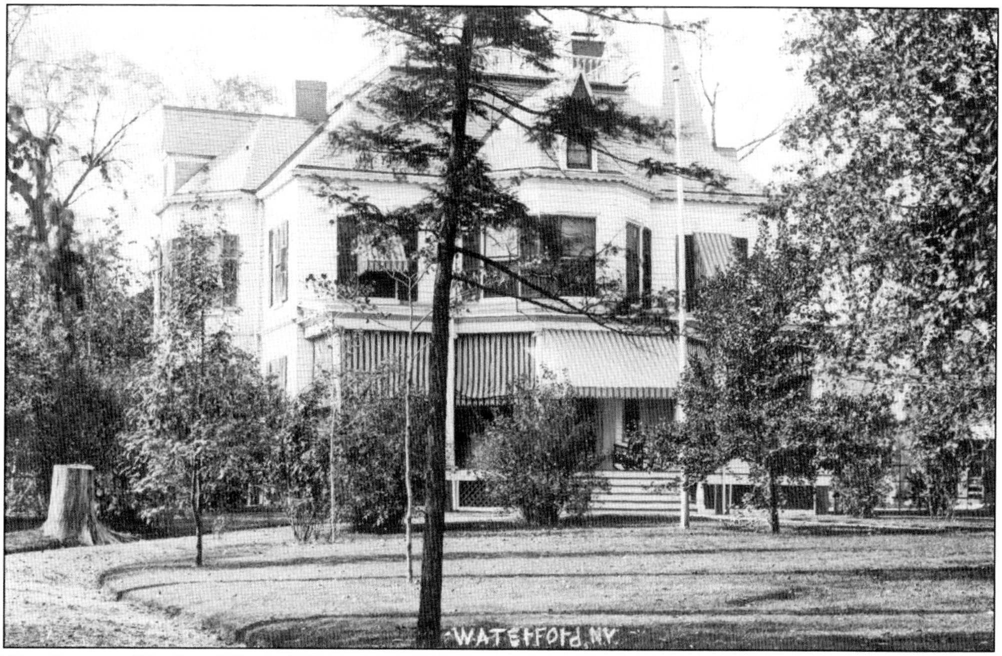

The home of Richard David Davis is another example of the elegance many Waterford residents were able to enjoy. Davis graduated from Yale, became a lawyer, and was elected as a Democrat to the 27th and 28th Congress. He served as chairman of the Committee on Revolutionary Claims. Afterward, he withdrew from political and professional life. He engaged in agricultural pursuits in Waterford until his death.

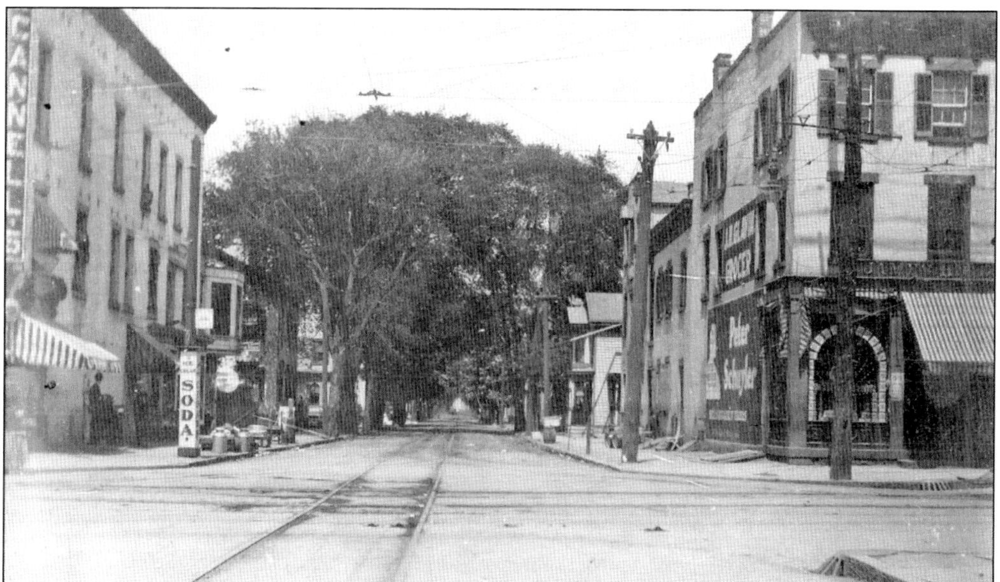

This view of the intersection of Broad Street and Third Street, looking north, is from about 1910. J.H. Glavin's Grocery store is on the northeast corner, advertising Peter Schuyler beef sausage. Scannell's Drug Store is on the northwest corner, advertising ice cream, soda, and cigars. Over the years, the terminology has been changed to pharmacy, so as not to be associated with the term "drug." (Courtesy of Merle Doud.)

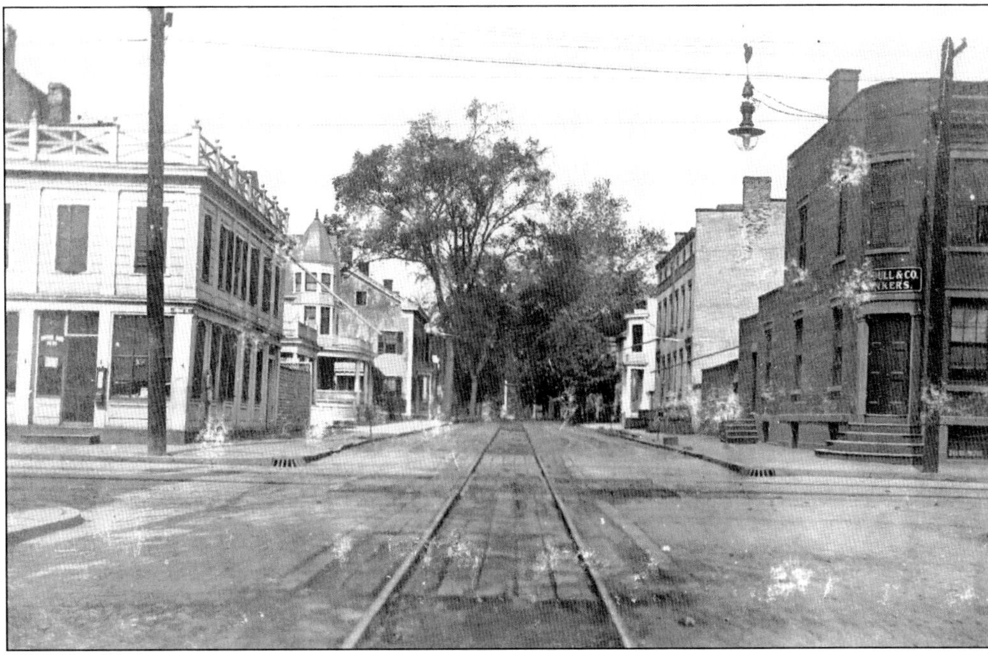

This is the corner of Broad Street and Second Street looking north. Pictured here sometime before 1909 is the S.C. Bull and Co. Bank on the northeast corner of the intersection. The white building in the background on the right is the current location of the Glavin and Glavin law office. In the early history of Waterford, Second Street was part of the main route from Albany to Saratoga and points north.

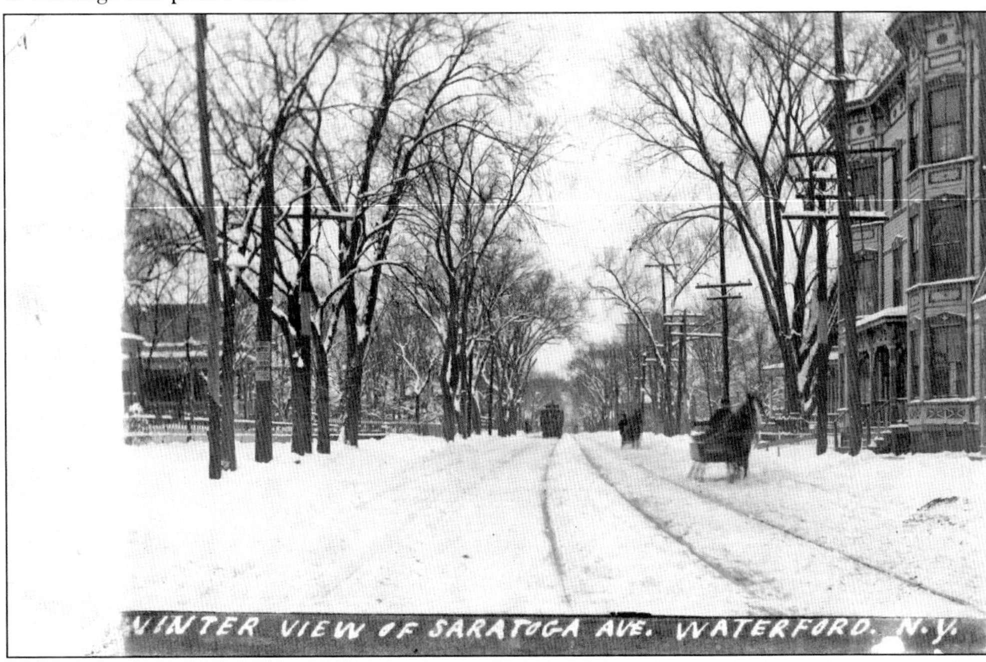

Pictured here around 1910 is Saratoga Avenue, boasting horse-drawn sleighs and new a mode of transportation, a trolley. Saratoga Avenue was once referred to as Mill Owner's Row, and the residents, usually well-to-do, were from both Cohoes and Waterford. (Courtesy of Michael D. Marchese.)

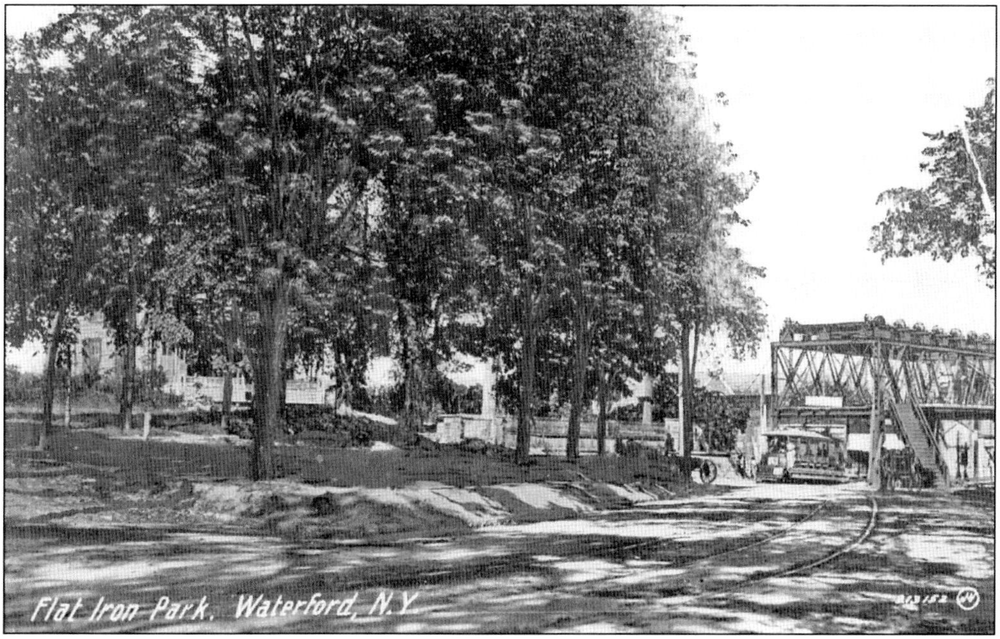

Flat Iron Park is a free-standing, formerly tree-lined park enclosed with a well, pump, and shrubbery. As Waterford grew, the well, which was located on Grogh Street, had to be closed because it was being run over as the trolley came through Waterford. In 1910, the state supreme court gave the park to the Village of Waterford. Its flatiron shape is smaller today, but it is still maintained by the village.

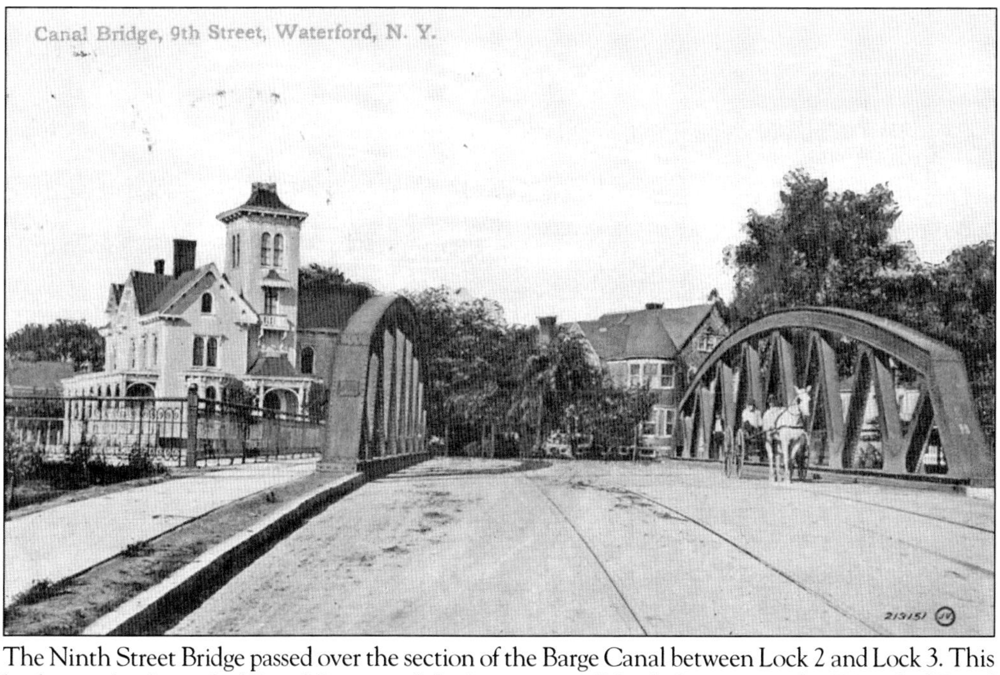

The Ninth Street Bridge passed over the section of the Barge Canal between Lock 2 and Lock 3. This bridge marks the end of Broad Street and the beginning of Ninth Street near the Waterford Rural Cemetery. The area of the bridge and the land that became the Barge Canal, the state maintenance shops, and the dry dock was once the Reverend Stephen Bush Farm. (Courtesy of Bill Paquette.)

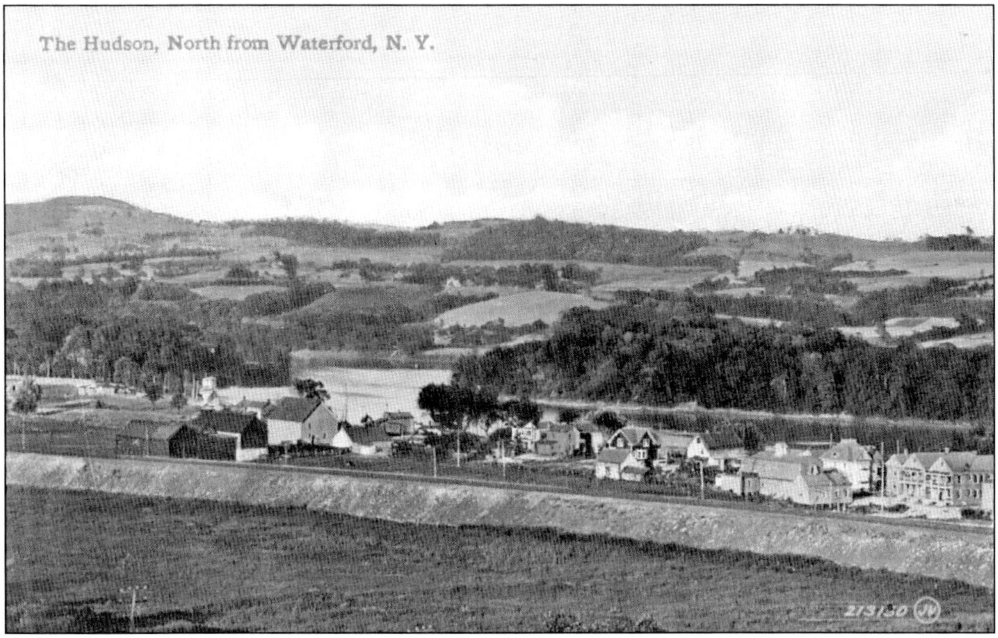

This bucolic view of the winding Hudson River and farmlands to the east could represent many views along this stretch of the river and road between Waterford and Mechanicville. The river was like a magnet to those who settled in the area, and the fertile farmland was ripe for the rural way of life that dominated this area in the 19th and early 20th centuries (Courtesy of Bill Paquette.)

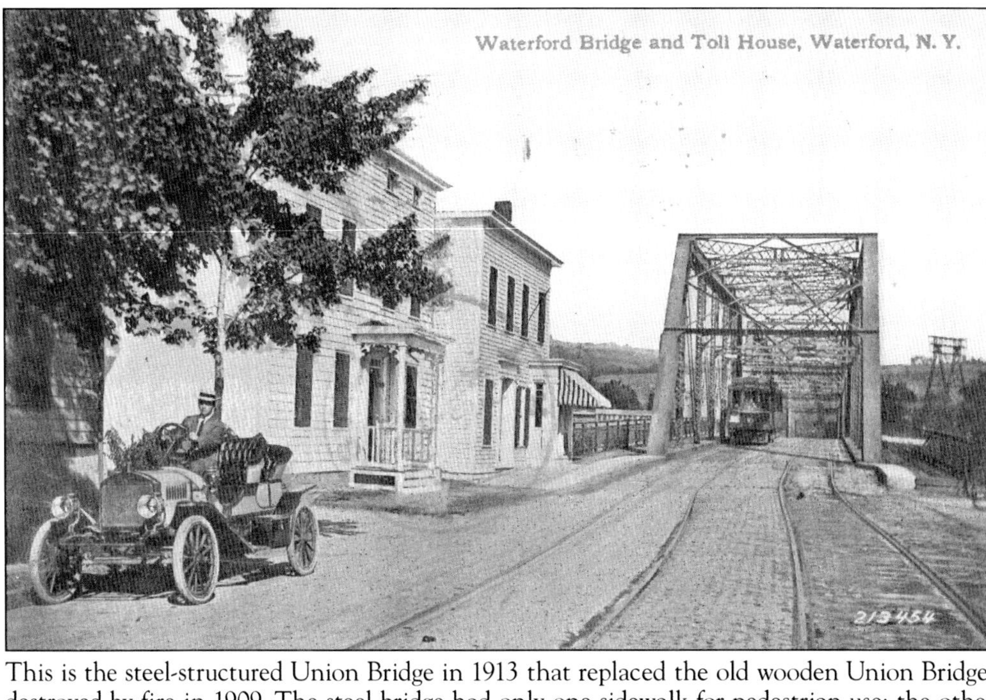

This is the steel-structured Union Bridge in 1913 that replaced the old wooden Union Bridge, destroyed by fire in 1909. The steel bridge had only one sidewalk for pedestrian use; the other was added later. The last building seen is the toll house. The village park is now on the site of the residential dwellings. The steel bridge is still in use today. (Courtesy of Fran Santspree Cullett.)

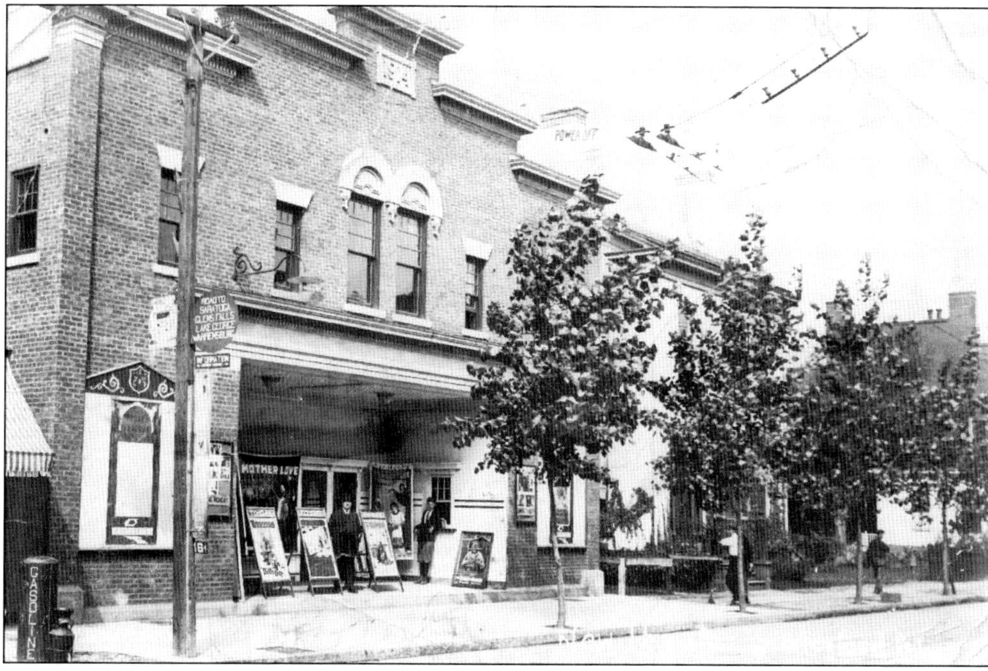

Pictured here is the Casino Theatre on Third Street. Built in 1914, the theater was open seven days a week showing a double feature and shorts. In later years, it became the Lyric Theatre. The manager's name was Charles S. Combs, and by the 1950s, it became known to the younger generation simply as Charlie's.

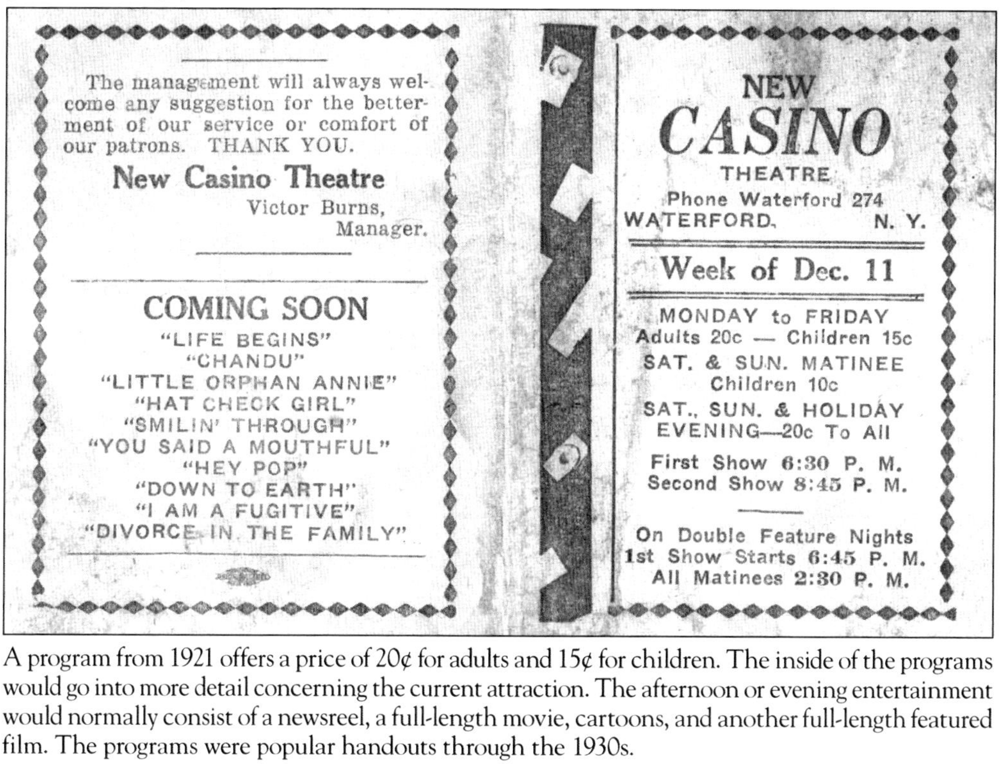

The management will always welcome any suggestion for the betterment of our service or comfort of our patrons. THANK YOU.

New Casino Theatre
Victor Burns,
Manager.

COMING SOON
"LIFE BEGINS"
"CHANDU"
"LITTLE ORPHAN ANNIE"
"HAT CHECK GIRL"
"SMILIN' THROUGH"
"YOU SAID A MOUTHFUL"
"HEY POP"
"DOWN TO EARTH"
"I AM A FUGITIVE"
"DIVORCE IN THE FAMILY"

NEW
CASINO
THEATRE
Phone Waterford 274
WATERFORD, N. Y.

Week of Dec. 11

MONDAY to FRIDAY
Adults 20c — Children 15c
SAT. & SUN. MATINEE
Children 10c
SAT., SUN. & HOLIDAY
EVENING—20c To All
First Show 6:30 P. M.
Second Show 8:45 P. M.

On Double Feature Nights
1st Show Starts 6:45 P. M.
All Matinees 2:30 P. M.

A program from 1921 offers a price of 20¢ for adults and 15¢ for children. The inside of the programs would go into more detail concerning the current attraction. The afternoon or evening entertainment would normally consist of a newsreel, a full-length movie, cartoons, and another full-length featured film. The programs were popular handouts through the 1930s.

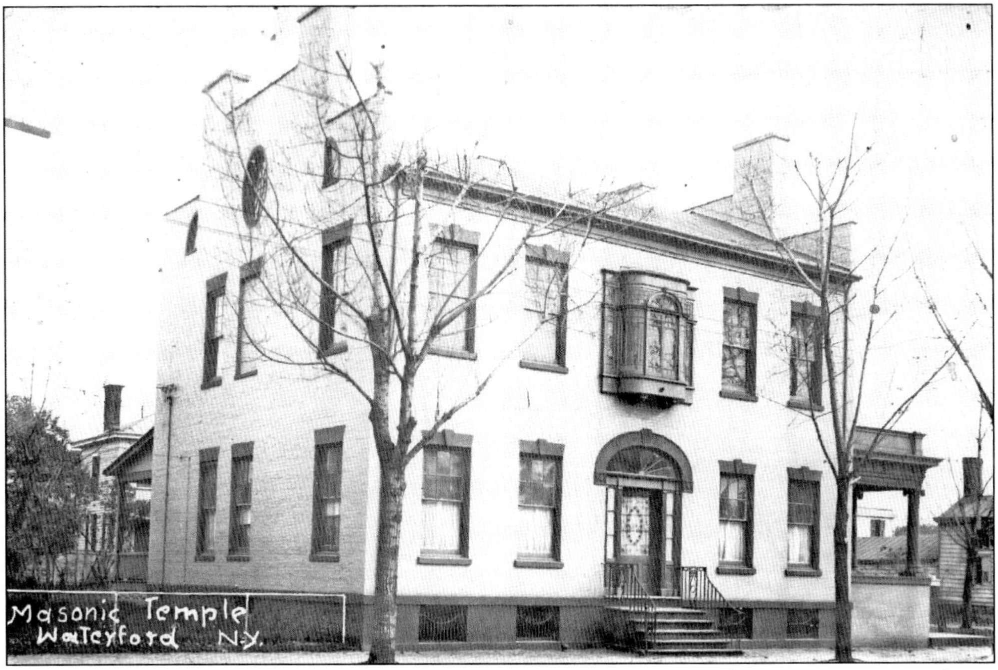

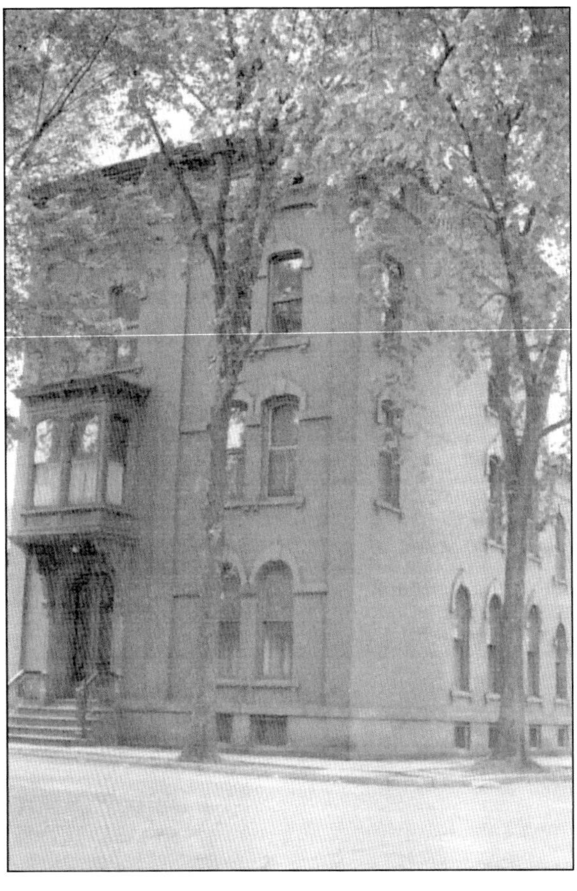

Clinton Lodge No. 140, Free and Accepted Masons, was instituted under dispensation on December 28, 1848, and its charter was granted on June 9, 1849. The first master was James M. Austin, a doctor of medicine. There were several locations during its history in Waterford—Waverly Hall, the Howard House, the first town hall, the Masonic hall built in 1876 by John Higgins, and finally the home of Gen. Samuel Stewart on Broad and First Streets in 1915. (Courtesy of Merle Doud.)

The Knights of Columbus Council No. 237 in Waterford formed in 1897, only 15 years after the national organization was started. The council, located on Third and Middle Streets, was one of the oldest in New York and consisted of 49 charter members at that time. Waterford's council was mostly Irish Catholics with some Franco American involvement. By virtue of the order's demographic, the first officers were of Irish decent. (Courtesy of Fran Santspree Cullett.)

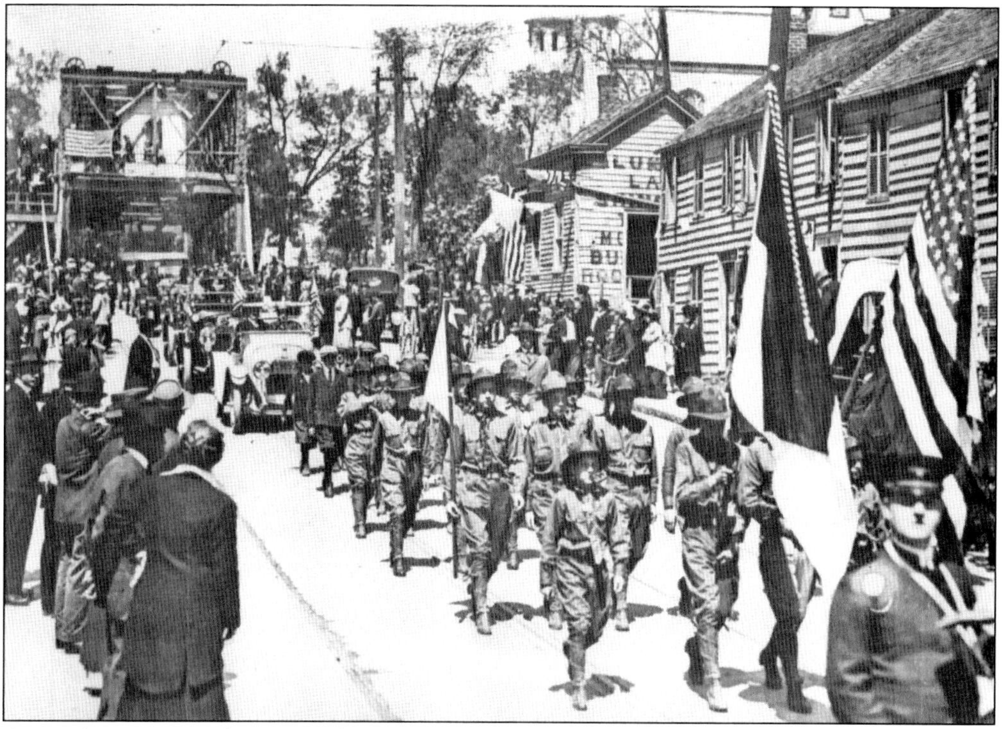

A parade is coming down Broad Street, escorting the gubernatorial party and Gov. Charles S. Whitman. The celebration pictured was the May 15, 1915, opening of the Barge Canal. Note the lift bridge over the old Champlain Canal, the bridge tender's house, and the stairway to permit pedestrians passage when the bridge was raised or open. Fitzsimons Lumber Company is shown on the right. (Courtesy of WHMCC.)

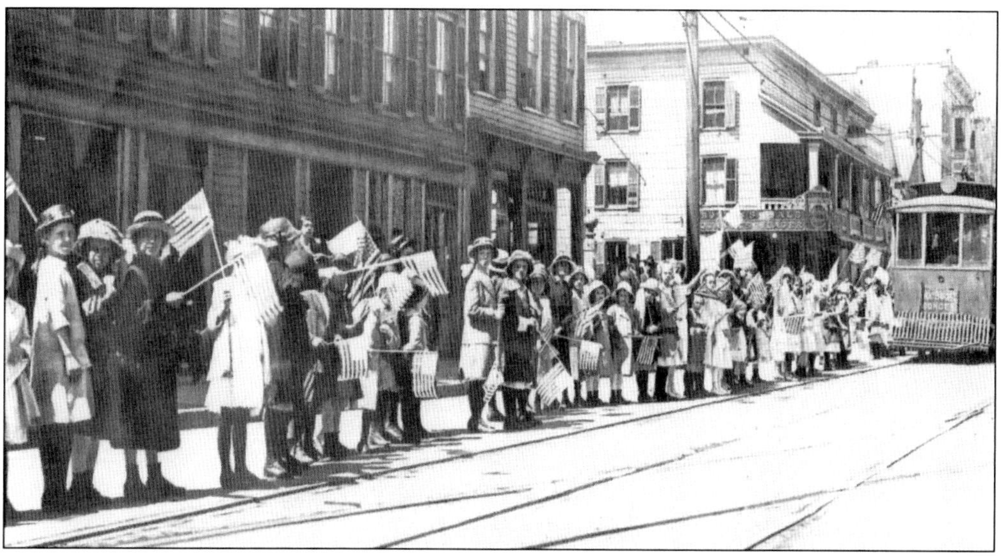

On May 15, 1915, spectators are waiting for the parade to pass by to celebrate the grand opening of the Barge Canal. The Clifton House is in the background at 90 Broad Street, and the market in the background is advertising Quandt's Beer & Ale. Also pictured is the Waterford Cohoes trolley. (Courtesy of Anna Marie Wilkes Lamos.)

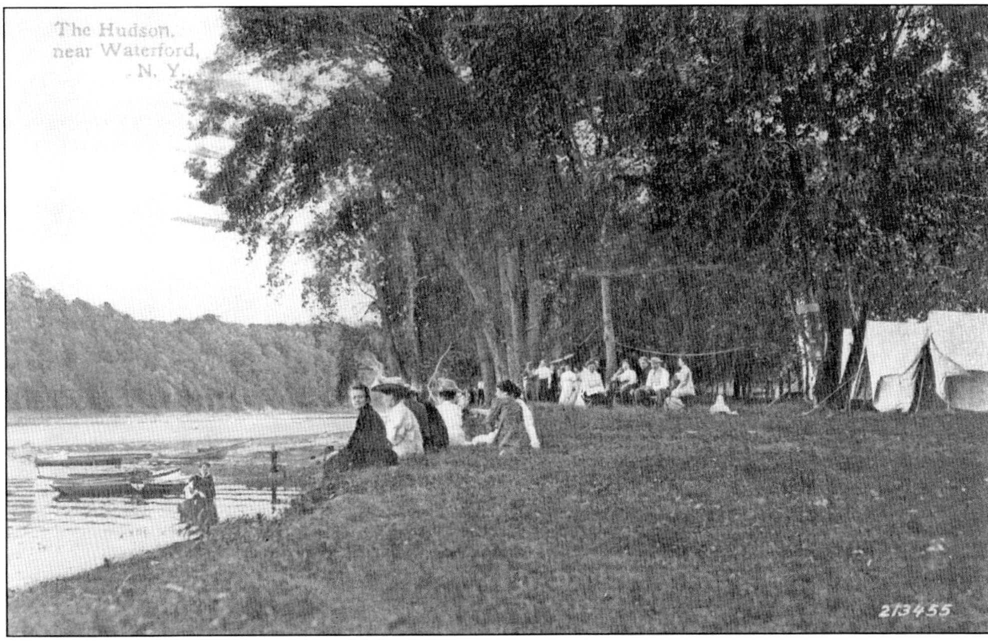

The confluence of the Mohawk and Hudson Rivers was a great place to hold church picnics, gatherings, and camp meetings. Peebles Island was a popular place to have these activities and partake in outdoor summer fun. In 1867, several organizations from Troy joined Waterford for a picnic at Peebles Island. The crowds were so great they required extra conveyances. Between 1850 and 1868, church camp meetings were also held at Fitzgerald's Grove. (Courtesy of Tracy Geel.)

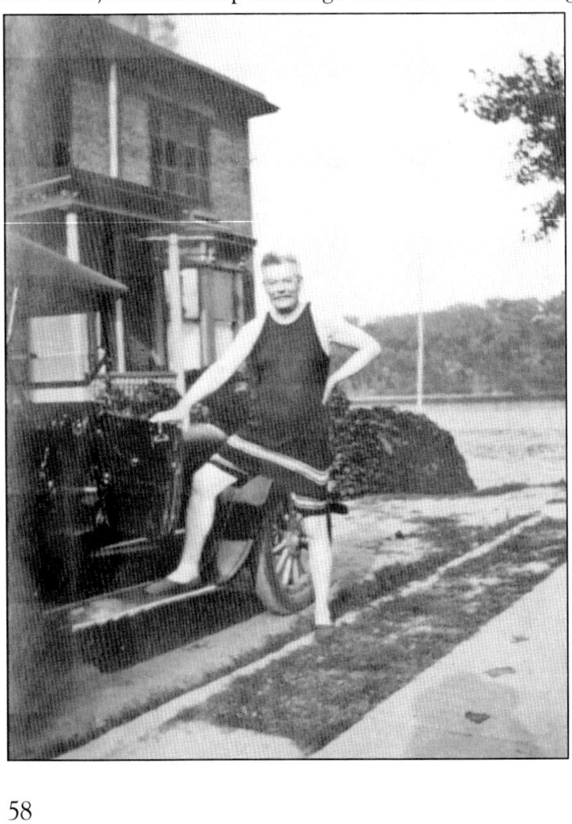

This is Charles Kavanaugh after a swim at Bliebtry's Beach on the Hudson River. He was president of the Kavanaugh Knitting Company, namesake of Kavanaugh Hook and Ladder Company, and involved in many civic projects in Waterford. He toured Italy, Egypt, and Southern Europe in 1922. The Kavanaughs were great supporters of community activities. (Courtesy of Russ Van Dervoort.)

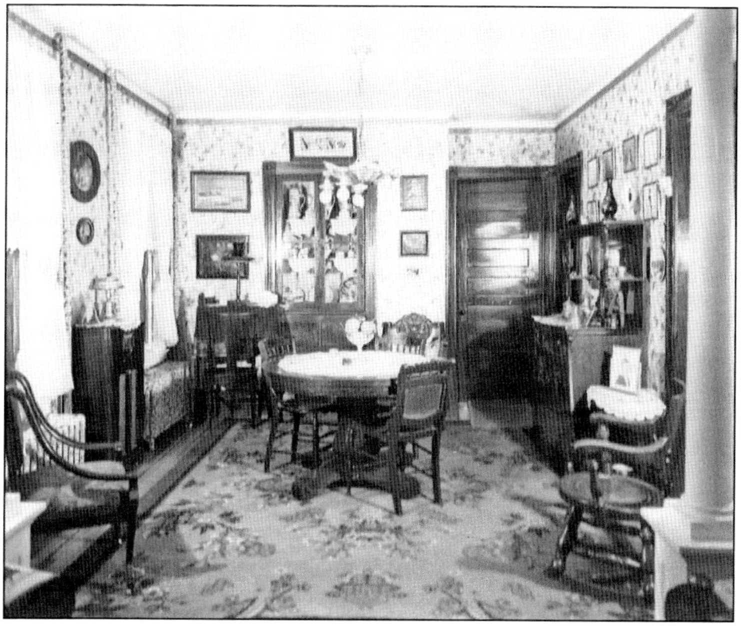

Pictured here is a typical dining room in the 1930s and 1940s: a golden oak pedestal table with chairs, a china closet holding the good china, and glassware. There is a buffet for serving meals. A chandelier above may have been gas powered, as evidenced by the pipes from floor to ceiling. A standing radio entertained with comedy, horror, and music. (Courtesy of Tracy Geel.)

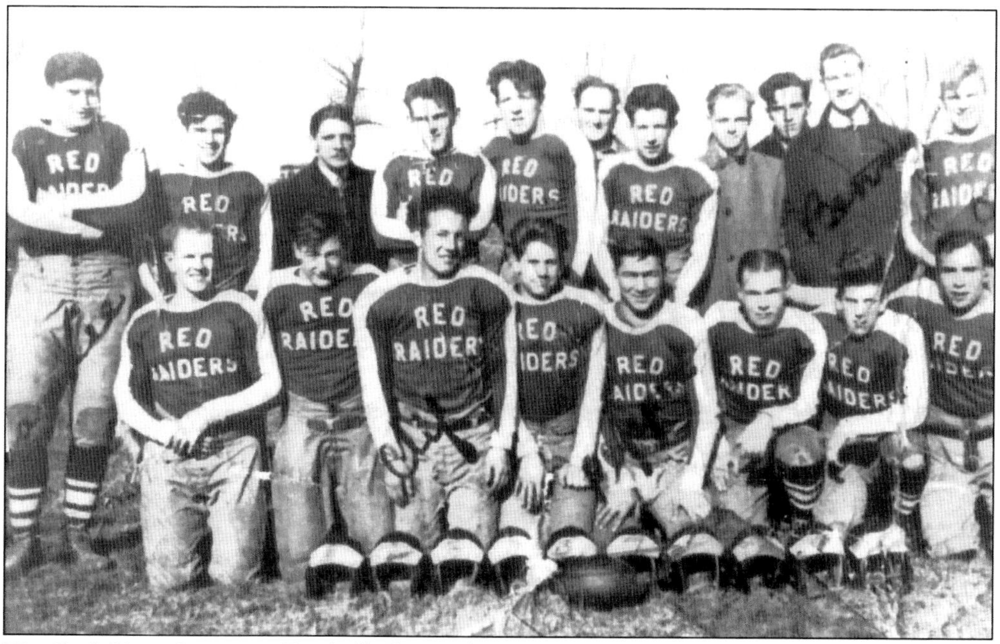

The Peck Hose Company Football Eleven changed its name to the Red Raiders in 1933. The Red Raiders were organized in 1939 as a semiprofessional football team in the Tri City Football League. The Red Raiders captured second place in the league championship in 1940. The team appears to have disbanded about the start of World War II in 1941, when many of its players enlisted in the military. (Courtesy of Donald Bowles.)

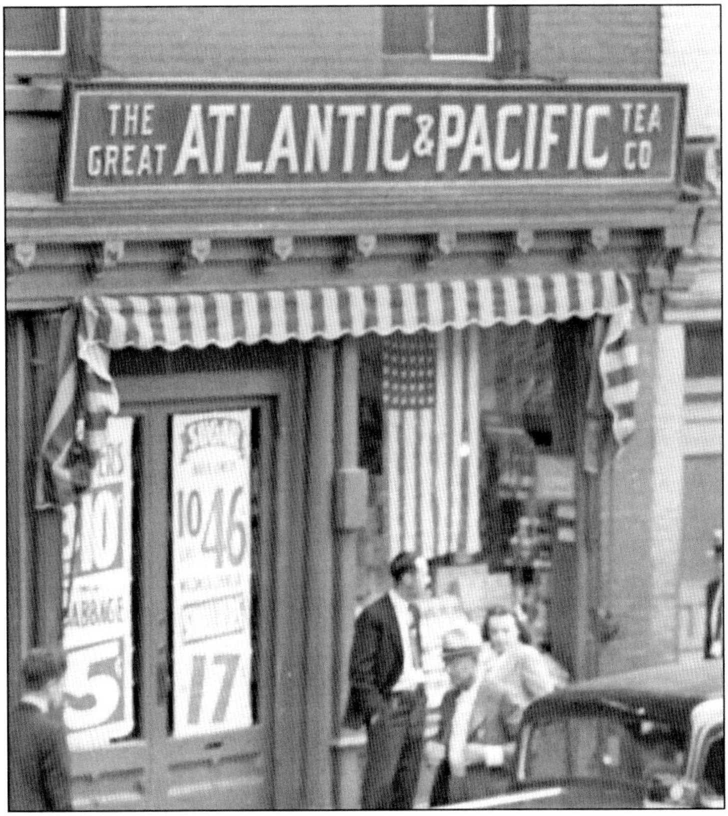

Pictured at left is the Great Atlantic & Pacific Tea Company, better known as the A&P, around 1940. Started as a tea company in 1859 by George Gilman, the company became the county's first grocery store chain. The first A&P in Waterford opened in 1918 at 31 Broad Street and remained there until 1923, when it moved to 61 Broad Street. At left is the 61 Broad Street location. (Courtesy of WHMCC.)

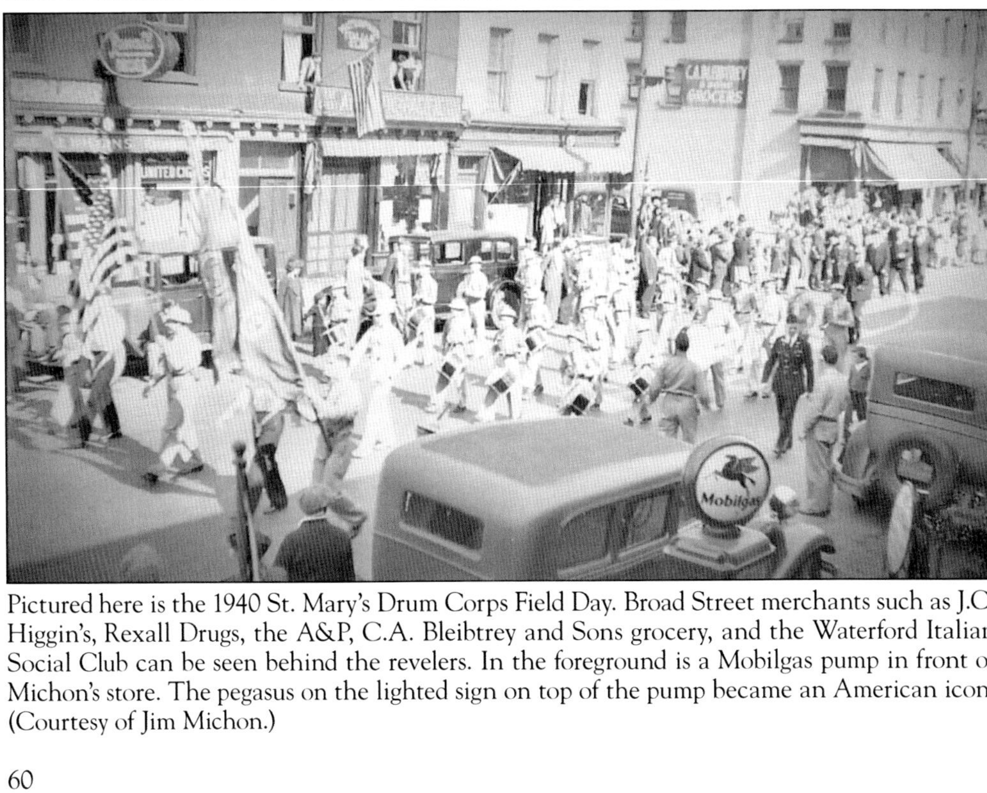

Pictured here is the 1940 St. Mary's Drum Corps Field Day. Broad Street merchants such as J.C. Higgin's, Rexall Drugs, the A&P, C.A. Bleibtrey and Sons grocery, and the Waterford Italian Social Club can be seen behind the revelers. In the foreground is a Mobilgas pump in front of Michon's store. The pegasus on the lighted sign on top of the pump became an American icon. (Courtesy of Jim Michon.)

Pictured here standing in front of his business around 1940, George N. Michon ran a newsstand and variety store in Waterford for almost 30 years. Selling a variety of items, it was also a place for old-timers to go and exchange stories both old and new. After Michon's death, the store was passed down to his wife, Rose, then to his son Warren, and eventually his grandson James. (Courtesy of Carol Ann Michon.)

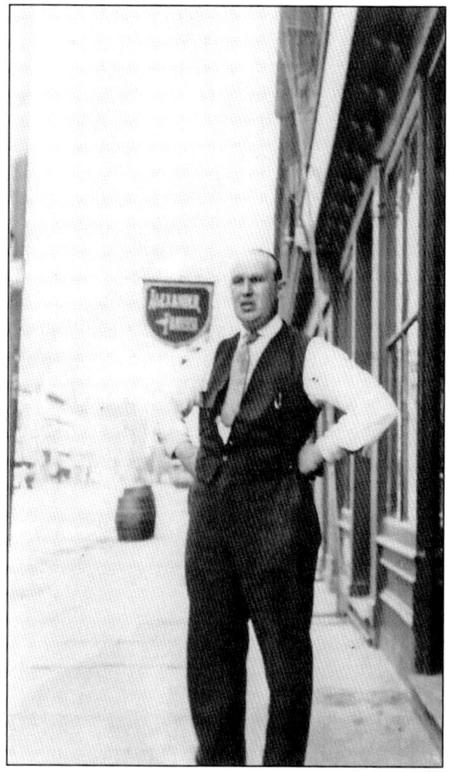

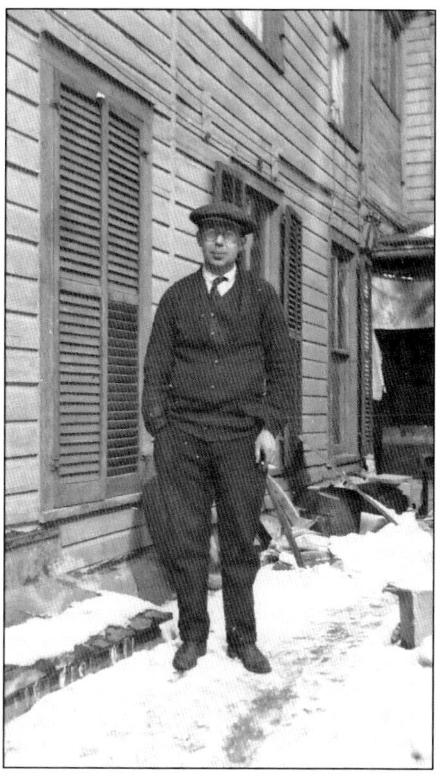

A. Warren Michon, born in 1896, was the son of George N. Michon. He took on his father's business, which offered a variety of items, including penny candy. Warren is remembered by many for his patience, standing at the candy window while the children would pick out each piece, one at a time, sometimes taking several minutes. (Courtesy of Jim Michon.)

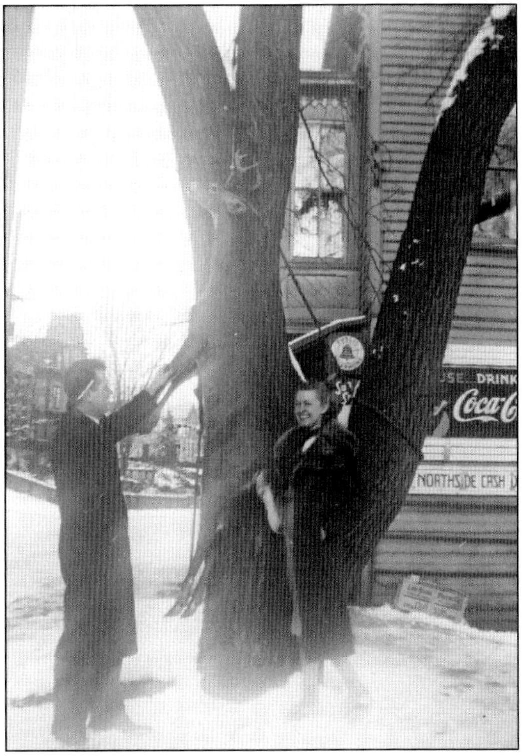

This property at 101 Saratoga Avenue was owned by Roelof Gerritsen Vanderwerken in 1680. In 1686, he owned 1,124 acres in Northside. Lawrence Vanderwerken owned and operated a general store until 1866, eventually passing it to Charles E. Vanderwerken in 1890. John Grochmal peddled groceries for Vanderwerken in the late 1930s and purchased the store in 1951. John's wife, Jess, is looking on as he butchers a deer. (Courtesy of Helen Grochmal Anderson.)

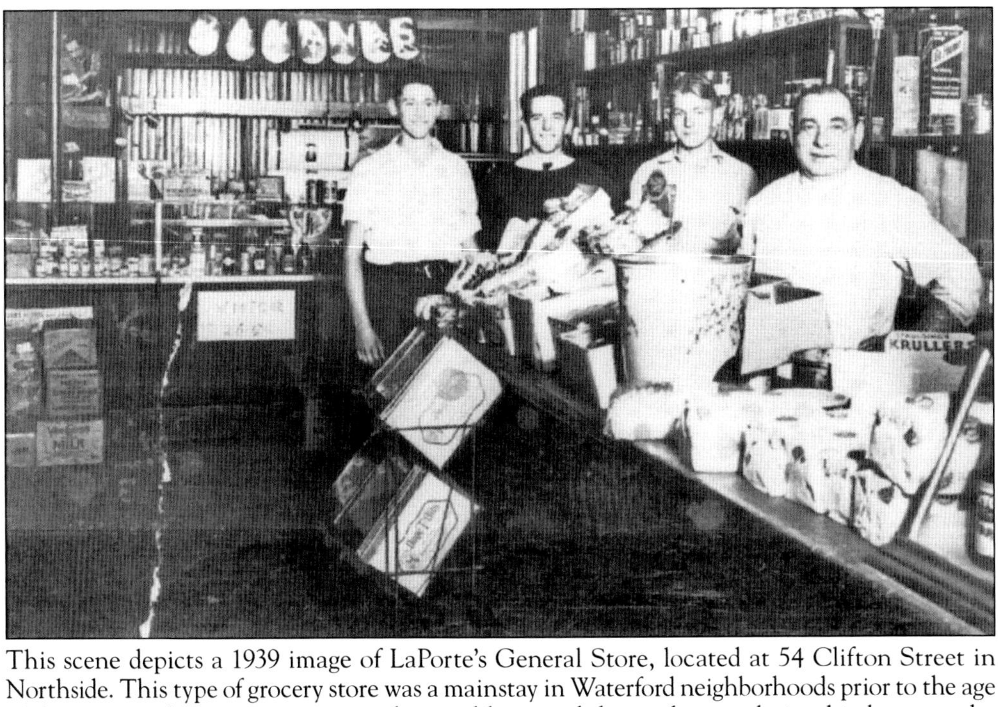

This scene depicts a 1939 image of LaPorte's General Store, located at 54 Clifton Street in Northside. This type of grocery store was a mainstay in Waterford neighborhoods prior to the age of the supermarket. Customers were also neighbors, and the symbiotic relationship between the store owner and the customer was the basis for the store's existence. Credit was often extended to the store's patrons. (Courtesy of Dennis Rivage.)

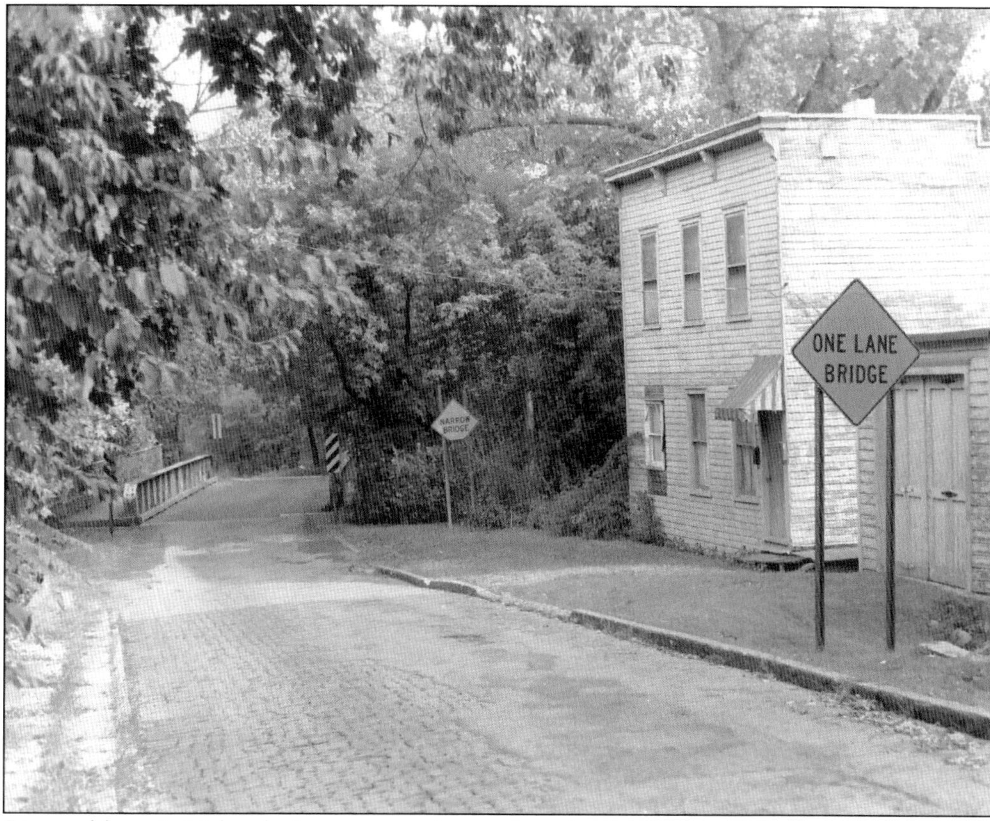

Pictured here is Mohawk Avenue, a major roadway in the 1800s, off Saratoga Avenue. The roadway crossed the Champlain Canal and made accessible all the mills and factories located in Dial City on King's Canal, known as "the ditch." This cobblestone road still stands, as well as the house. The last remaining factory left on the ditch is the Mohawk Paper Mill Inc., which was established after 1829. (Courtesy of WHMCC.)

Standing on the corner of Hill Street and First Avenue in Northside around 1945 is the Reverend Aldis Lomas, looking at the Wesleyan Methodist Church. Behind the reverend is an obscure small store, managed by Harry and Dan Walsh. A young girl, Anna Wilkes, used to peddle papers from the store, possibly one of the youngest papergirls. (Courtesy of Anna Marie Wilkes Lamos.)

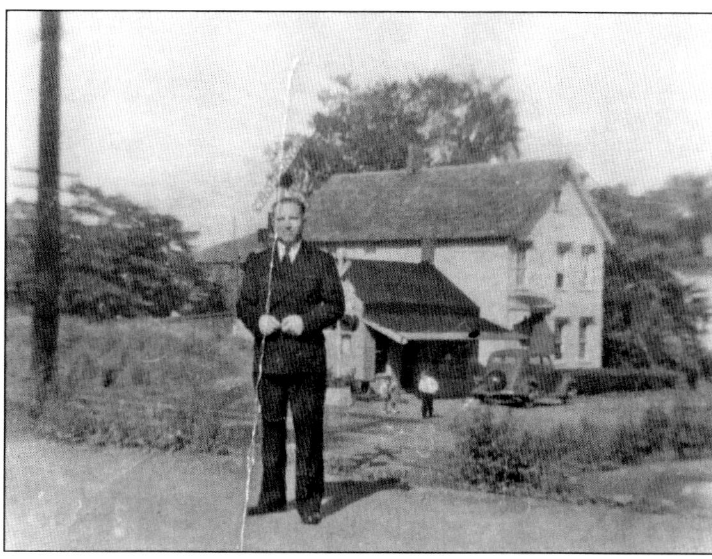

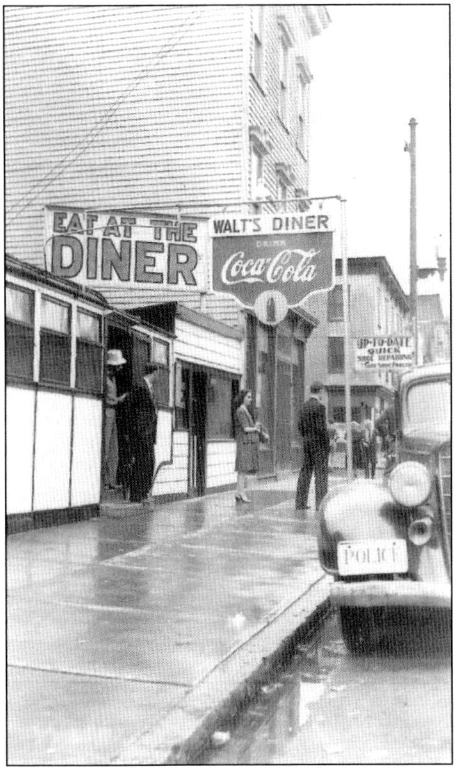

Walt's Diner was located at 78 Broad Street. Its predecessor was the Night Lunch Wagon. The wagon was said to have been used to create the diner. It was owned by George Waldron from 1929 until his death in 1940. It was then operated by his wife, Bertha, until 1942. Bertha then sold the diner to Walt Burns, who operated it until 1952. Before being renamed Walt's Diner, it was known as Waldron's or George's. (Courtesy of Dennis Rivage.)

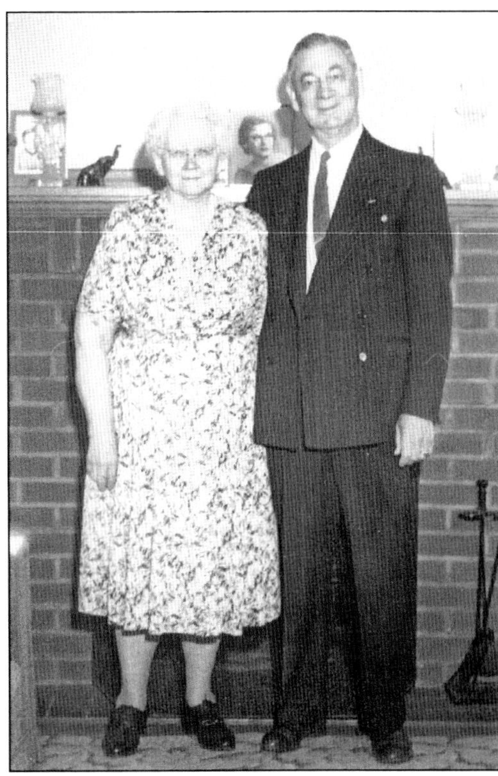

Sydney Ernest Hammersley and his wife, Florence Adalyn McCreedy, are pictured here celebrating their 50th wedding anniversary. Married in 1911 and living in Waterford, they raised three girls, Florence, Frances, and Doris. Colonel Hammersley was chief cannon inspector at the Waterliet Arsenal, where he was employed for 40 years. The Hammersleys are both buried in the Waterford Rural Cemetery. (Courtesy of Donald E. Child.)

Three

SCHOOLS AND CHURCHES

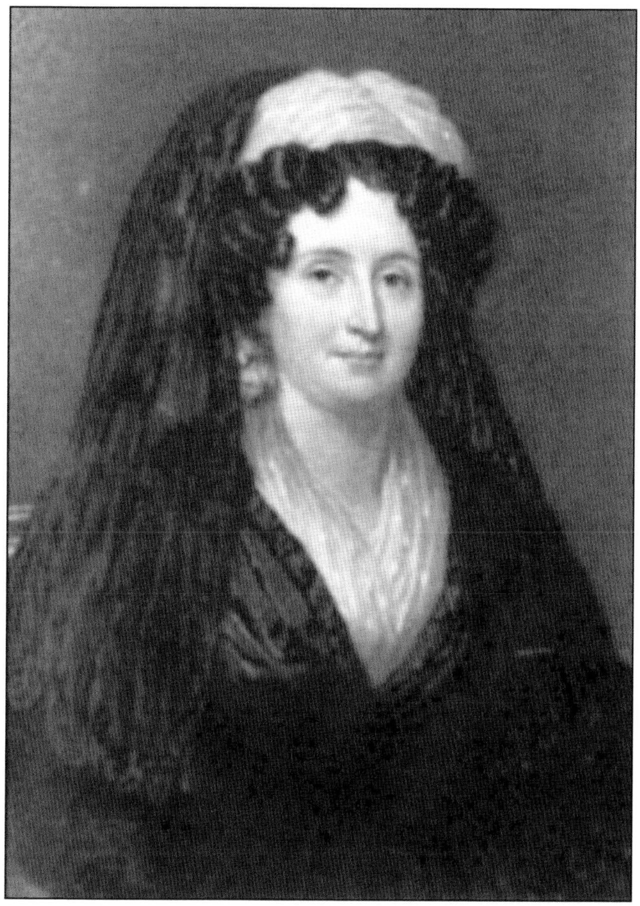

Emma C. (Hart) Willard (February 23, 1787–April 15, 1870) was an American women's-rights advocate who founded the first women's school of higher education. In 1819, after moving to New York State, she opened the Waterford Academy. In 1820, as expenses grew and funding grew scarce, she wrote to an acquaintance: "We have a petition for funds now pending in the Legislature which has passed the Senate for the sum of $2000 but I shall not be surprised if the House rejects it. Economy is the order of the day." Willard was rejected for funding by both Waterford and the state. In 1821, a group of businessmen in the city of Troy offered to fund Emma Willard's school. The school originally opened as the Troy Female Seminary and eventually became the Emma Willard School. It still remains in Troy, a very prosperous and successful young women's boarding school.

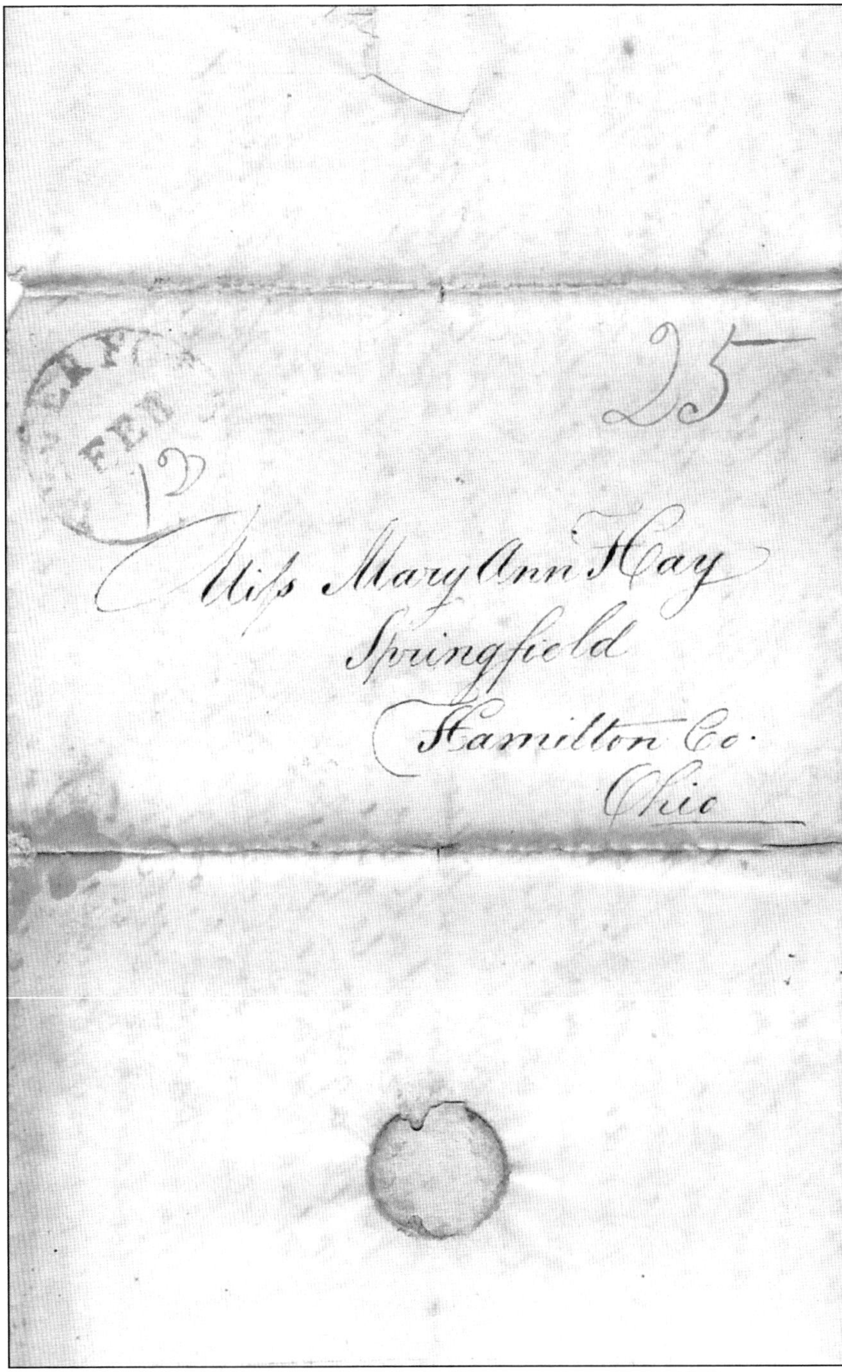

The above was written by Emma Willard to Mary Ann Hay of Springfield, Ohio. Note there is no stamp on the letter. It was referred to as a stampless cover or prestamped mail. A stampless cover generally refers to any item of mail sent before the issuance of postage stamps. The sender would drip hot wax on the paper and fold it in such a manner as to seal the letter. The postmaster would determine the cost to mail the letter depending on the distance. The covers existed, without envelopes, until January 1, 1856.

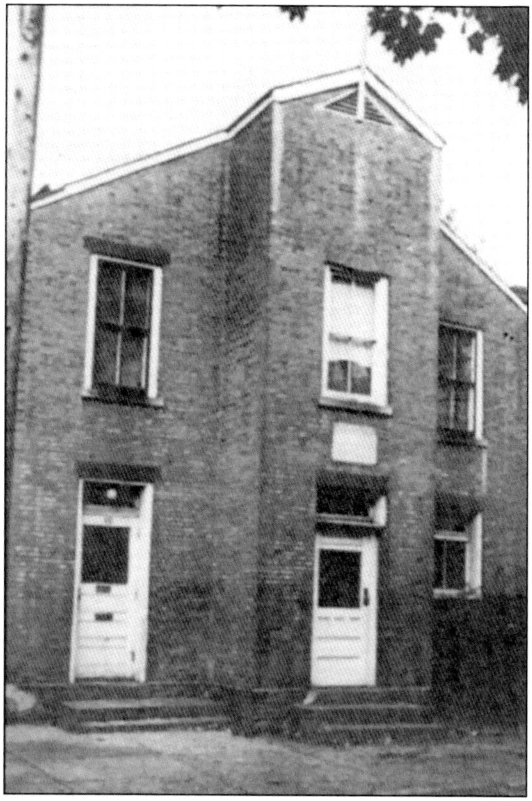

Classic Hall, built in 1813, was a private school for young men. The school was located at 48 First Street in Waterford, and the building still stands there today. There is a plaque over the front door written in Latin that reads "esto Monumentum Aere Perenins," which means, "Let this be a monument more lasting than bronze." (Courtesy of Ward Patton.)

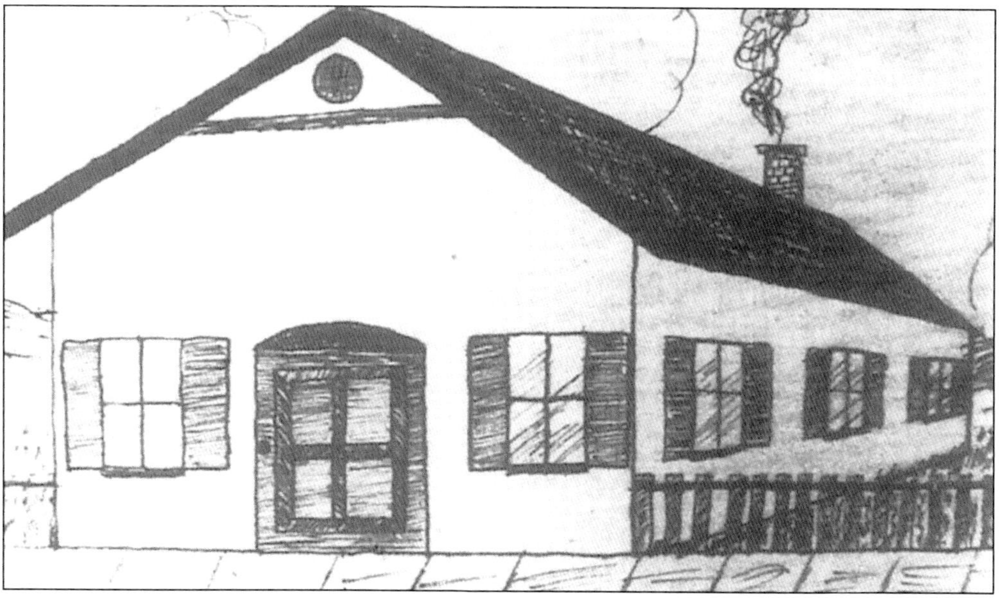

Dial City School No. 3 served residents from about 1845 to 1891. The school taught students from grades one through five. In or about 1862, there were two teachers at the school, a Miss Wheeler and a Miss Thurber. If the boys became unruly, the teachers sent for the principal, and he punished the ruffians with willow switches that he made from branches. The school was discontinued in 1891. (Courtesy of WHMCC.)

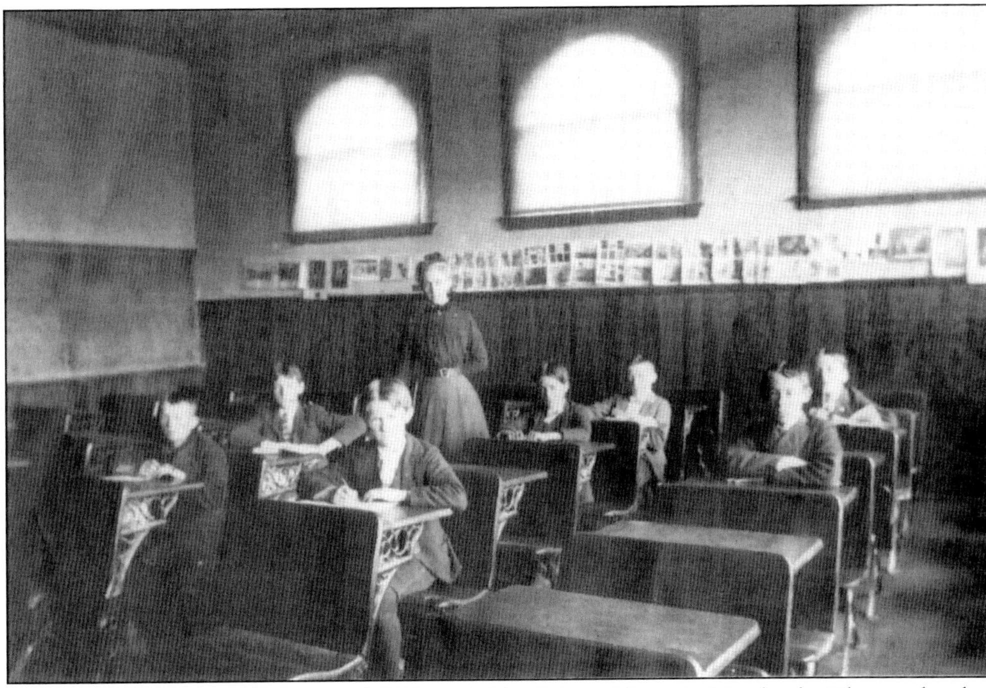

This photograph was taken around 1900 at Public School No. 2 in Northside. The teacher has been identified as a Miss Rogers and one student as Paul Holz. Northside was a vibrant and colloquial community and had its own churches, fire protection, and schools. Many who settled in Northside were French Canadians, and French was spoken in the churches and schools. (Courtesy of Anna Marie Wilkes Lamos.)

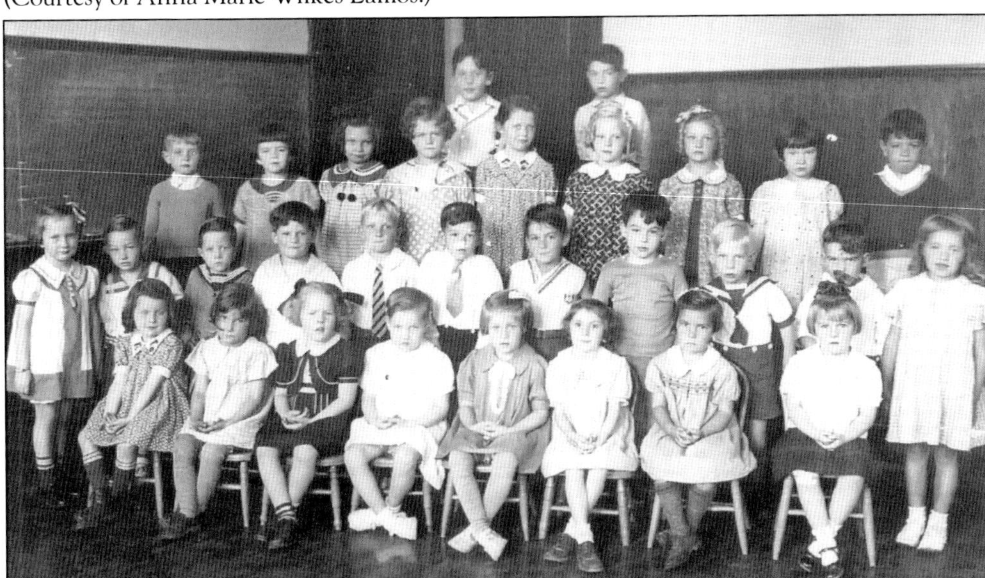

This class from around 1936 was part of Public School No. 2, located on Saratoga Avenue in Northside. It was a three-story building with grades going from kindergarten through sixth grade. In the days before school buses, everyone walked to and from school, including the trek home for lunch. Anna Marie Wilkes is seated second from the right. (Courtesy of Anna Marie Wilkes Lamos.)

Pictured here in 1937 are students of Briggs School No. 3, located on the Hudson River Road. This was an elementary school, and many students attended from outside the Waterford Union Free School District. The residents from outside the district petitioned the school to become part of the Shenendehowa School District. (Courtesy of Russ Van Dervoort.)

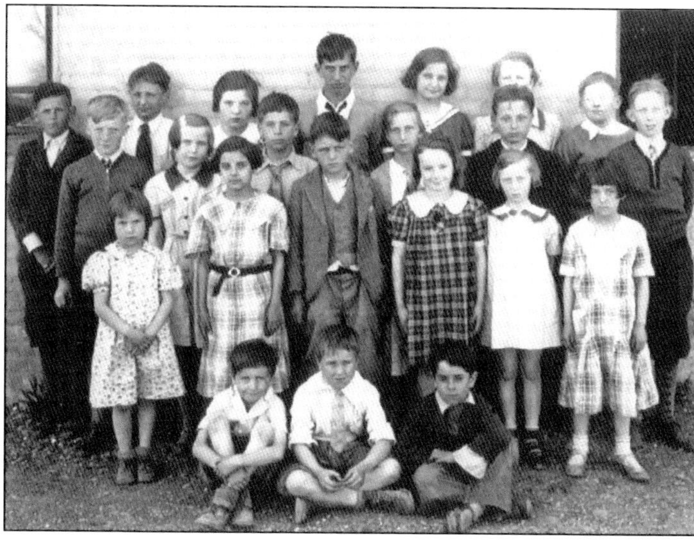

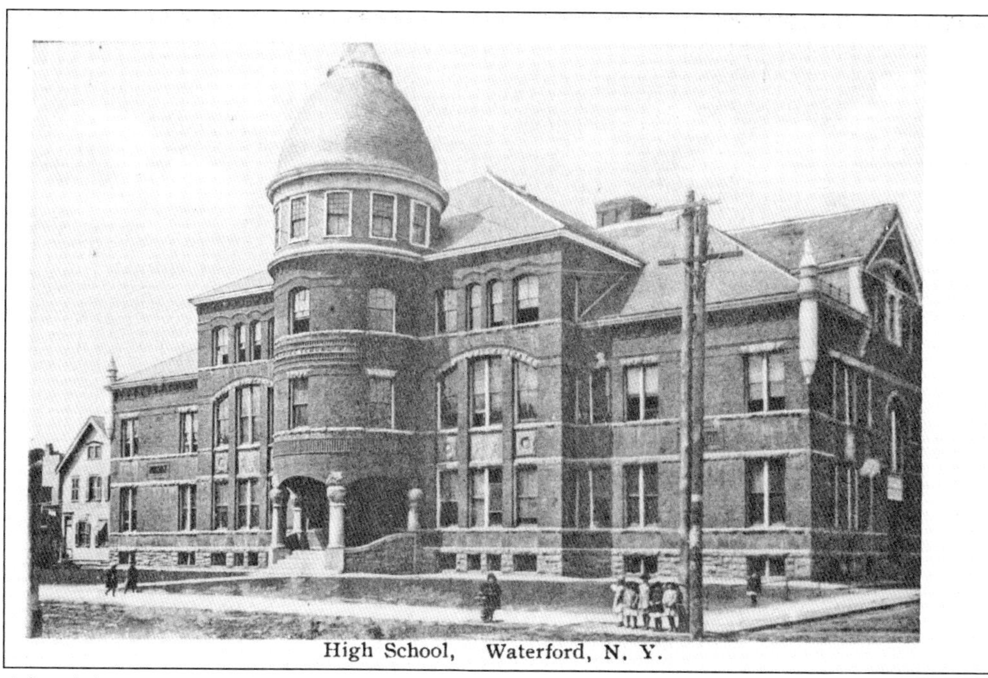

After defeat in 1888 and a name change to Union Free School District No. 1, the 1889 vote for a new school carried 200-110. It was erected on Fourth and Division Streets. The cornerstone was laid on July 17, 1890, and the school opened in September 1891. There was one big obstacle: the grounds were a cemetery. The deceased were exhumed and reburied in the Waterford Rural Cemetery. (Courtesy of Ward Patton.)

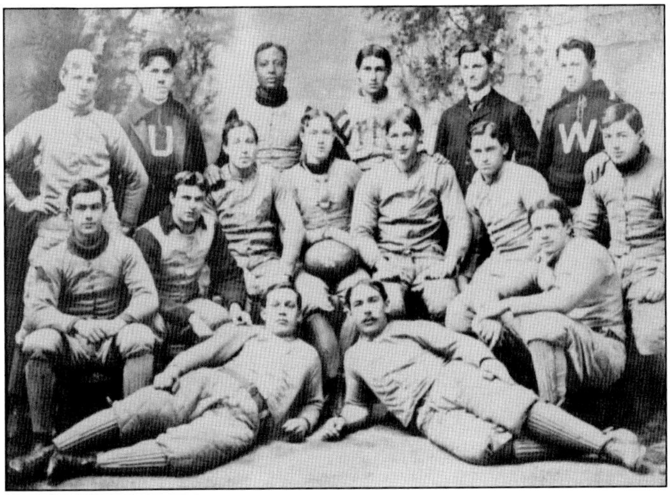

Pictured here is the 1896 Waterford football team. They are (first row, from left to right) Fred "Frenchy" Park and Herb Parker; (second row, in no particular order) Harry Davidson, Will Tierney, Milo Martin, Will Laughlin, Lew Savage, two unidentified, and Will Davidson; (third row, from left to right) Arthur Harriman, William Smith, Epps, Howard MacHaffie, D.B. McCarthy, and Currier. (Courtesy of WHMCC.)

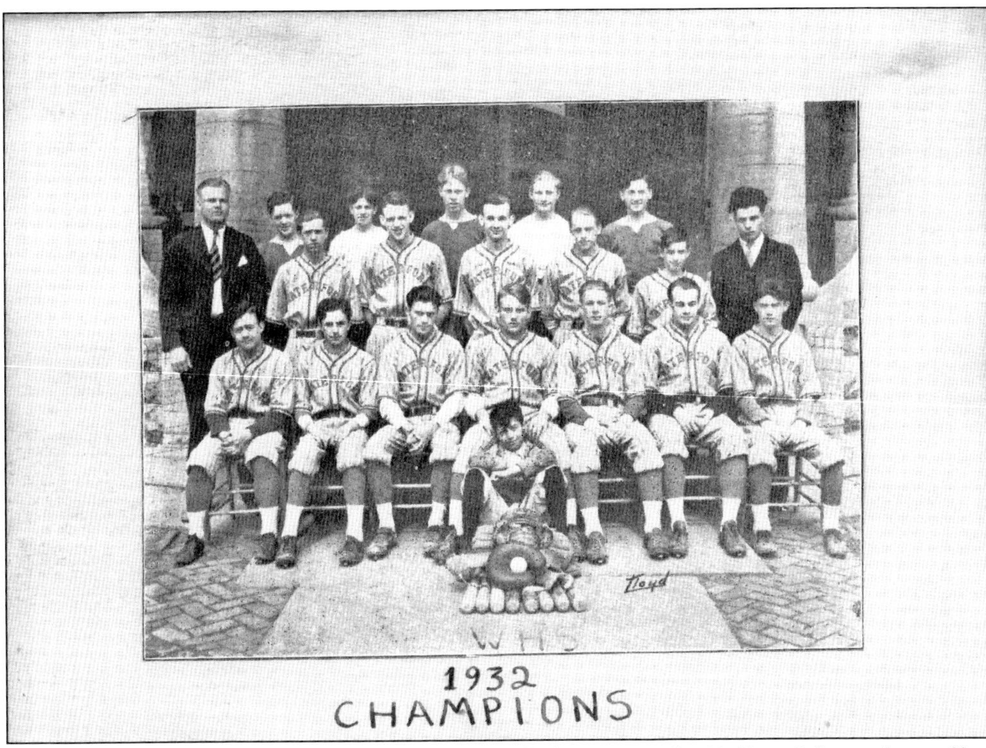

Pictured here are the Waterford High School baseball champions of 1932. From left to right are (first row) Merico Catallo, the mascot, behind the bats and other equipment; (second row) Lawrence Currier, Armanda DePalma, Anthony Catallo, Joseph Willetts, Leonard Johnson, Morman Dowtielle, and John Diviney; (third row) coach Frederick Morris, Thaddeus Bartnick, Maurice Larkings, Warren Collins, Nelson Costello, Leo Bessette, and manager Harry Jackson; (third row) Carl Sorenson, W. Benardo, Casmir Gula, Tony Drombony, and Al Pallozi. (Courtesy of Jeff Diviney.)

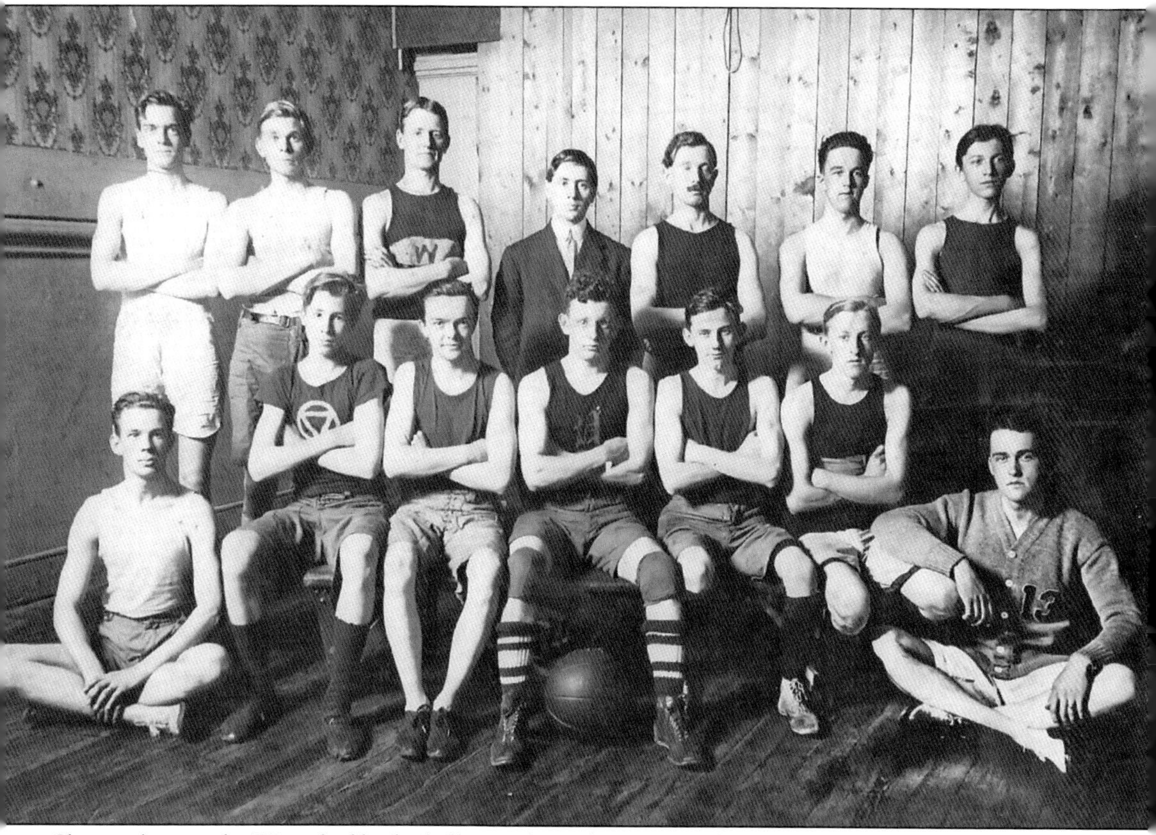

Shown above is the Waterford basketball team from about 1910. The basketball team was organized in 1904 by T. Harry Stephens. It was the first basketball team organized in Waterford, New York. Members of the team are, from left to right, (first row) Frank Hayner, unidentified, Irwin Holton, Red Collins, Harold VanArnum, Edward Hawley, and Merton S. Carlton; (second row) Howard Parsons, Allen Geramine, James G. Anderson, Howard Turner, T. Harry Stephens, Jack Rebman, and Joseph Pratt. In 1924, five of the original players from the 1904 team played on the Waterford High School team. Although they lost 30-19, the younger team was impressed with their skills. (Courtesy of Helen Grochmal Anderson.)

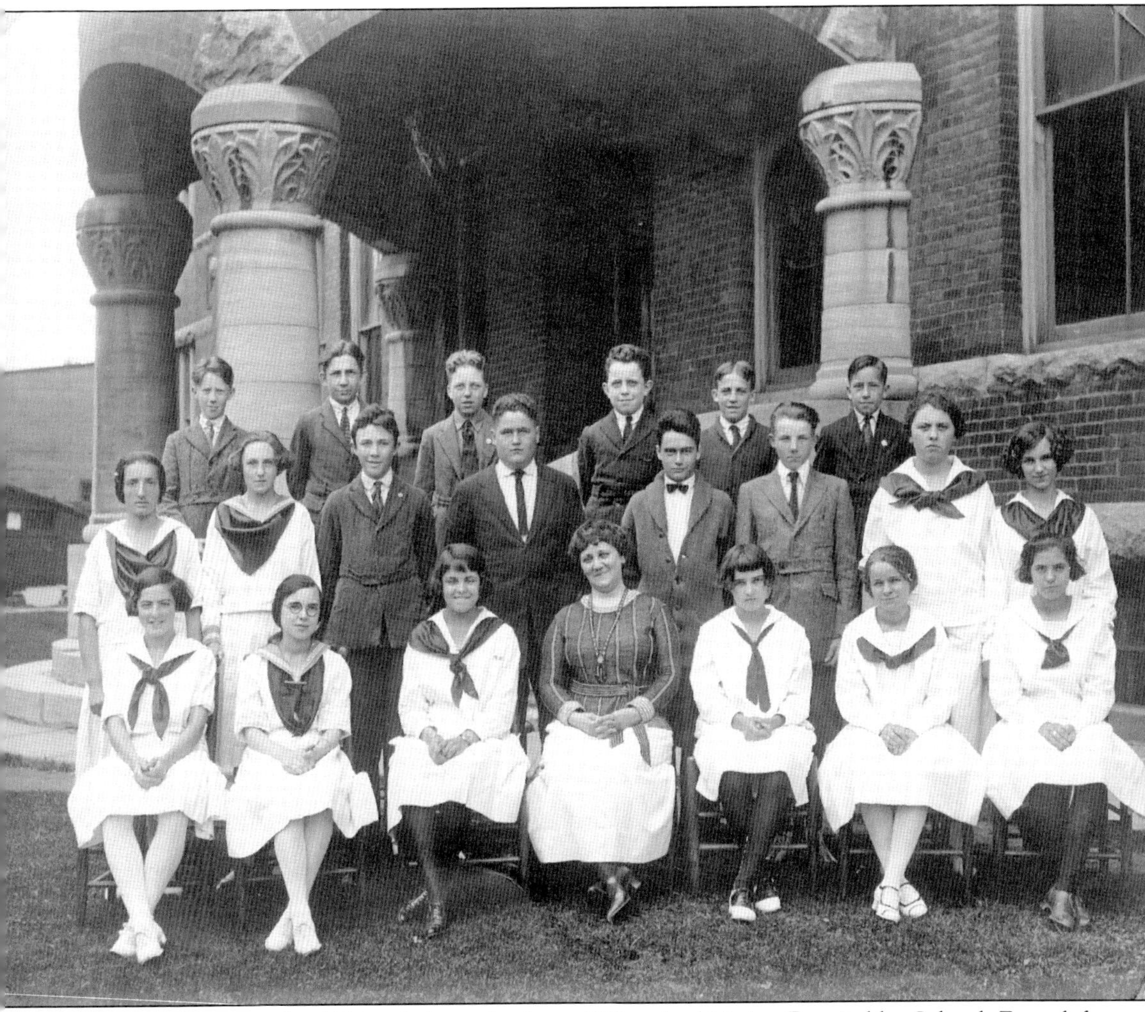

Pictured here is the 1922 eighth grade class of Waterford Union Free Public School. From left to right are (first row) Helen Halpin, unidentified, Sally Allen, Lydia Yoemans Fountain West (teacher), Mary Dwyer, and two unidentified girls; (second row) Jennie Fannucci, two unidentified students, Ralph Whitehurst, Alvah Lange, unidentified, Lillian Hayner, and Anna VanOrden; (third row) Charles Haggerty, Charles Gibbs Charles Ackenbrach, Frank Fitzpatrick, Joseph Bills, and unidentified. The photograph was taken in front of the Union Free School No. 2. This school handled kindergarten through 12th grades and was located in the center of the village. This was conducive for businesses along Broad Street, which was less than a block away. (Courtesy of WHMCC.)

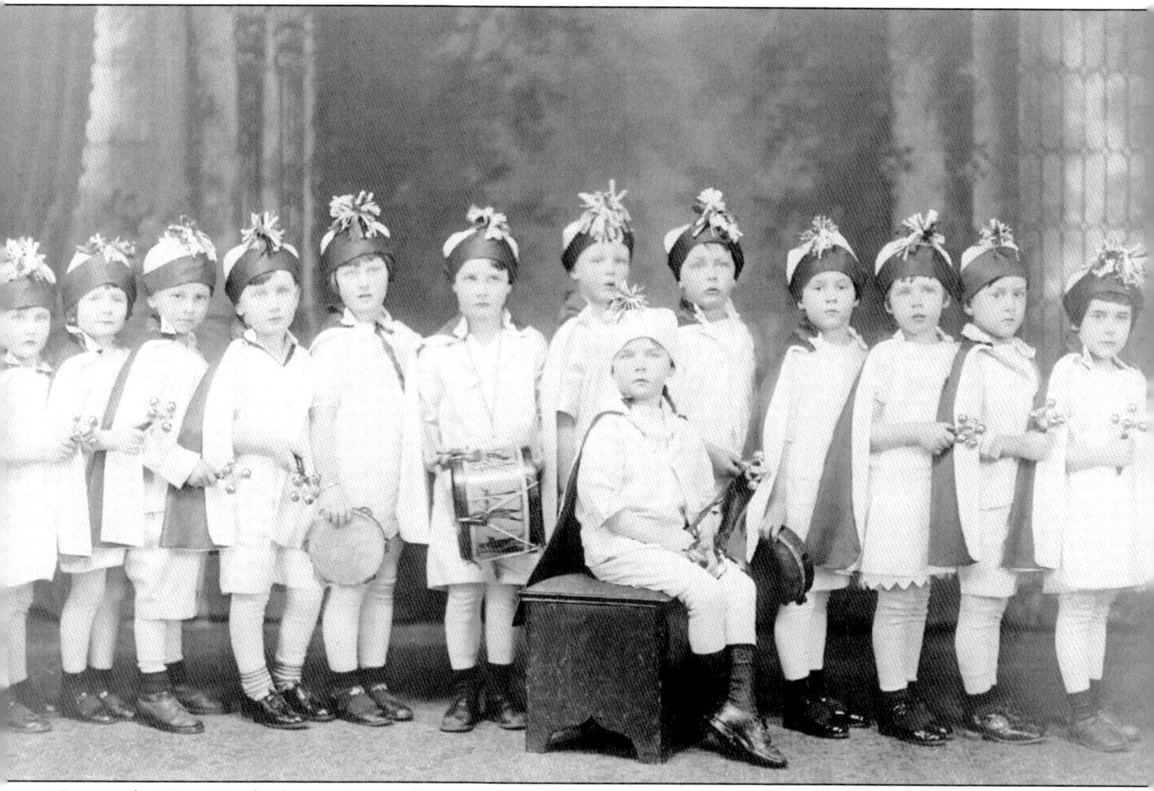

Gertrude Van Linda (not pictured) taught the 1929 kindergarten class of School No. 1. From left to right are Elinor Condon, Mary Cane, Peter Medick, Robert Bleibtrey, Virginia Martin, Clyde Cook, Richard McTuff, Gordon Harter, Dorothy Gero, Aileen Roda, Walter Sorenson, and Viola Winnie. Seated in the center is John Mullen. School No. 1 was located in Northside, a neighborhood that ran from the Waterford Rural Cemetery to the Cohoes Bridge. It appears that the class is involved in some sort of a musical production and in full costume. One can only imagine what was going through their young minds at the time and how their lives evolved in years to come. (Courtesy of WHMCC.)

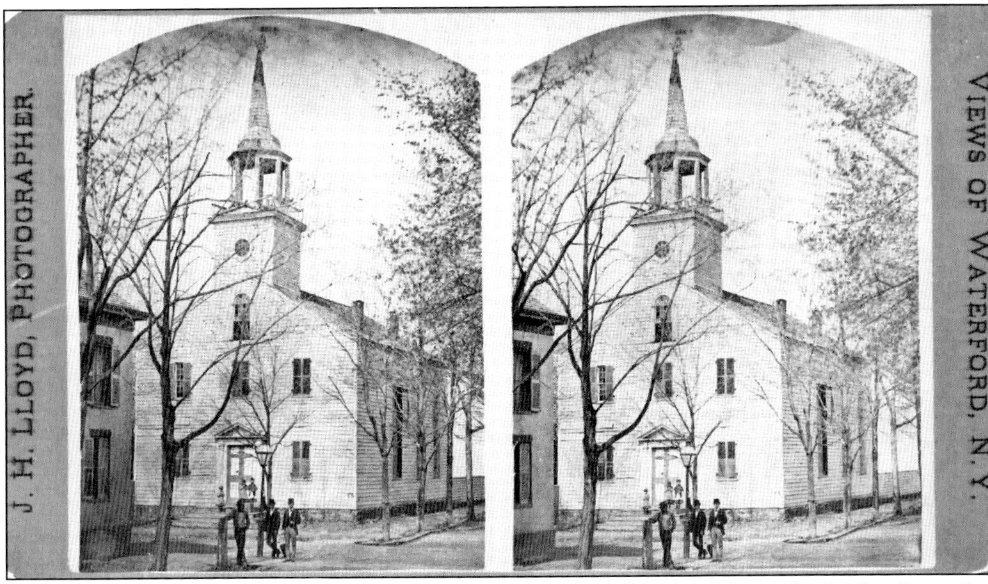

The Reformed Dutch Church is referred to as the mother church of Waterford. The date of its actual construction is believed to be before the American Revolution. Originally built 1.5 miles north of Broad Street, the church was dismantled in 1797 and reassembled on the southwest corner of Middle and Third Streets. The Dutch church remained there until 1876, when it was demolished after the effects of a fire two years prior.

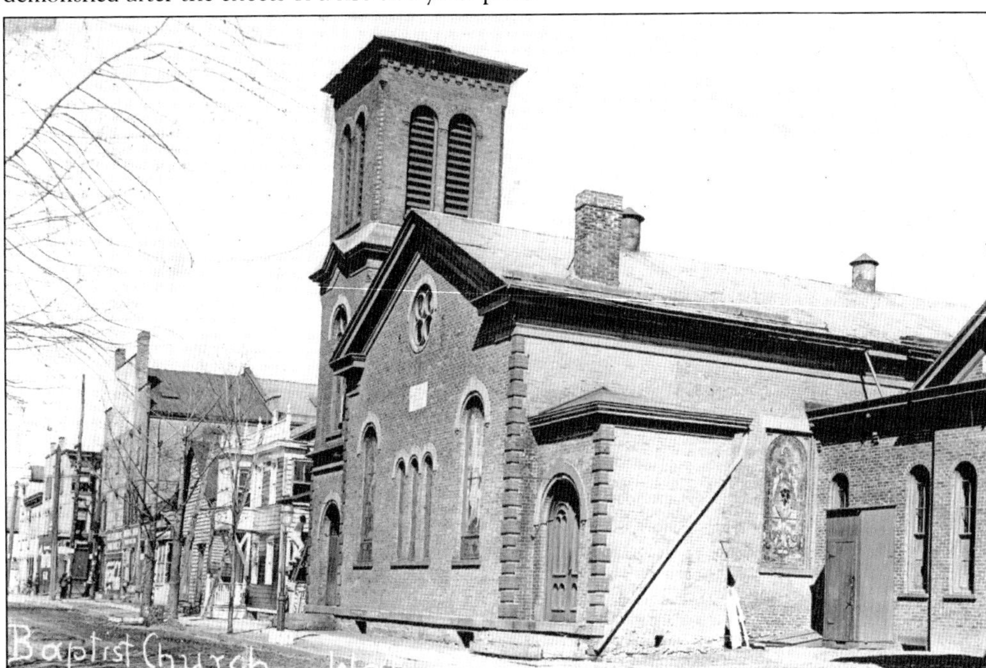

Between 1812 and 1815, the Baptists first gathered at the home of Deacon Whitney and then moved into the old schoolhouse. The first Baptist church was destroyed in the great fire of 1841. In 1842, under the direction of Dea. George Hurd, a new meetinghouse was erected; it was remodeled in 1867. It was updated again in the 1950s and serves to this day.

The Grace Episcopal Church was organized on September 17, 1810. The original church was burned in the great fire of 1841. The following is a quote on an old postcard: "This is the Grace Episcopal Church I attend here. Bertha Barclay's works is 'The Rosary' 'The Mistress of Shenstone,' 'The Following of the Star' etc. They are light, they digest easily. I guess that is one reason I like her. Sincerely, Gertrude Hammersley." (Courtesy of Merle Doud.)

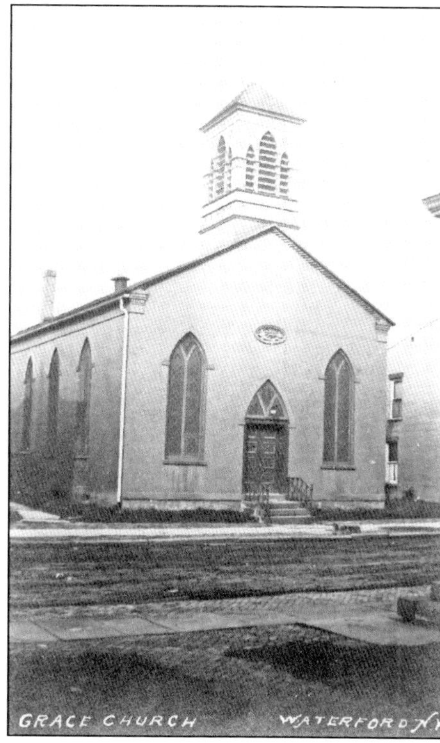

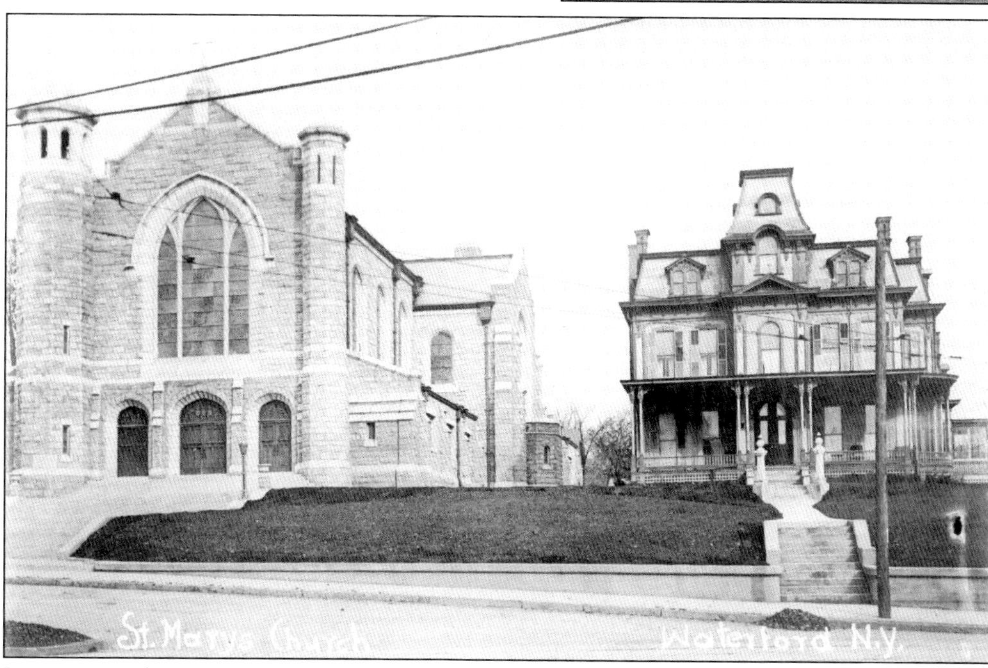

In 1911, population growth prompted St. Mary's of the Assumption to develop plans for a larger church. By 1913, the English Gothic–style church was completed on the corner of Broad and Sixth Streets. The first pastor of this beautiful structure was Rev. Alfred H. Valiquette, OSA. It was referred to as the "little cathedral of the north." In 2013, St. Mary's celebrated its 100th anniversary. (Courtesy of Dennis Rivage.)

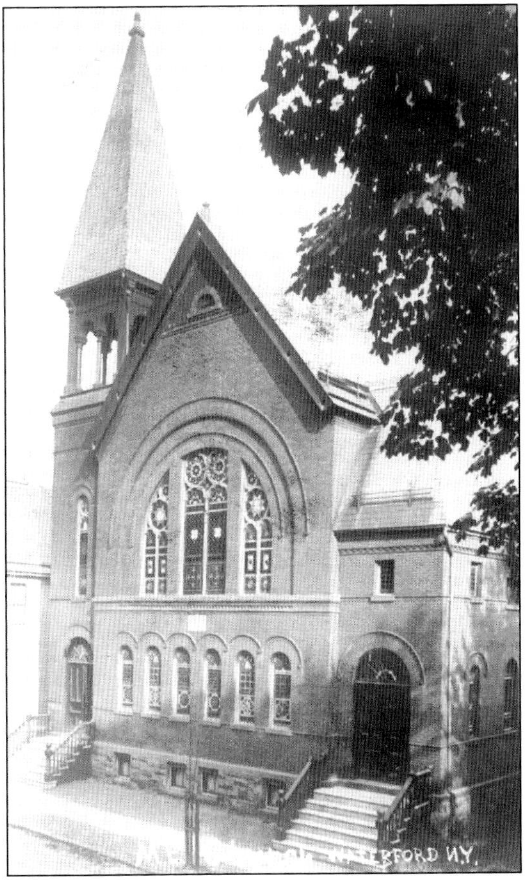

The Methodists first convened in Zadok King's family home on South Street in 1802. The first Methodist church, built in 1832, was located on lower Third Street between Middle and South Streets. This church was later demolished and rebuilt on the same site in 1895. In 1963, the congregation convened to a new church on Middletown Road that still serves the Methodists today. (Courtesy of J. Bert Mahoney.)

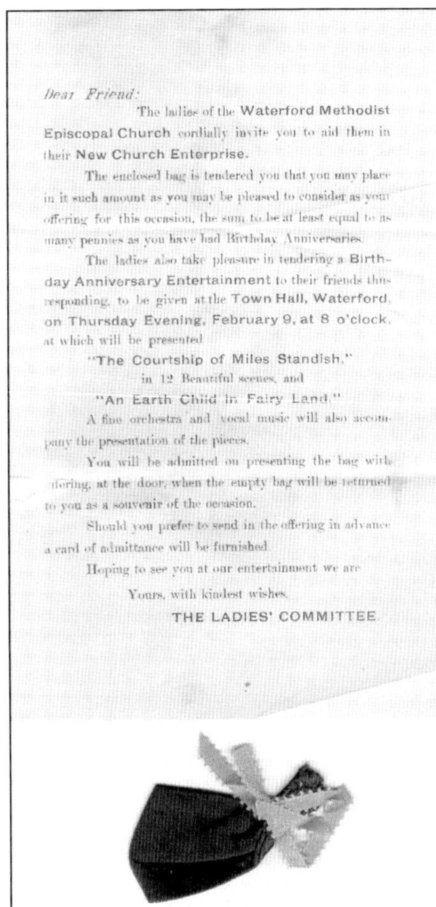

Dear Friend:

The ladies of the **Waterford Methodist Episcopal Church** cordially invite you to aid them in their **New Church Enterprise.**

The enclosed bag is tendered you that you may place in it such amount as you may be pleased to consider as your offering for this occasion, the sum to be at least equal to as many pennies as you have had Birthday Anniversaries.

The ladies also take pleasure in tendering a **Birthday Anniversary Entertainment** to their friends thus responding, to be given at the **Town Hall, Waterford, on Thursday Evening, February 9, at 8 o'clock,** at which will be presented

"The Courtship of Miles Standish,"

in 12 Beautiful scenes, and

"An Earth Child in Fairy Land."

A fine orchestra and vocal music will also accompany the presentation of the pieces.

You will be admitted on presenting the bag with offering, at the door, when the empty bag will be returned to you as a souvenir of the occasion.

Should you prefer to send in the offering in advance a card of admittance will be furnished.

Hoping to see you at our entertainment we are

Yours, with kindest wishes,

THE LADIES' COMMITTEE.

At right is an invitation to attend the new Waterford Methodist-Episcopal Church enterprise. The new church was organized in 1832 and located at 15 Third Street. The Ladies' Committee is asking attendees to fill the bag with pennies equal to their ages.

In 1826, the Presbyterians purchased a lot on Third and Division Streets and built their church. Dr. Blatchford served as pastor until his death in 1828. As a result of a flood in 1913, part of the Presbyterian church collapsed and had to be demolished. The church was rebuilt and the cornerstone laid on August 2, 1914. The bell from the original church was saved from the flood. (Courtesy of Helen Grochmal Anderson.)

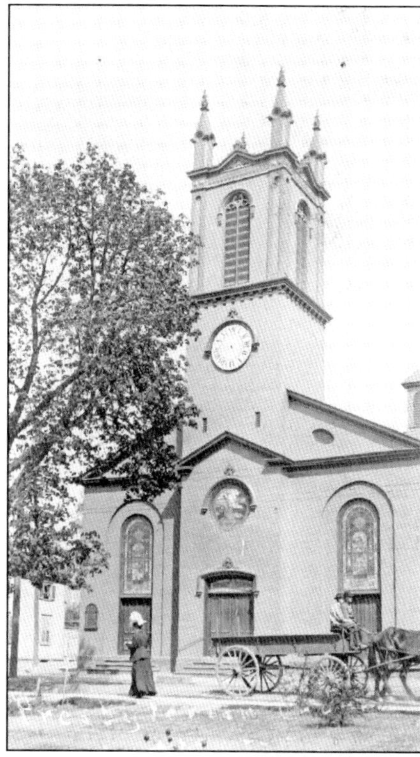

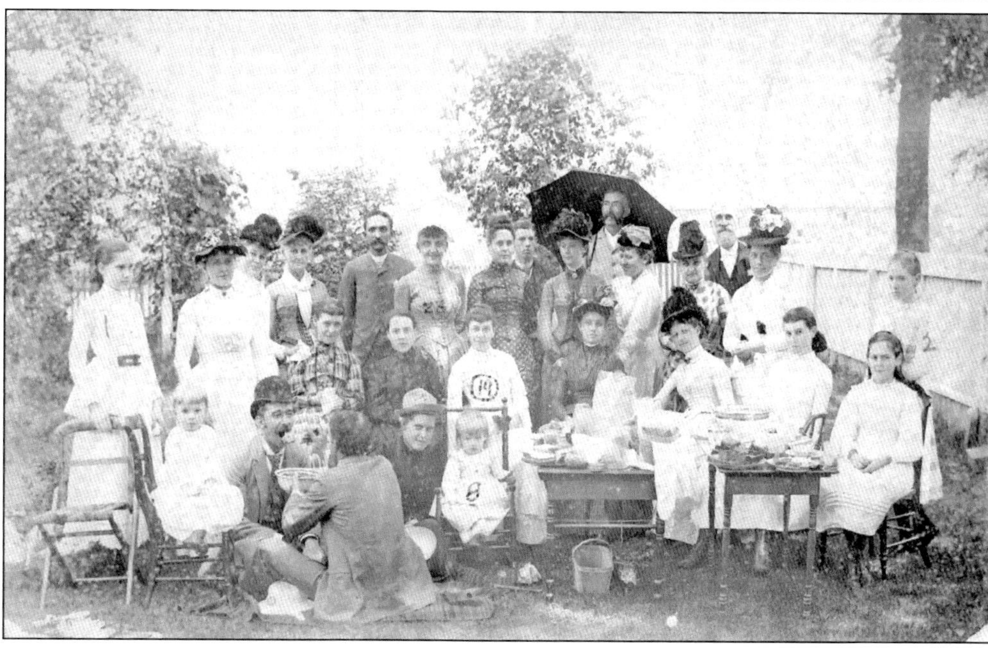

Pictured here at the parsonage on Monday July 1, 1889, and Fred Platt, Mr. and Mrs. Burton, a Mrs. Platt, a Mrs. Flack, a Mrs. Johnstone, Charlie Stewart, Bert Riggs, Ned Johnstone, Eunice Burton, Elsie Riggs, Ella Riggs, Olin Brady, H. Brady, Sophie Brady, a Mrs. Brown, Libbie Burdick, Allie Backus, Cora Burnap, a Miss Packard, a Mrs. Norton, Florence Eddy, and L. Edith Waldron (Courtesy of WHMCC.)

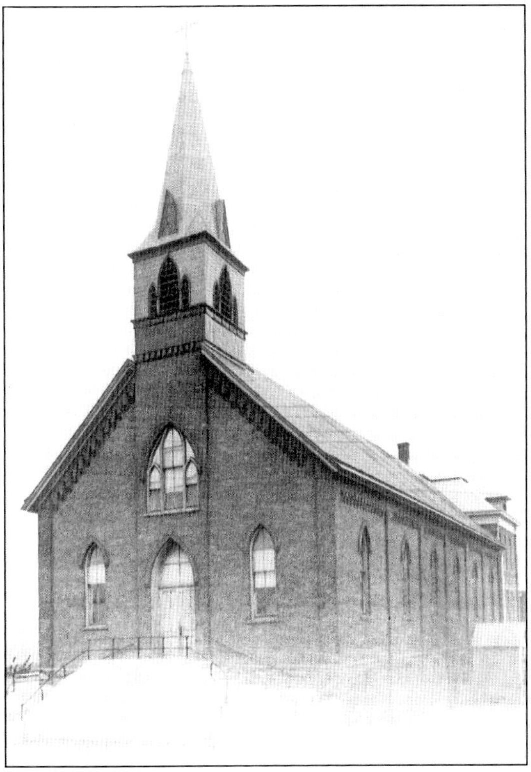

Prior to 1887, Roman Catholic services in the Northside neighborhood were conducted by a priest from St. Joseph's Church in Cohoes. In 1887, as the community grew, St. Anne's Roman Catholic Church was established. During a major fire in Northside, local lore states that Fr. Eugene Rey brought out the blessed sacrament from St. Anne's Church and stood in the path of the flames, which did not come any farther, saving the church from any damage. (Courtesy of Russ Van Dervoort.)

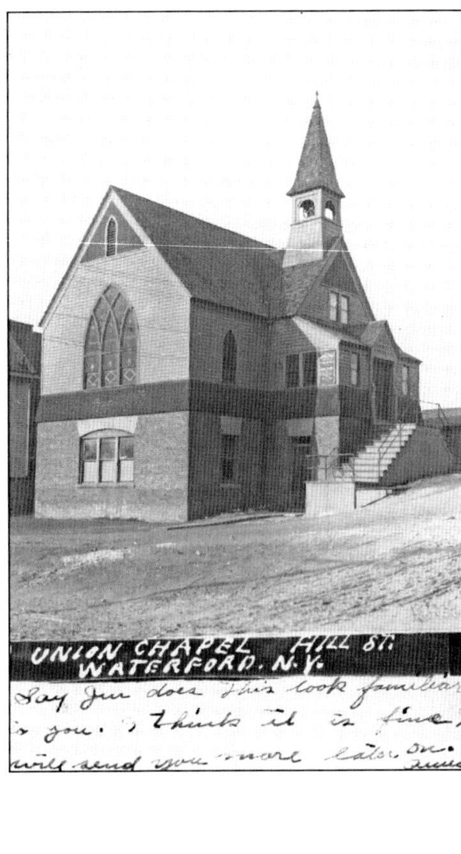

Pictured here is the Union Chapel, built in 1895. The chapel is located at the southwest corner of Hill Street and First Avenue in Northside. The name was changed to the Wesleyan Methodist Church in 1945. The churchgoers now hold services in the former St Anne's Church, and the Union Chapel is now a private residence. (Courtesy of Tracy Geel.)

Four

TRANSPORTATION

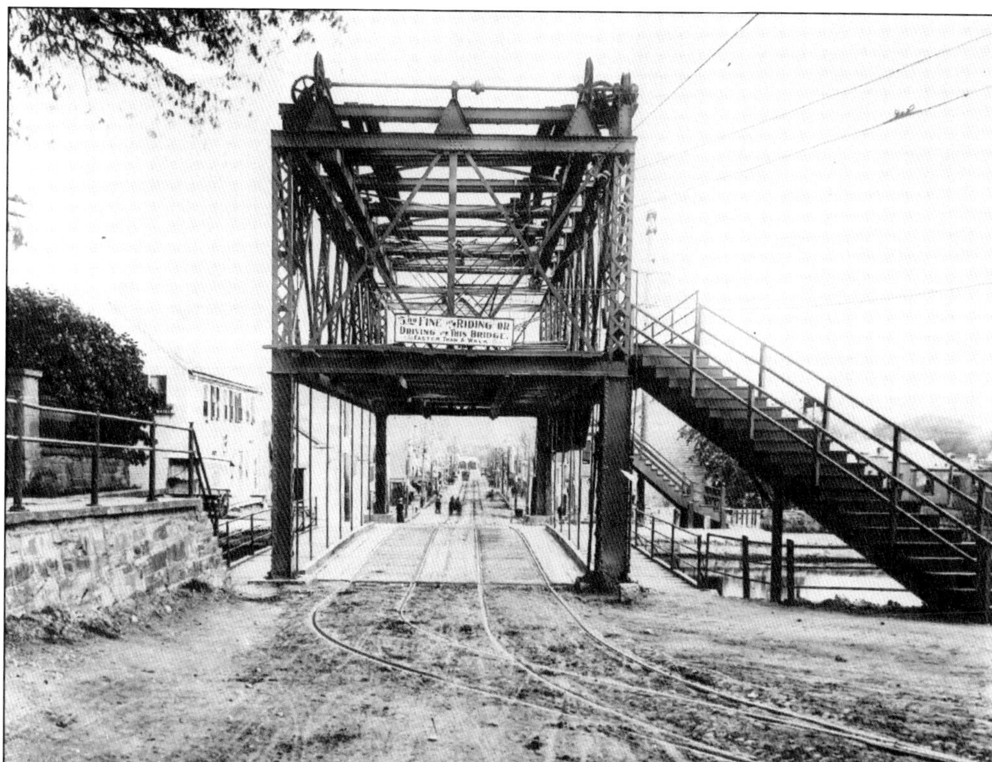

On April 22, 1867, an act was passed in the New York State Senate and Assembly to authorize the construction of an iron bridge over the Champlain Canal on Broad Street. The iron bridge would replace the wooden one, and it had to be of sufficient length to permit the widening of the canal to allow the free passage of boats of the same size as those navigating the Erie Canal. The sign in the middle of the bridge read, "$5.00 Fine for Riding or Driving on This Bridge Faster Than a Walk." Looking east on Broad Street, the entrance to the Union Bridge over the Hudson River to Lansingburgh can be seen. (Courtesy of WHMCC.)

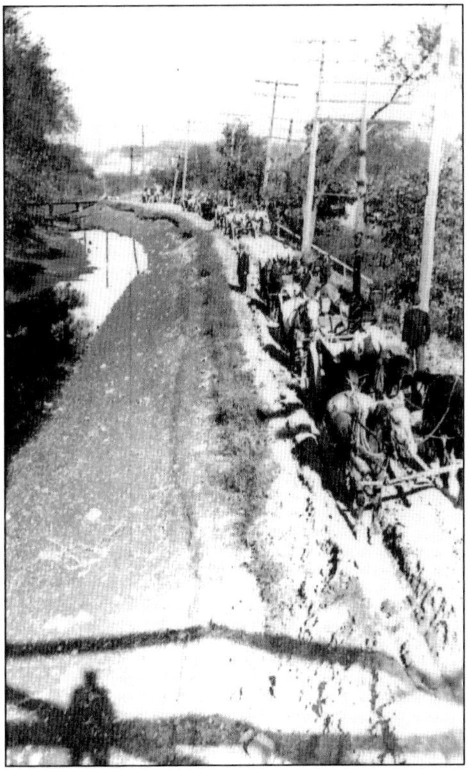

Pictured here is construction on the Northside section of the original Champlain Canal during the late 1880s. This section is north of the Mohawk River and Lock 4. This section of the canal was never widened from the original 44 feet. During this improvement, the intent was to create more depth to the canal. Many industries in this area utilized the waters from the canal to power their operations. (Courtesy of Mike Cicchinelli.)

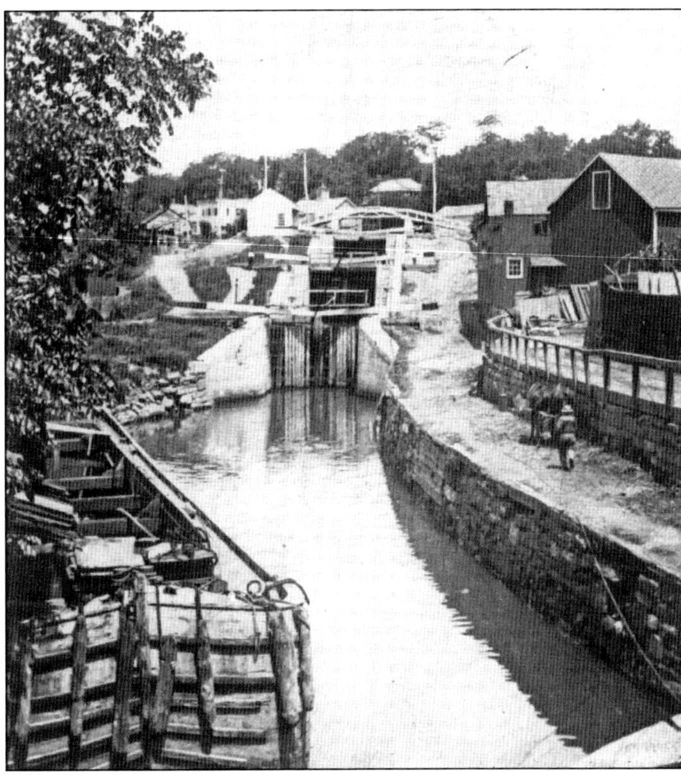

The side-cut locks were the gateways to the Champlain Canal at Waterford. This is the site where canal boats would be raised from the river level up to the canal or lowered from the canal to the river. The Erie Canal could also be accessed from Waterford at this point by traveling south on the Champlain Canal to Cohoes at the junction of the two canals. (Courtesy of J. Bert Mahoney.)

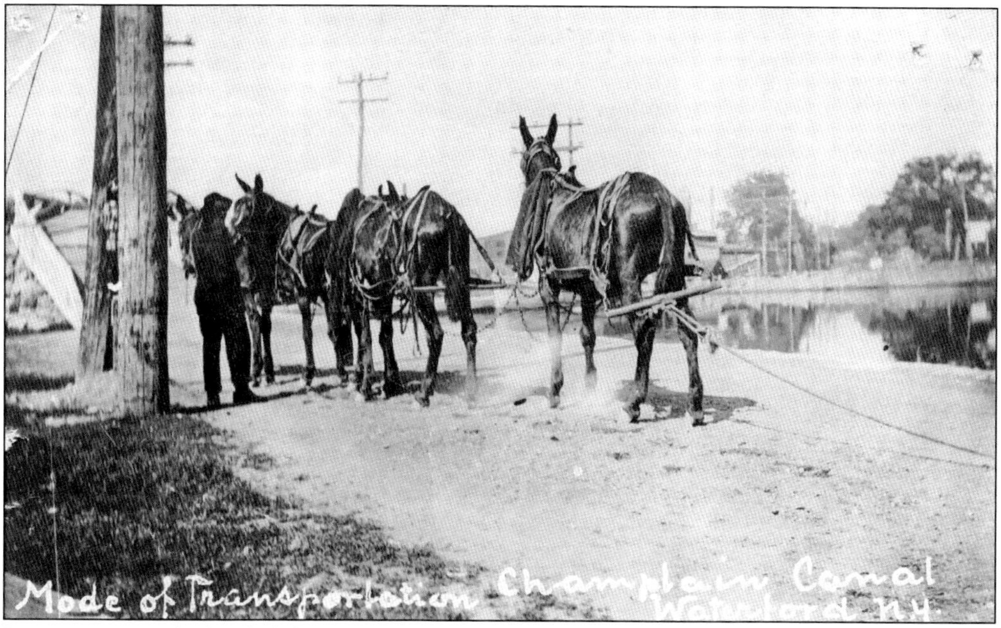

Two or more mules hauled the canal boats with 70 to 90 yards of heavy rope. The men, women, and children who guided the animals were called "hoggee" (ho-gee). Many of the mule drivers were crippled, and some sported wooden legs, stumping along behind their patient but stubborn charges. Many of these unfortunate men were aging Civil War veterans. This industry engendered the word towpath, meaning a trail on the bank of the canal.

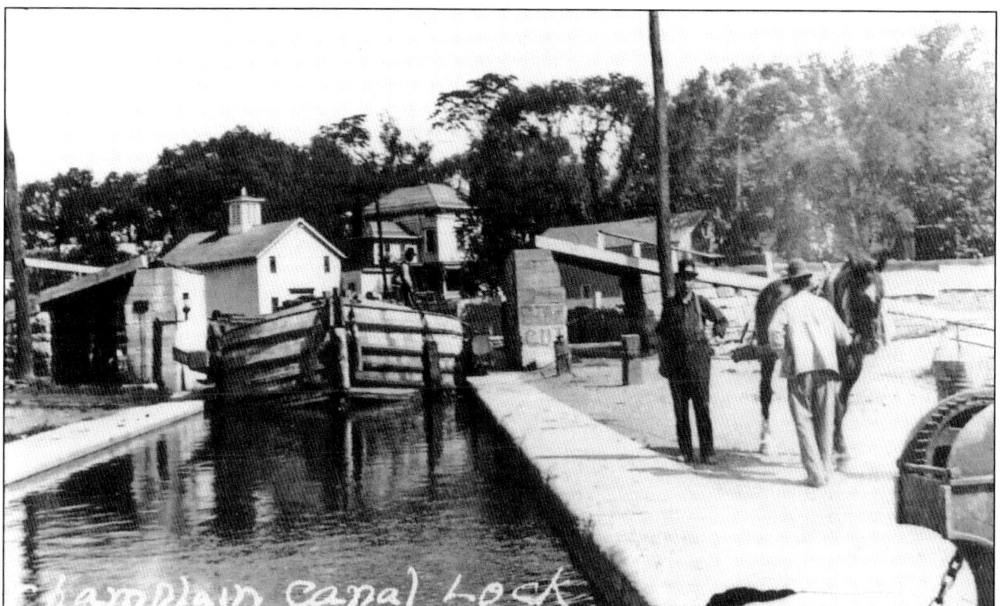

A canal boat is exiting the Champlain Canal to be locked down into the Mohawk River before entering the Hudson River and becoming part of a tugboat tow to points south. Note the ramps to the right and left of the canal boat. That is a removable bridge, with the center section removed, to allow boat passage. (Courtesy of Bill Paquette.)

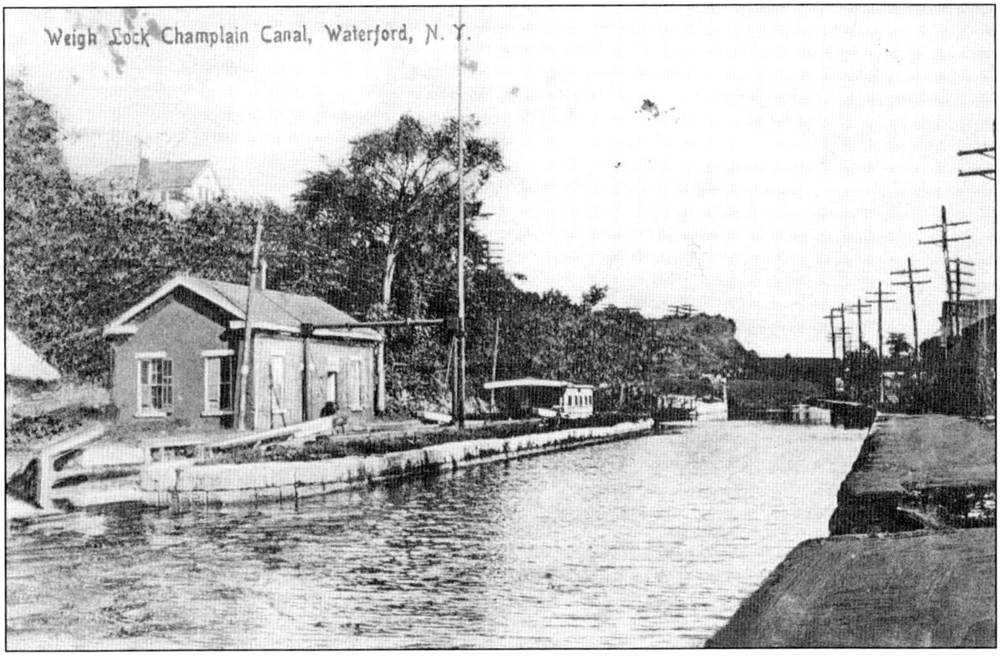

In this 1898 image, looking north from the bridge at Division Street (Slade's Hill), the Champlain Canal can be seen. On the left is the weigh lock and Nealor's Inland Seaman's Union Store. Also in the distance, one can see the Black Bridge, which carried the Delaware & Hudson Railway over the Champlain Canal and the adjoining towpath. (Courtesy of Mike Judge.)

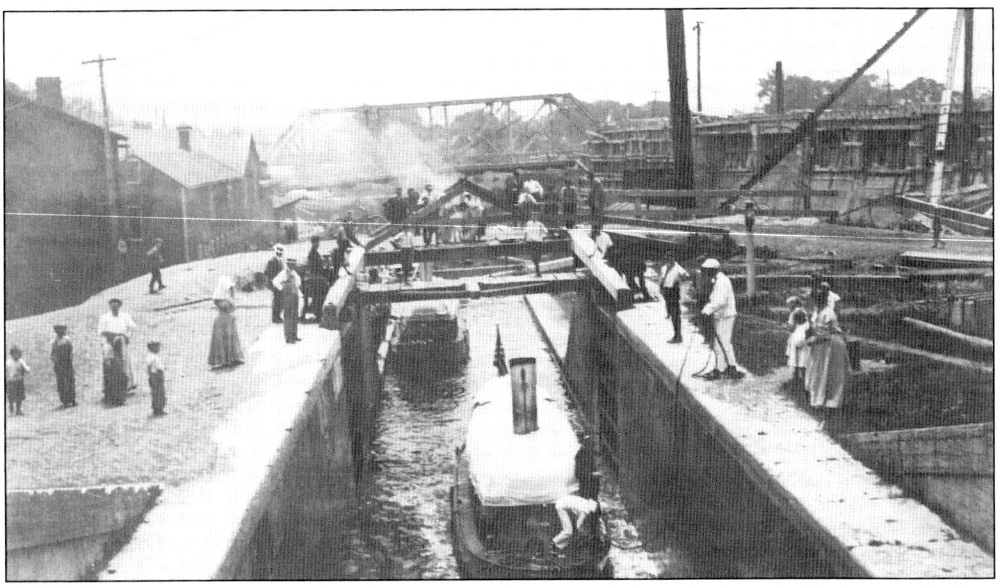

Torpedo boats are pictured here in the Champlain Canal side-cut locks in July 1909. In the late 19th century, many navies started to build torpedo boats 30 to 50 meters in length, armed with up to three torpedo launchers and small guns. They were relatively inexpensive and could be purchased in quantity, allowing mass attacks on fleets of larger ships. These are returning from Vergennes, Vermont, for the anniversary observance of Samuel de Champlain's discovery of the lake.

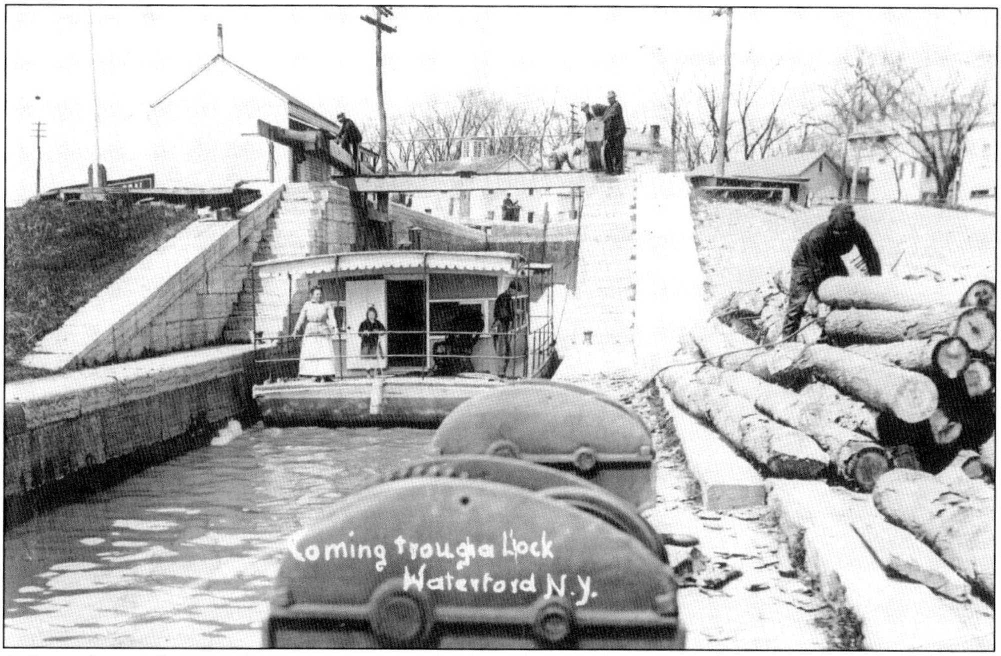

A houseboat, the *Rudder Grange*, enters the last chamber of the side cuts. The craft will rise to the canal level, turn right out of the lock, and proceed to the Waterford Weigh Station. There it will take up residence until 1918. Nearly all boats on the canal had living quarters on board. The Van Dervoort family had 11 family members working on the canal with several tugboats. The *Rudder Grange* was office and home. (Courtesy of Russ Van Dervoort.)

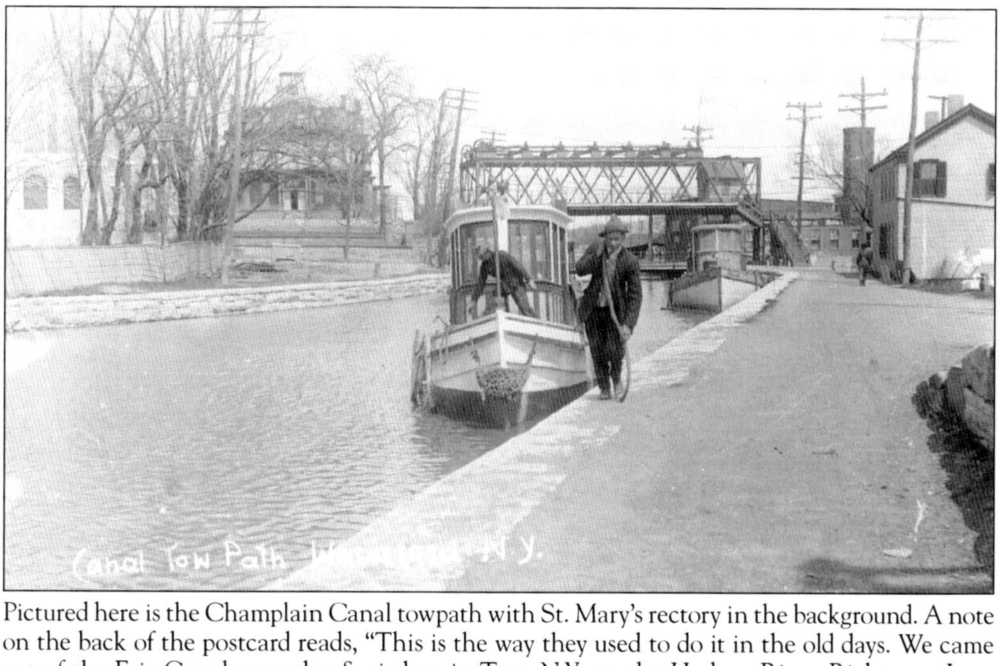

Pictured here is the Champlain Canal towpath with St. Mary's rectory in the background. A note on the back of the postcard reads, "This is the way they used to do it in the old days. We came out of the Erie Canal yesterday & tied up in Troy, N.Y. on the Hudson River. Right now I am writing this going down the Hudson, watching, and enjoying the most gorgeous scenery—what a life." (Courtesy of Tracy Geel.)

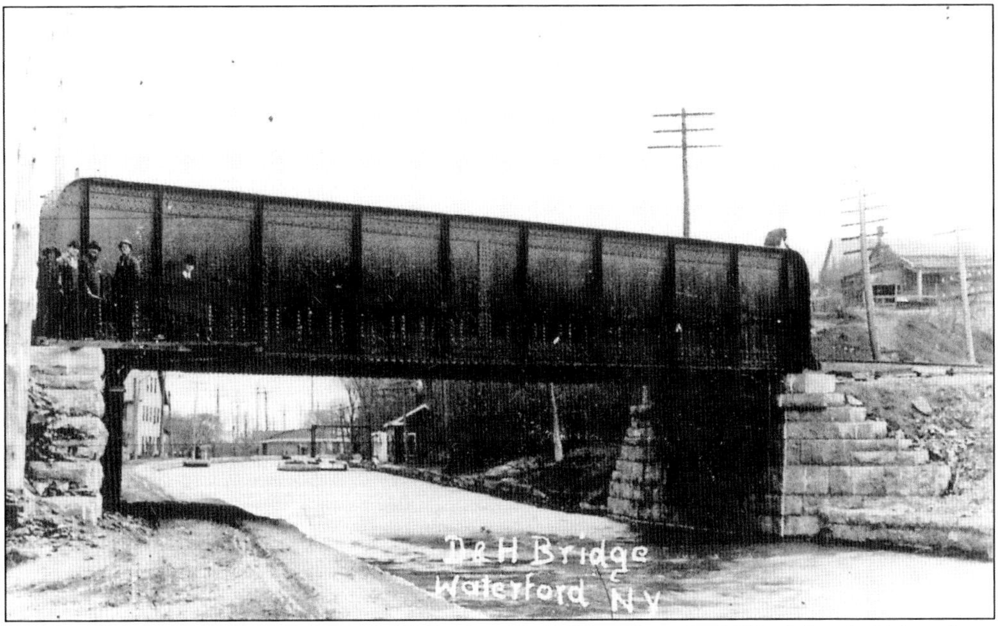

This is an interesting perspective of a different view of the Waterford Weigh Lock. Taken from just past the Black Bridge and looking toward Division Street, a close examination will reveal men posing on the bridge. Note the building behind the telephone pole it is believed to be Titcomb Distilleries, producers of Waterford whiskey. The buildings on the towpath were three stories high, and only the top floor was visible on the towpath. (Courtesy of Dennis Rivage.)

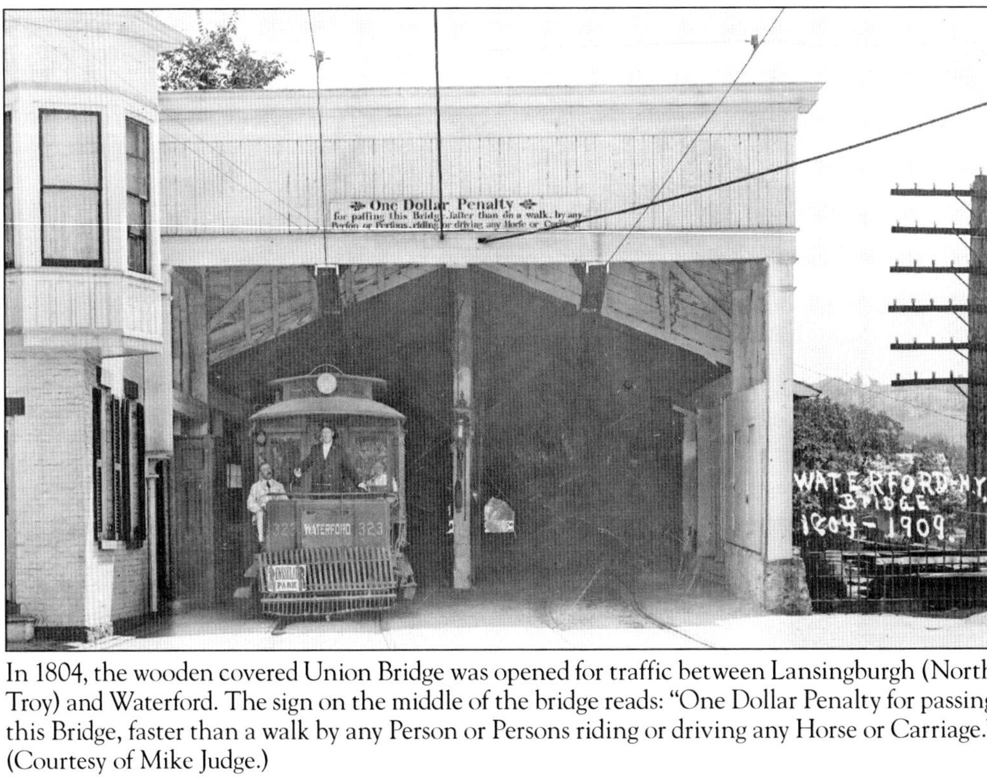

In 1804, the wooden covered Union Bridge was opened for traffic between Lansingburgh (North Troy) and Waterford. The sign on the middle of the bridge reads: "One Dollar Penalty for passing this Bridge, faster than a walk by any Person or Persons riding or driving any Horse or Carriage." (Courtesy of Mike Judge.)

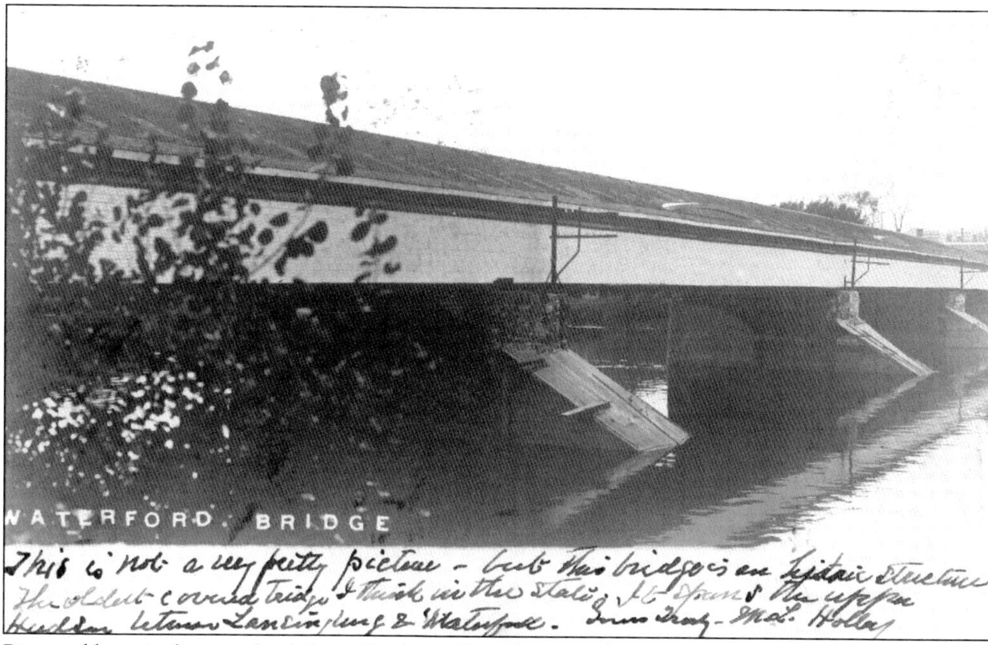

Pictured here is the wooden Union Bridge, officially opened on December 11, 1804, and destroyed by fire July 10, 1909. This four-span structure was 750 feet in length. The bridge was capable of carrying the 25-ton trolley cars of the Hudson Valley Trolley Company between Waterford and Lansingburgh. The bridge was replaced by a steel bridge, using the same abutments. (Courtesy of Frank McClement.)

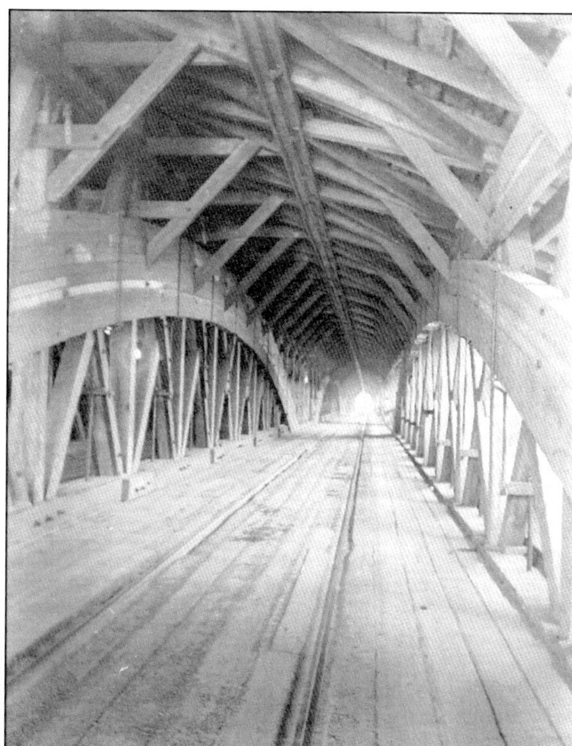

The interior and upper structure of the Union Bridge was all wood, built of red and white pine. One can appreciate the massive use of wooden beams, trusses, and oak planks used for the flooring from this offering. This covered bridge burned in 1909. Since it was made of unprotected, aged, and tinderbox dry wood, it presented a huge fire and conditions that the firefighters could not overcome. (Courtesy of Patricia Wilcox.)

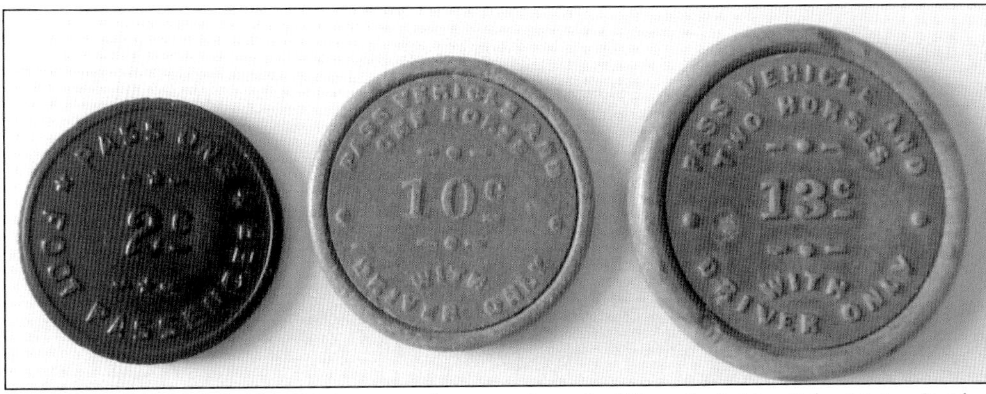

Shown are three of the four Vulcanite tokens used on the Waterford side of the Union Bridge. From left to right are a 2¢ pass for one individual on foot, a 10¢ pass for a one-horse vehicle and driver, and a 13¢ pass for a two-horse vehicle and the driver. The reverse of all three reads "Commutation Union B. Co. Waterford, N.Y."

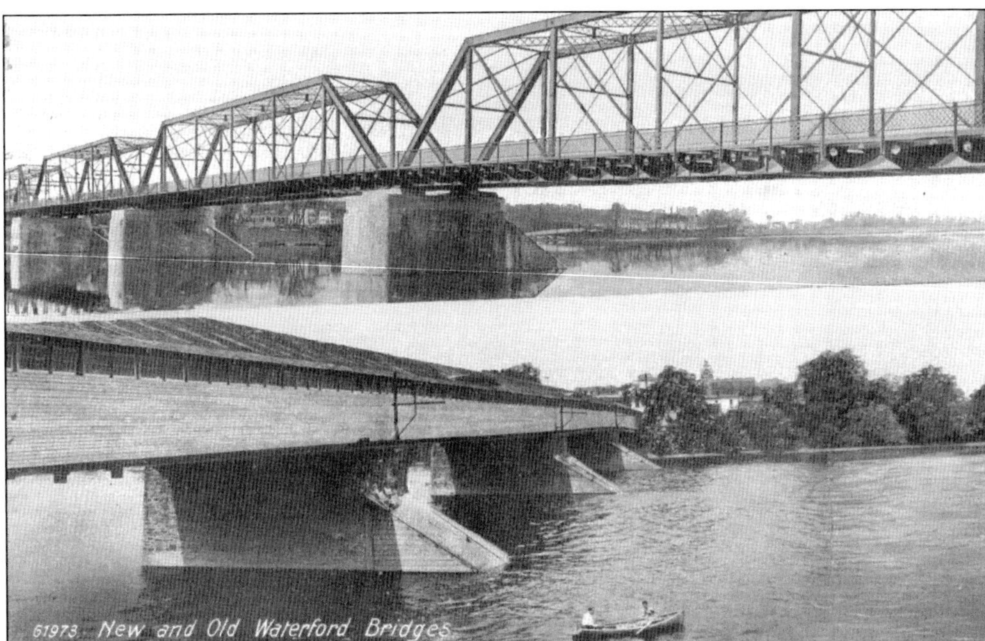

Note the piers supporting the wooden bridge and the added concrete structure erected at an angle into the upriver, or upstream. These additions were usually constructed with a wedge shape and served to break up ice jams during the spring thaw or divert large debris in times of flooding. The steel bridge shows the downriver, or downstream, side of the piers. These were often arched, allowing the ice or debris to flow easily past the pier.

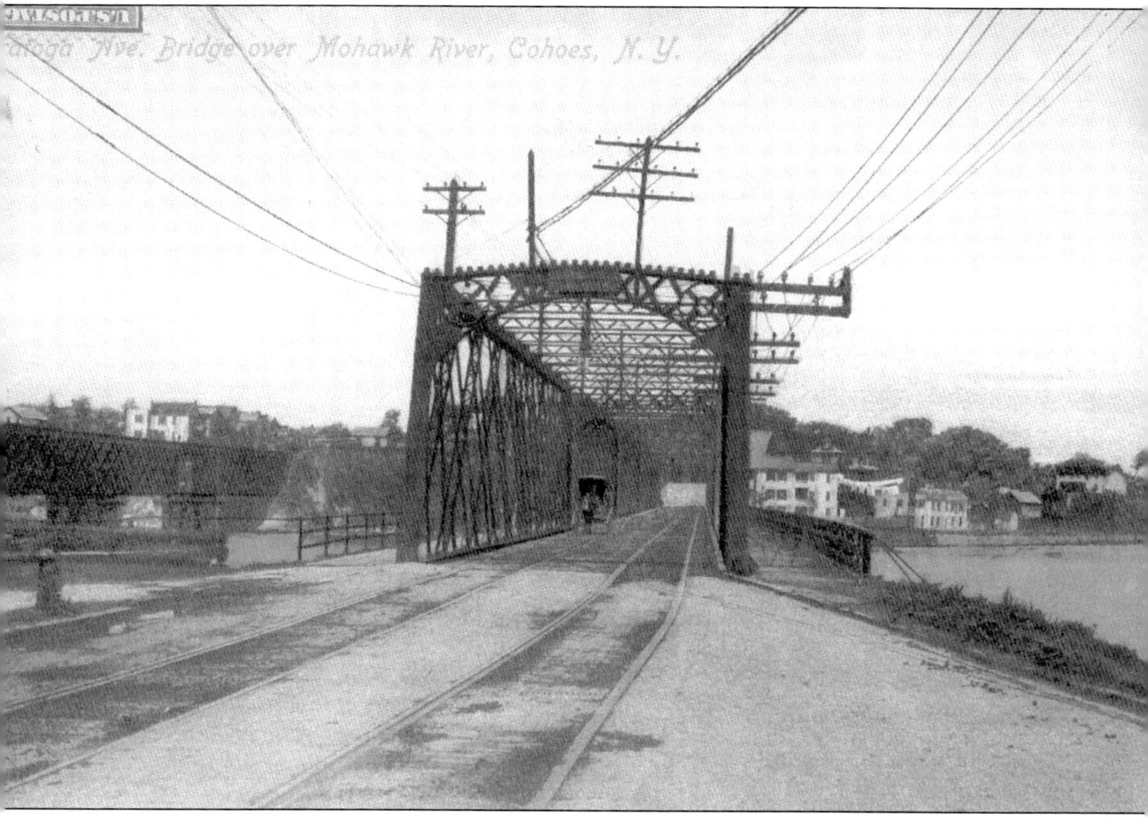

Pictured here in 1909 is the Saratoga Avenue iron bridge crossing over the Mohawk River, connecting Cohoes and Waterford. To the left the railroad bridge can be seen. Note the walkway (towpath) on the right side of the bridge; starting in Cohoes, it was the beginning of the southern end of the Champlain Canal. The mules would tow the boats out of Champlain Canal Lock 3 in Cohoes, then cross the bridge with their lines attached and tow the canal boats into Lock 4 in Waterford to continue their journey north to Whitehall, Lake Champlain, Vermont, and Canada. (Courtesy of Elaine Neveu McAllister.)

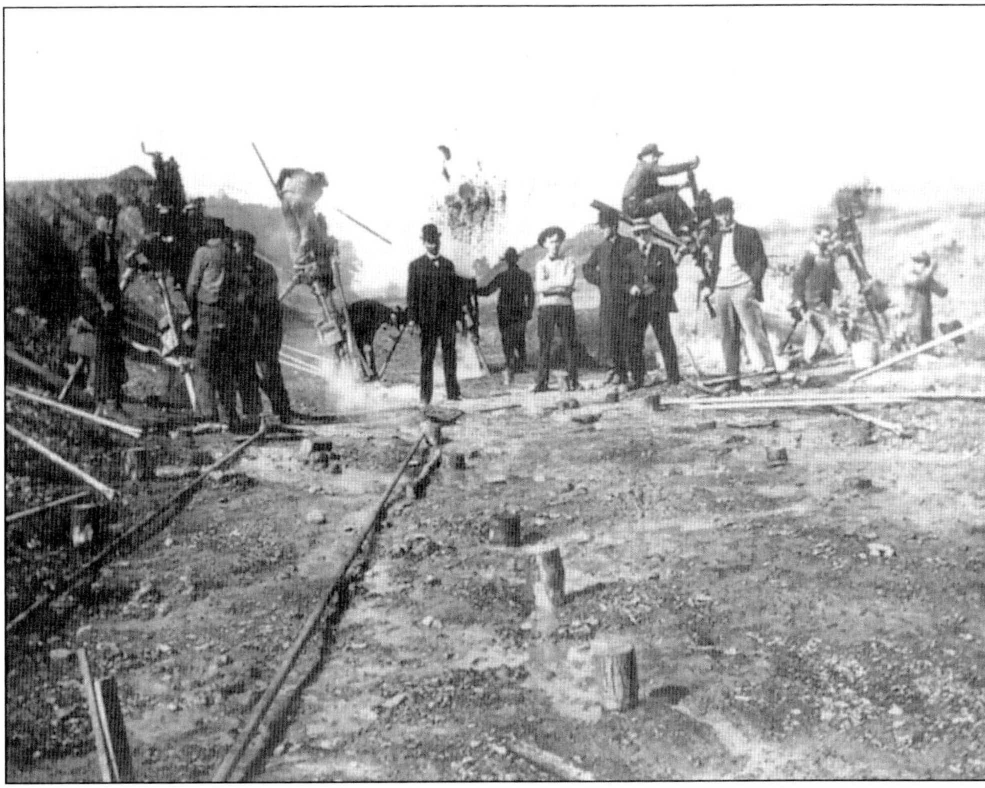

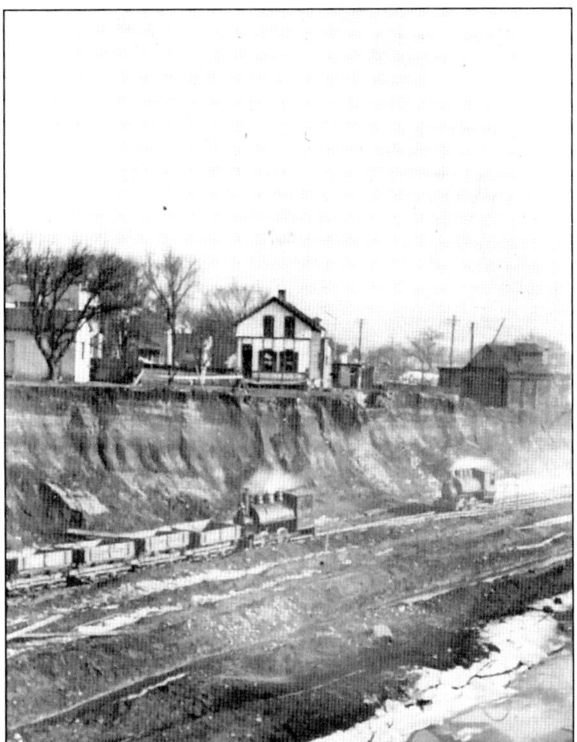

In 1903, New York State voters passed a referendum to finance and build the Barge Canal. By 1905, construction was under way for what would become known as the Flight of Locks, connecting the Hudson and Mohawk Rivers. After ground was broken and excavation began, a construction railroad had to be laid to supplement the building operation. Here, canal engineers are laying out that railroad. (Courtesy of Hugh Holton.)

Seen here is the construction railroad in use in the bed of the canal between Locks 2 and 3. Many buildings in Dial City, Sixth Street, West Street, now Seventh Street, and Eighth Street were moved or demolished for this project. Bush's Farm, located on present-day Ninth Street, was sold to make way for the canal. Waterford was changing, and not all were happy with these changes. (Courtesy of Hugh Holton.)

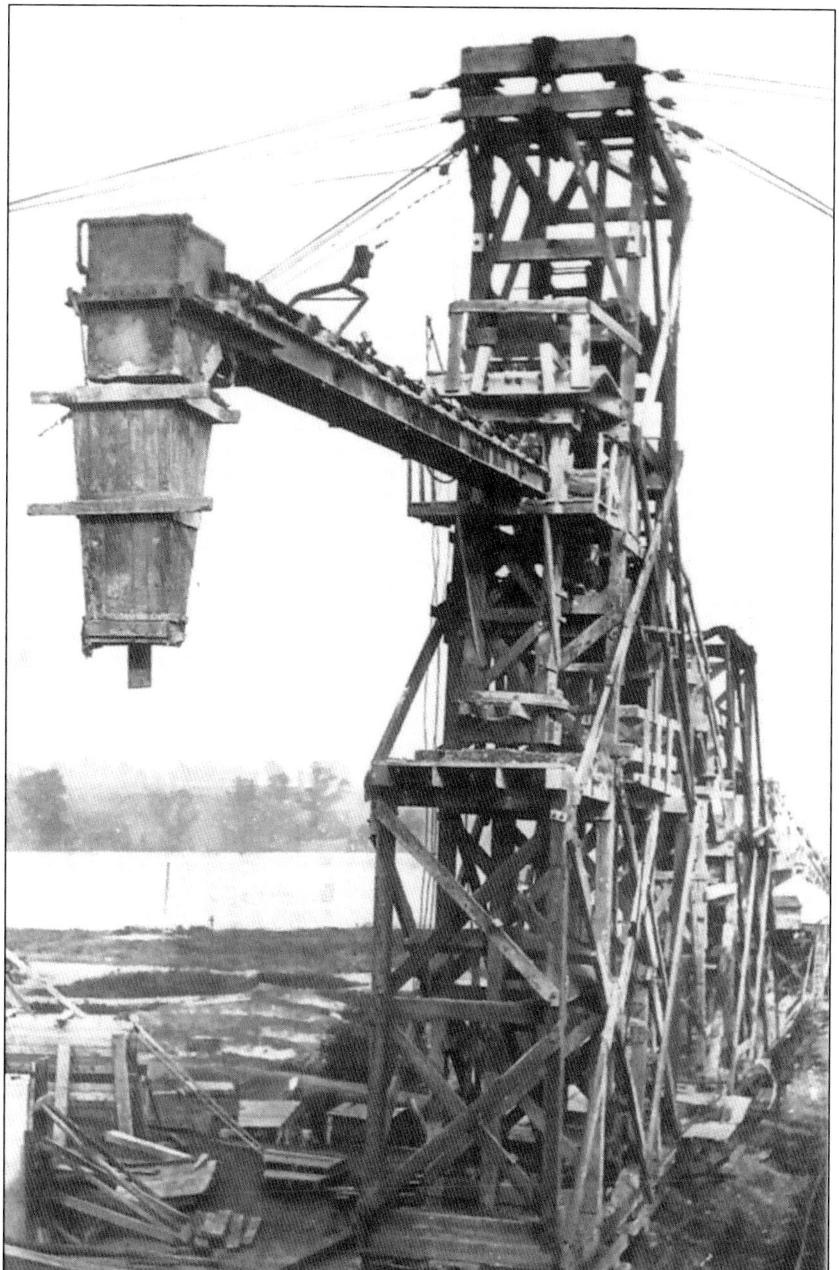

This was a cement elevator constructed on site for the building of the Barge Canal Flight. *Scientific American* magazine lauded the project: "This new waterway is the greatest canal improving project ever attempted and one of the greatest undertakings in the History of the World." This new undertaking was so important, in that it employed a relatively new construction method and product, that a concrete-testing lab was established in the basement of the New York State capitol. The lab geared up for the most extensive analysis of the comparatively new material to be done at a state level. The flight makes one great 169-foot climb from the Hudson River at Waterford to the Mohawk River in the Crescent area, 2.6 miles away, through five great locks. They are the greatest series of high-lift locks in the world. (Courtesy of James T. Lefebvre. DC.)

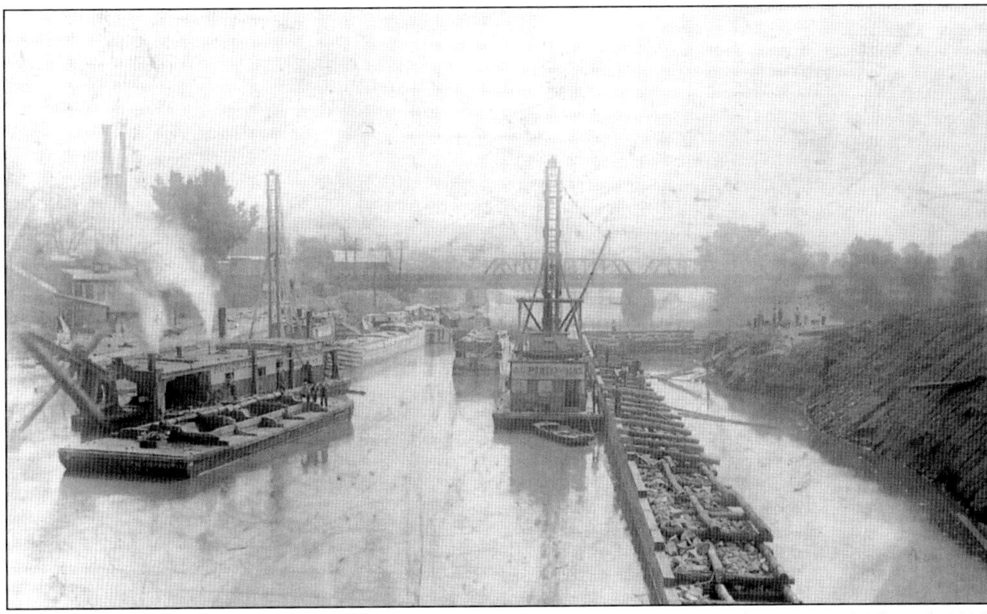

The people of Waterford experienced life-altering changes between the years 1905 and 1915. During this period, the Waterford Flight system of locks was being constructed. In this scene, the Waterford Harbor area is being deepened and widened, and the terminal approach wall is under construction. Tin shacks (shanty towns) housed the workers, and noise and dynamite blasts were everyday occurrences. (Courtesy of Frank McClement.)

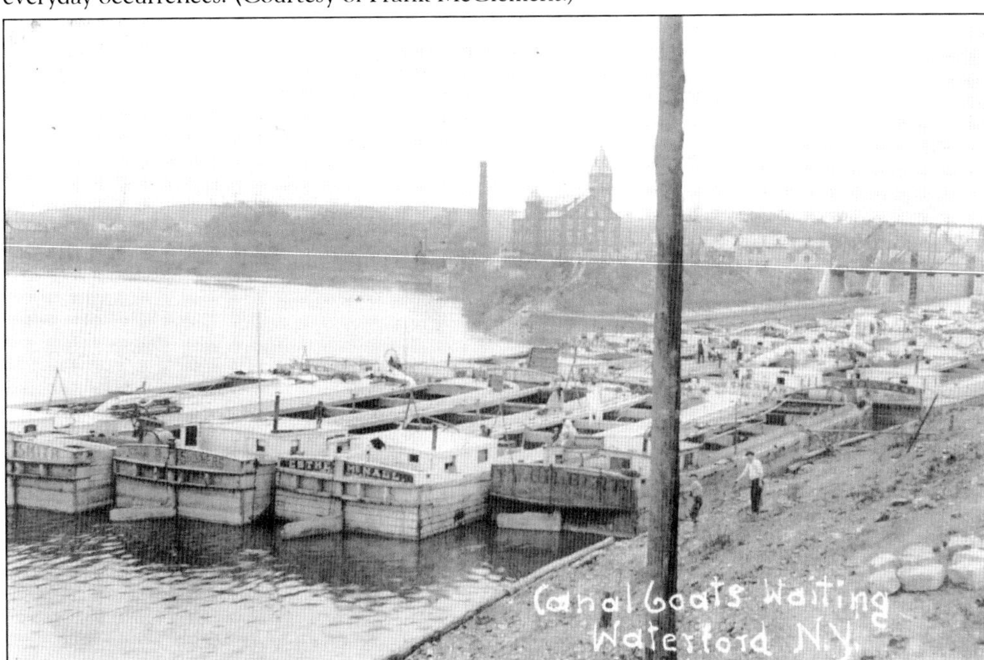

Canal boats waiting to enter the locks were a common Waterford sight from 1823 to 1918. These boats are all going to need two mules to continue their journey on the Champlain Canal. This means there are at least 240 mules nearby to accommodate the towing of these boats. (Courtesy of Mary Michon.)

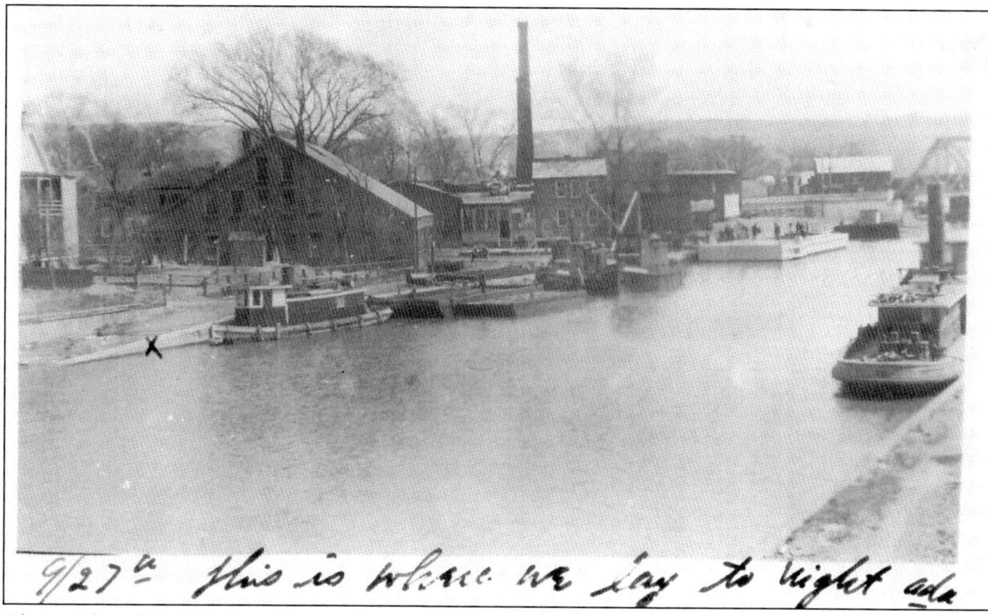

The sender of this Michon Postcard states, "This is where we lay tonight." Lay was a common term for the times when a tugboat crew would stop overnight. Waterford was, and still is, a favored place to stop because of its accessibility to a wide range of supplies, fulfilling a wide range of boaters needs and desires. (Courtesy of Bill Paquette.)

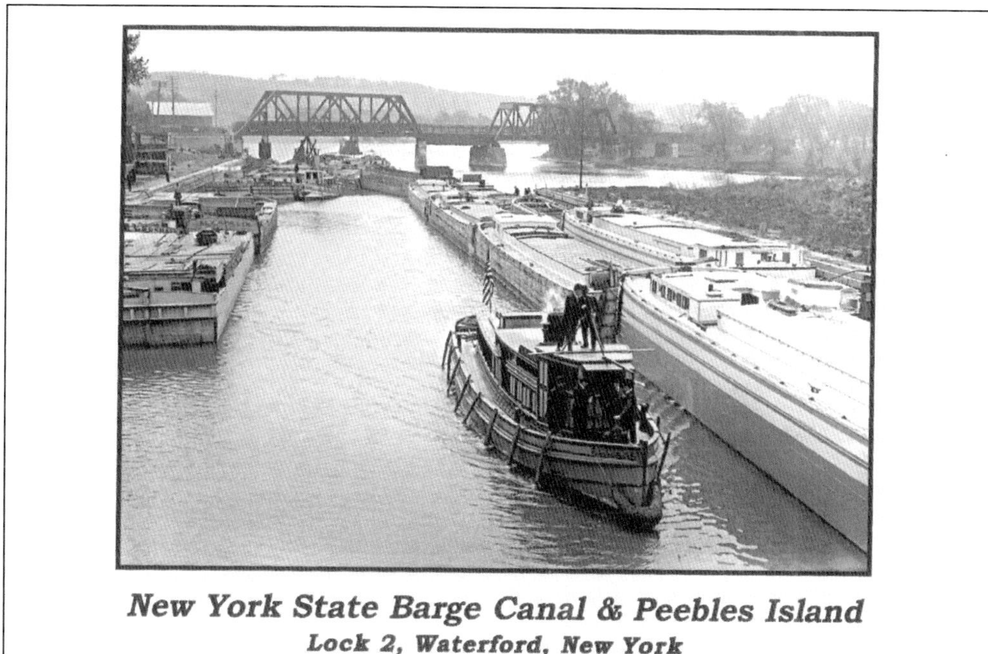

On May 15, 1915, New York State was ready to open the Barge Canal from Waterford to Rexford. This was a momentous occasion. Note a movie photographer on top of the tugboat pilot house. Unfortunately, that film is gone. The boats to the right in this photograph are taking part in the ceremonial opening of the Barge Canal while those to the left are awaiting entrance to enter the original Champlain Canal. (Courtesy of Russ Van Dervoort.)

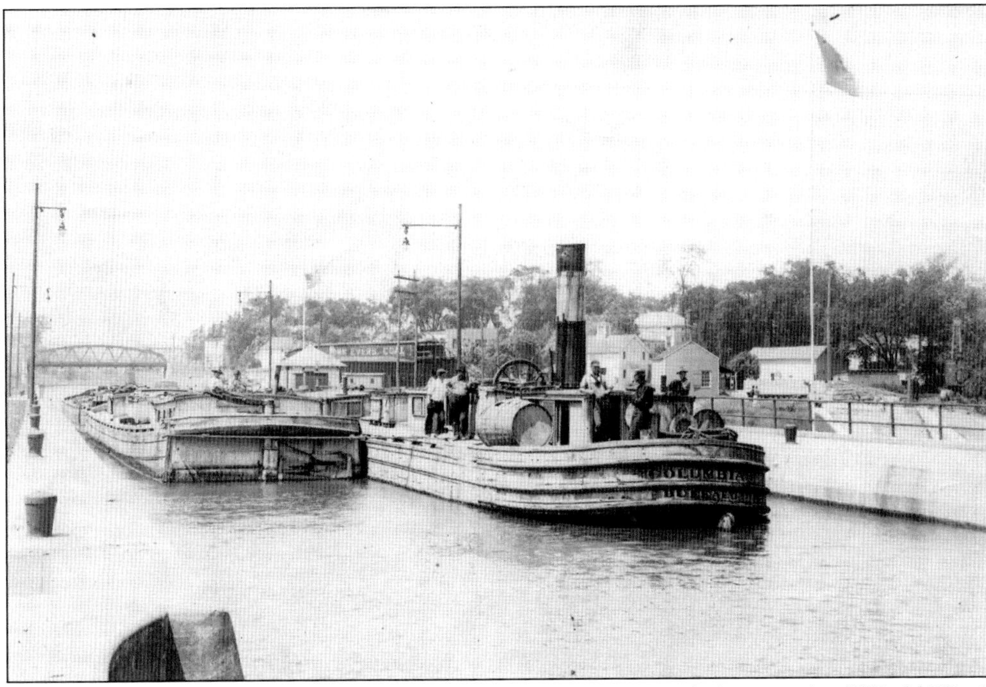

Pictured here around 1918 is Lock 2 on the new Erie Barge Canal. As a result of World War I, boats able to take advantage of the canals new dimensions had not yet been built. Here a steam-powered canal boat is propelling two others through the system. Proper boats to fully utilize the new canal would not be available until the mid-1920s. (Courtesy of Russ Van Dervoort.)

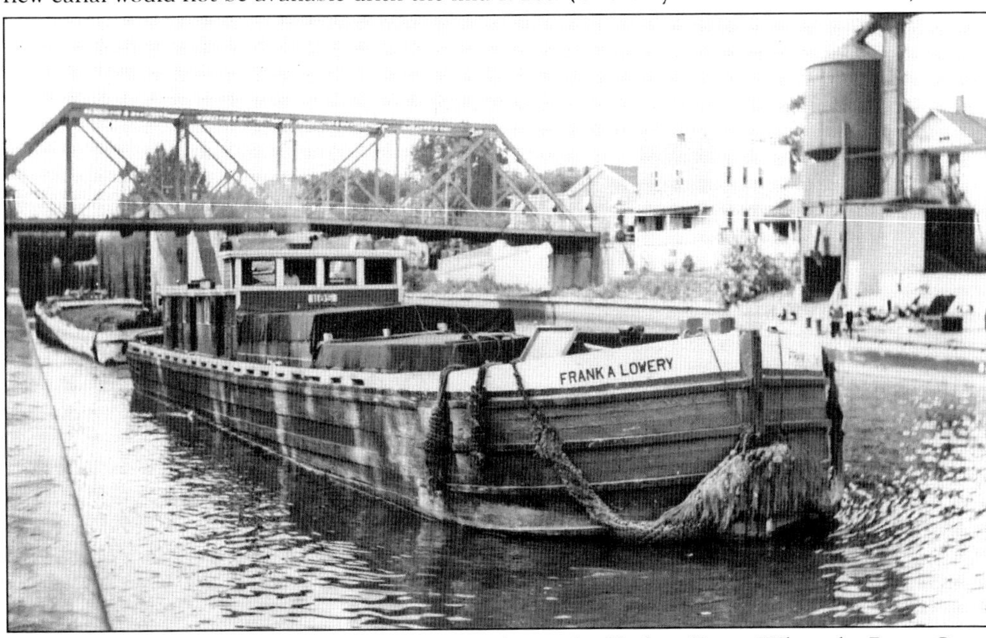

The *Frank A. Lowery* is pictured here exiting Lock 2 to the Hudson River. When the Barge Canal opened in Waterford, the harbor area became a terminal. Note the storage tower on the terminal wall; there were three of these in place until about 1950. Walking the promenade today, it is difficult to imagine these structures being in place. (Courtesy of Talia Futia.)

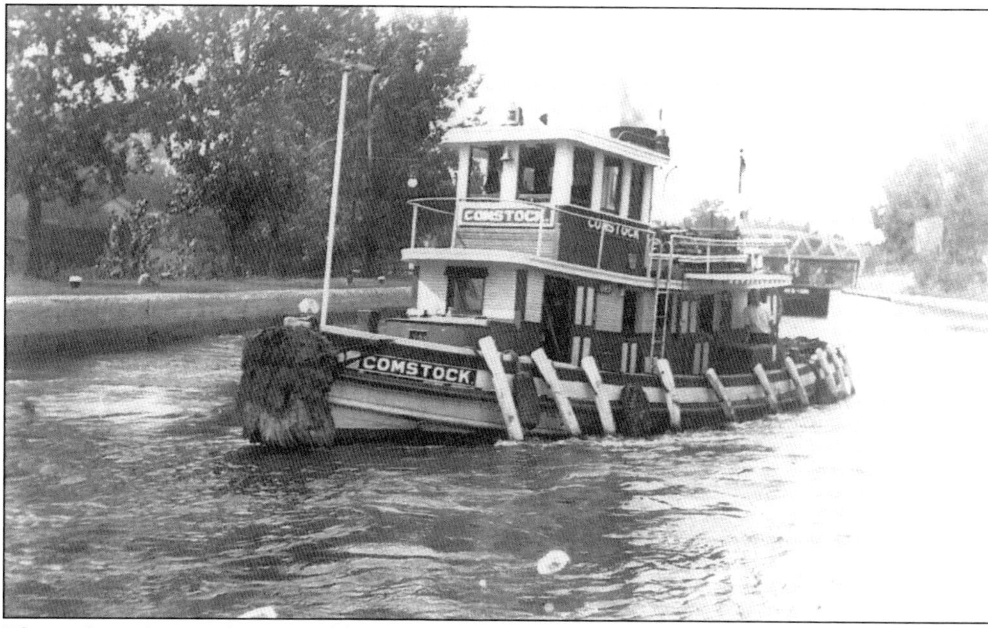

The tugboat *Comstock*, pictured here around 1940, is working the Barge Canal below Lock 3. It was built in 1911 and acquired by the Van Dervoort family of Waterford in 1921. The *Comstock* was utilized until 1942, assisting other tugboats moving scows through the lock system and working the Hudson and Mohawk Rivers. The captain, Louie Van Dervoort, notes in his logbook that during the 1926 season, the *Comstock* took on 82,410 pounds of coal, or an average of 638 pounds of coal daily.

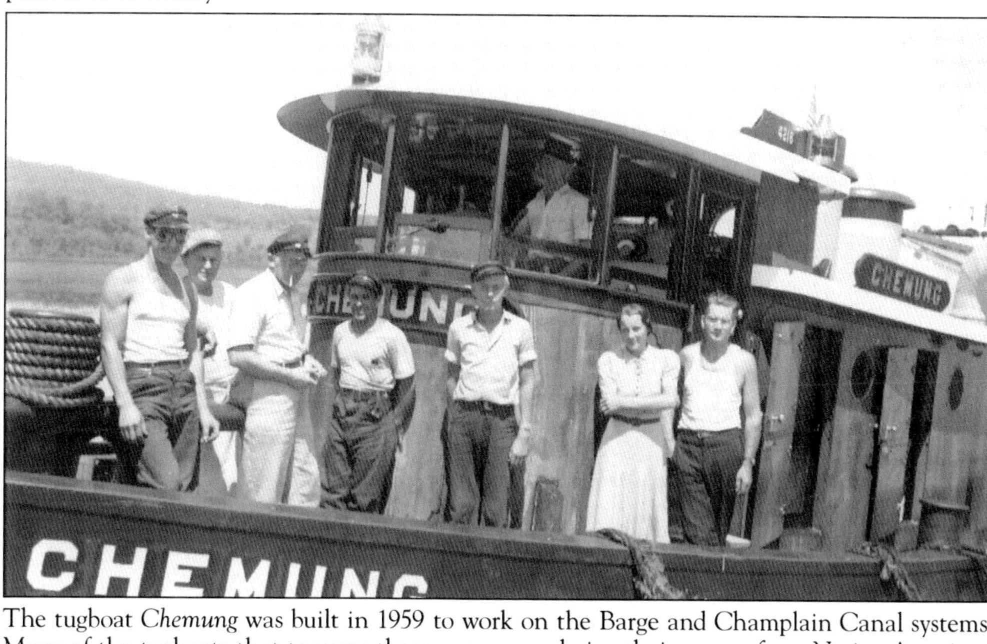

The tugboat *Chemung* was built in 1959 to work on the Barge and Champlain Canal systems. Many of the tugboats that traverse these waterways derive their names from Native American roots. Chemung means horn or antler in the language of the Seneca tribe. Norm Paquette (center) served on many tugboats of that era, as did so many other Waterfordians. He retired as a captain. (Courtesy of Bill Paquette.)

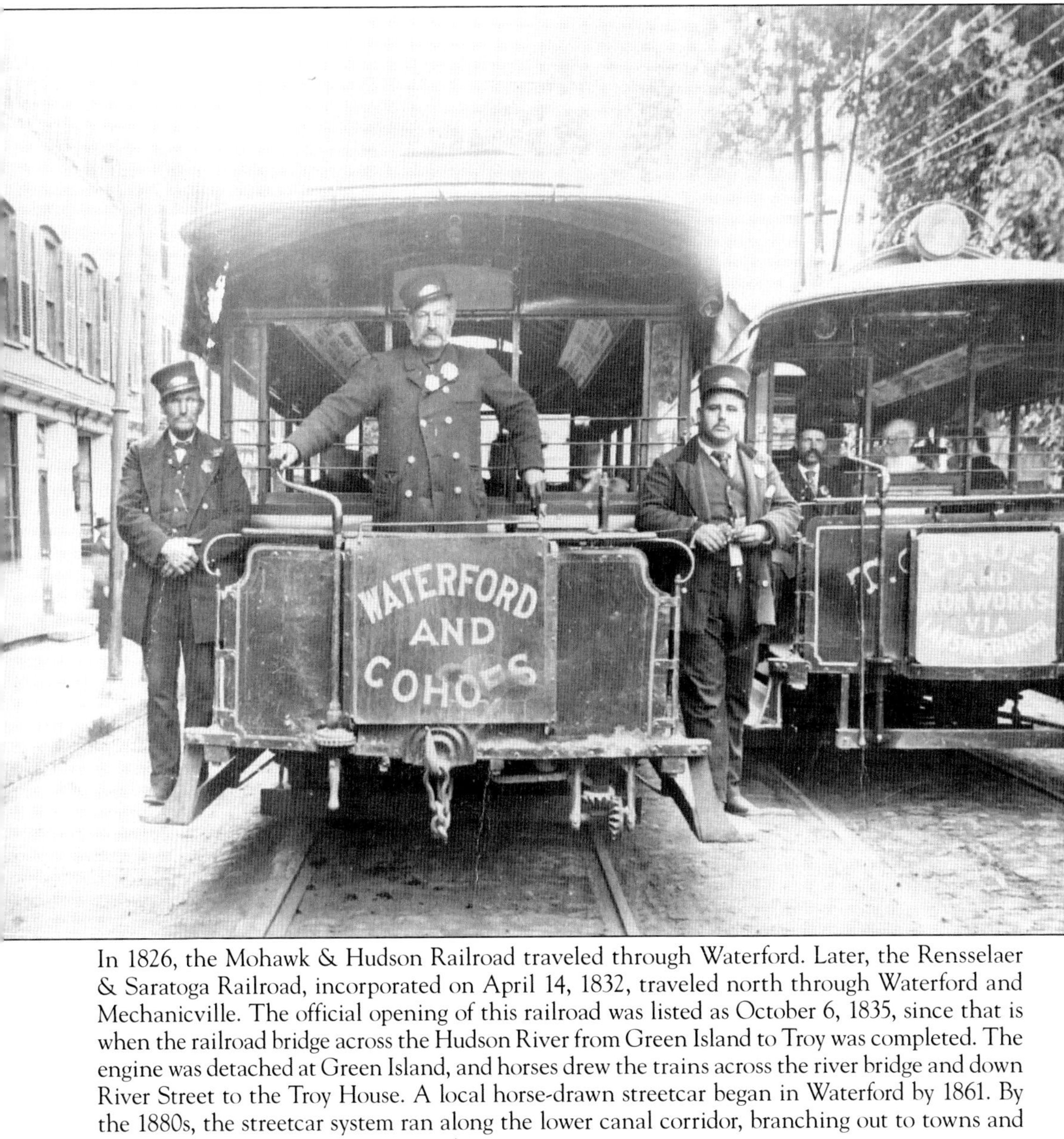

In 1826, the Mohawk & Hudson Railroad traveled through Waterford. Later, the Rensselaer & Saratoga Railroad, incorporated on April 14, 1832, traveled north through Waterford and Mechanicville. The official opening of this railroad was listed as October 6, 1835, since that is when the railroad bridge across the Hudson River from Green Island to Troy was completed. The engine was detached at Green Island, and horses drew the trains across the river bridge and down River Street to the Troy House. A local horse-drawn streetcar began in Waterford by 1861. By the 1880s, the streetcar system ran along the lower canal corridor, branching out to towns and villages. (Courtesy of Dennis Rivage.)

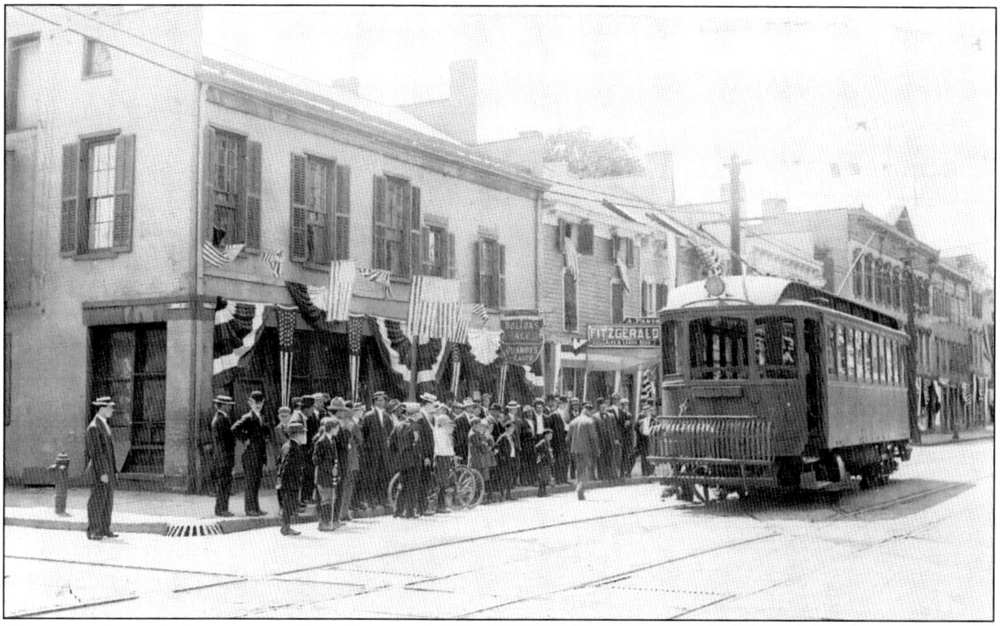

A group of people has gathered at the southwest corner of Broad and Third Streets. What appears to be a Fourth of July or other holiday celebration turns out to be a crowd of onlookers. Upon further inspection of the photograph, the motorman is out of the trolley inspecting the car. The trolley actually jumped the track, and the undercarriage is lying on the ground beneath the trolley.

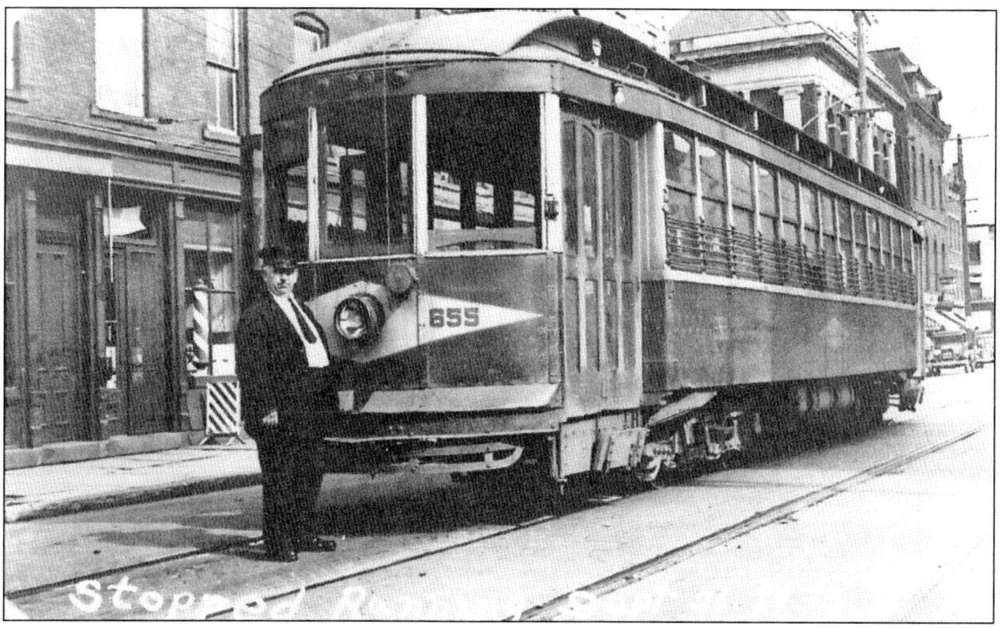

The Waterford Trolley was known as the Green Line. In the late 19th and early 20th century, the trolley was a main method of transportation between villages, towns, and cities. They were convenient, inexpensive, and fairly reliable. The trolleys were stored in Lansingburgh and ran across the Union Bridge into Waterford. Waterford saw the last of the trolley runs in 1933. (Courtesy of Bill Paquette.)

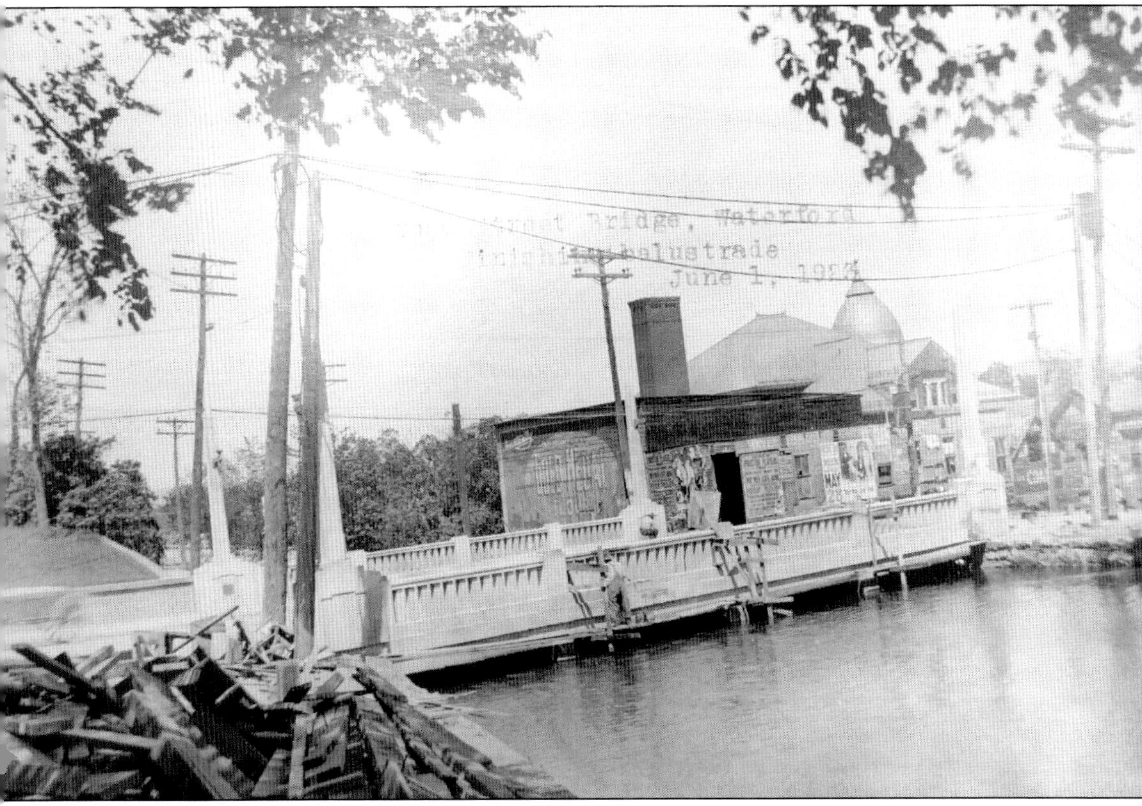

This newly constructed bridge over the Old Champlain Canal on Broad Street was for many years an iron lift bridge. By 1922, the lift bridge was no longer needed, as the Champlain Barge Canal was open, and it was replaced with the bridge pictured here. The old iron bridge was the cause of many delays when it was open for the passage of the canal boats. The removal of the lift bridge was a welcomed change for many Waterfordians of that era, while many others who relied on the passage of the canal boats for a living were not so pleased. Workers can be seen on the scaffolding putting the finishing touches on the bridge along with a large pile of rubble left over from the removal of the old iron bridge. (Courtesy of Donald Bowles.)

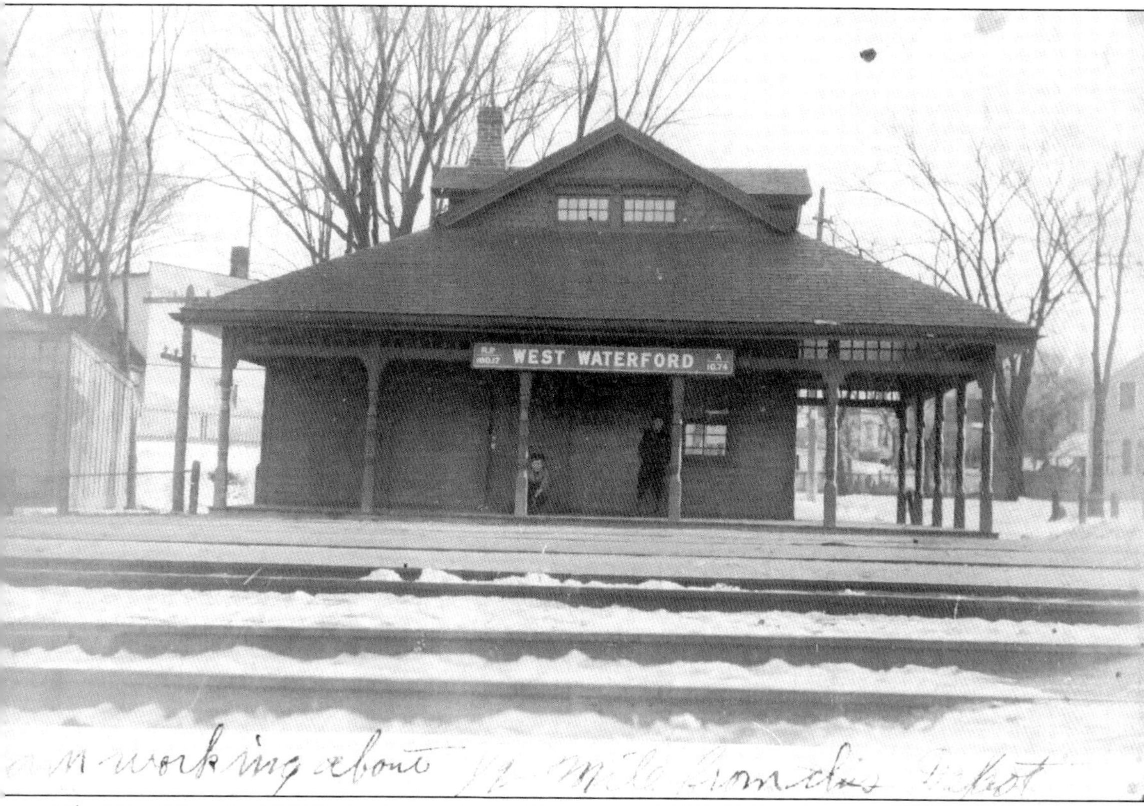

The West Waterford D&H Station is pictured here around 1910. R. Brink wrote, "[I] am working about 1/2 mile from this depot. I rode around on the engine yesterday and went to work this morning. I have to go to work at 4 A.M. and work until 12. I have to get up at 3 oclock and that is harder work than the rest of it. I have to carry my breakfast in a pail, have a good place to board." (Courtesy of Gwen E. Terry Piacente.)

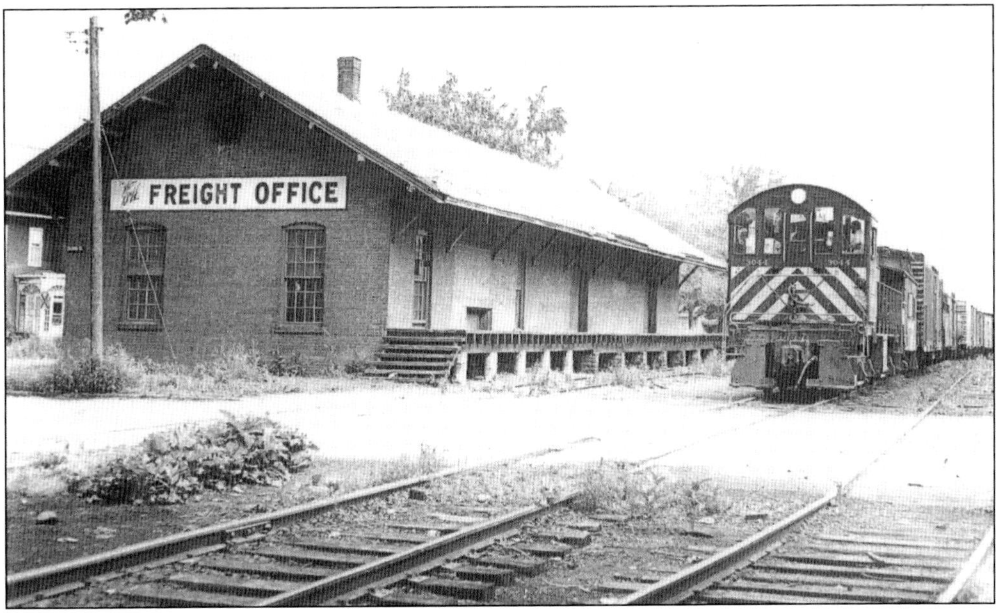

The Waterford freight station, located on upper Third Street, served as both a passenger and freight station. It was built in 1896 and served the Rensselaer and Saratoga Line running from Troy via Waterford to Ballston Spa. It was also used by the Delaware & Hudson Railroad. The Waterford station closed in the 1970s. It became a restaurant in the late 1980s and today houses the Waterford Public Library. (Courtesy of Mike Marchese.)

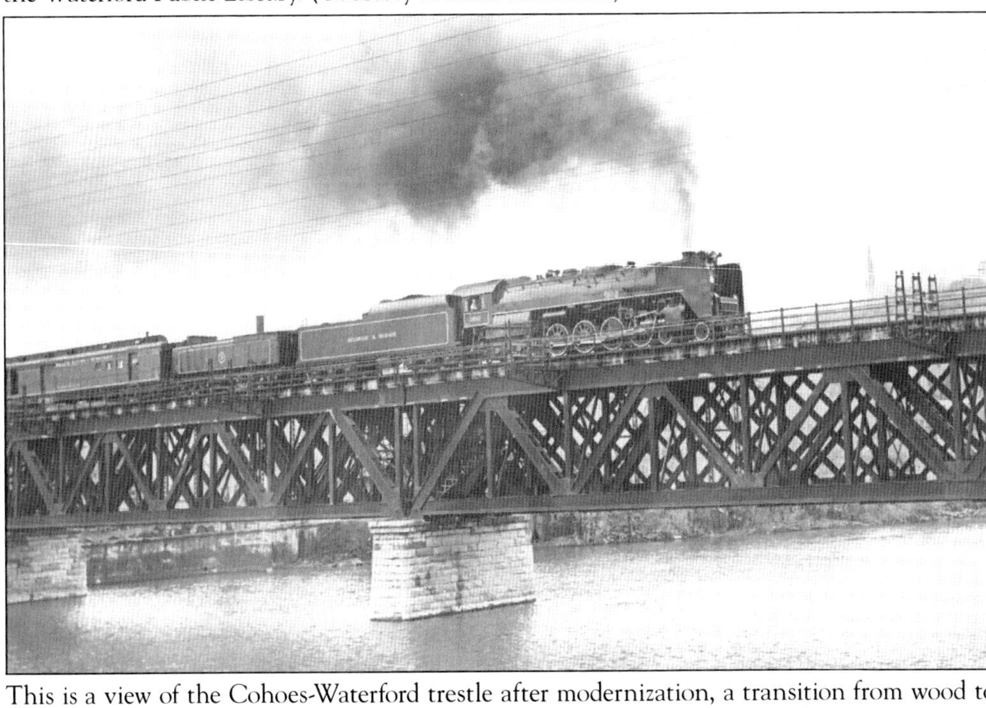

This is a view of the Cohoes-Waterford trestle after modernization, a transition from wood to steel. One can see a much more substantial and busier train on the bridge. This passenger train made stops in Waterford until the late 1960s; during this era, the railroads were affecting the freight tonnage being transported through the canals. (Courtesy of Dennis Rivage.)

Five

DISASTERS

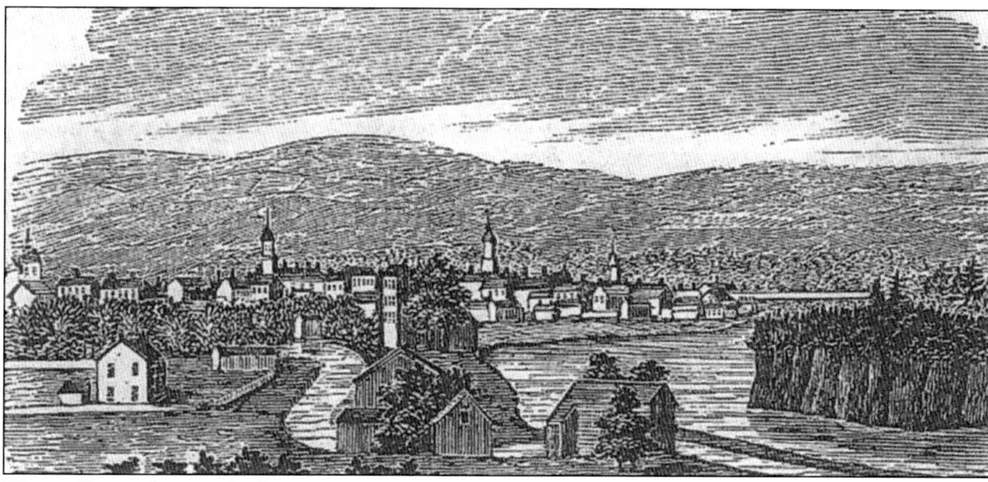

The Village of Waterford was incorporated on March 25, 1794, and the Town of Waterford was incorporated on April 17, 1816. It has a population of about 1,600 residents and is pleasantly situated at the junction of the Mohawk and Hudson Rivers, 10 miles north of Albany. This annexed view was taken on the road to Cahoos (Cohoes) Falls, about a mile west of the village. Here, there are four churches: Presbyterian, Methodist, Episcopal, and Dutch Reformed; an academy; and a bank. It is favorably located for trade on the lines of the Champlain Canal and Rensselaer & Saratoga Railroad. It also derives considerable importance from the navigation of small vessels on the Hudson River. There is an outlet here from the canal by three locks, each 11 feet, to the Mohawk River. The agricultural and manufactured products exported from the village annually amount to about $1 million. The waterpower used in the large manufacturing establishments at this place is derived from the Mohawk River. Since the drawing for the above engraving was made, a destructive fire broke out July 11, 1841, destroying a large portion of this flourishing village.

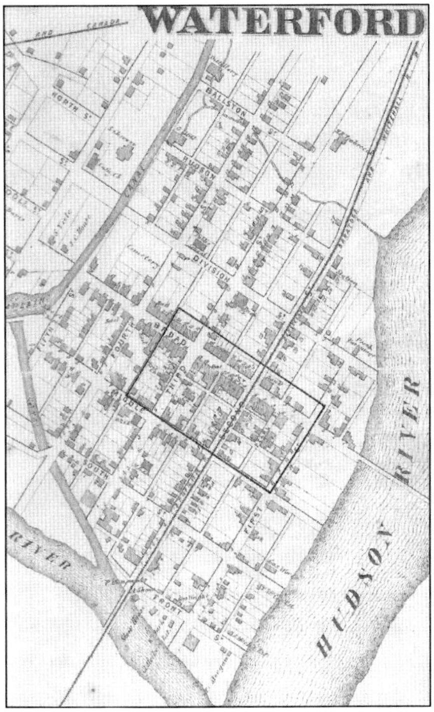

The area of Waterford outlined in black here was devastated by the fire of July 11, 1841. A letter dated August 15, 1841, from E.J. Smith reads, "The fire commenced in the barns and spread with great rapidity-The Episcopal Church and the houses on each side of it were on fire-The flames raged with unabated fury.-I called two or three men who assisted in carrying water on to the roof which was repeatedly on fire-the fire crossed the railroad." There were 178 stores, storehouses, and dwellings destroyed.

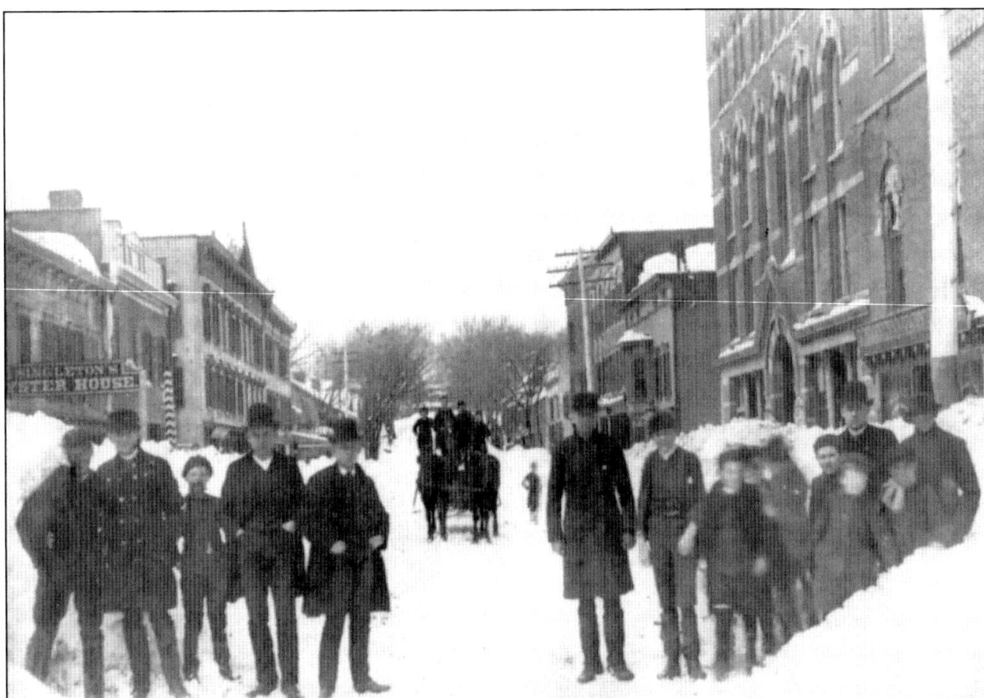

The great blizzard of 1888 began on March 11 and lasted through March 14. It was the most severe blizzard in the history of the United States at that time. Some 20 to 60 inches of snow fell in the state of New York. Drifts were 30 to 40 feet high. Rail service was halted, and roads were impassable for up to a week. (Courtesy of Ann Marie Wiles Lomas.)

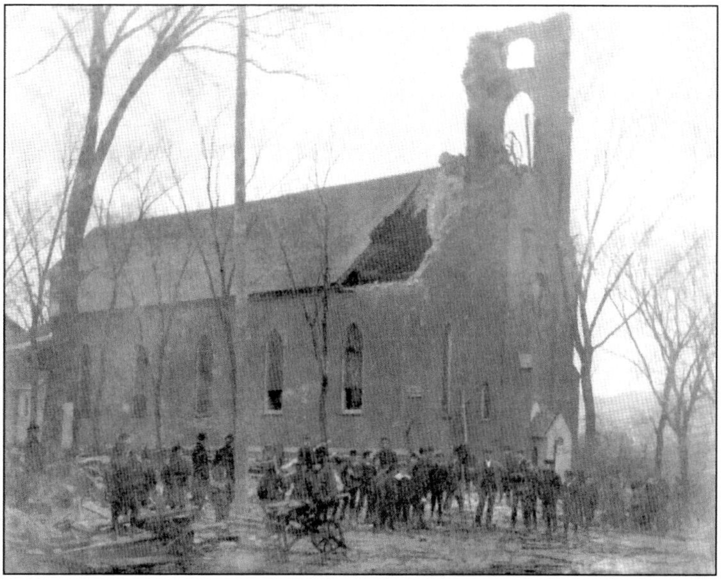

The original St. Mary's Church is at the northeast corner of Sixth and Division Streets. Shown is the damage caused by a tornado in 1894. Built in 1848, it still stands at its original location after being replaced by the present St. Mary's Church in 1913. (Courtesy of James T. Lefebvre, DC.)

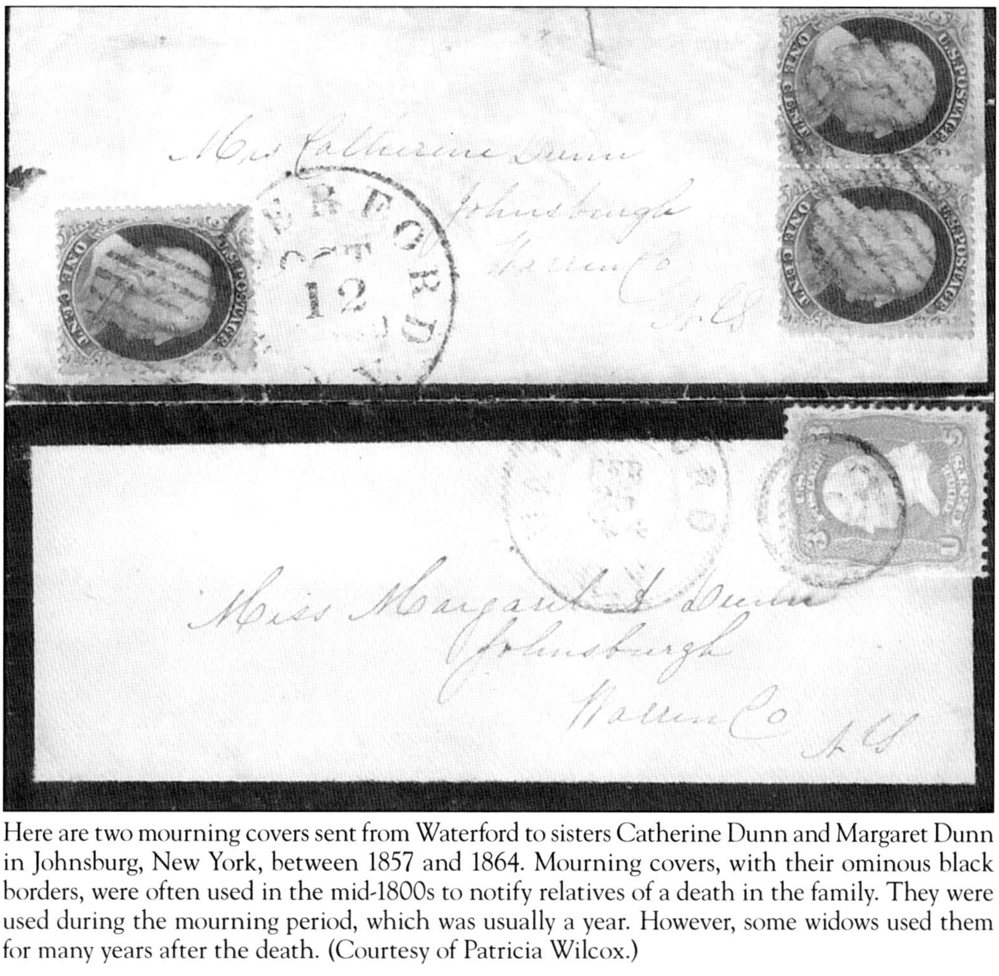

Here are two mourning covers sent from Waterford to sisters Catherine Dunn and Margaret Dunn in Johnsburg, New York, between 1857 and 1864. Mourning covers, with their ominous black borders, were often used in the mid-1800s to notify relatives of a death in the family. They were used during the mourning period, which was usually a year. However, some widows used them for many years after the death. (Courtesy of Patricia Wilcox.)

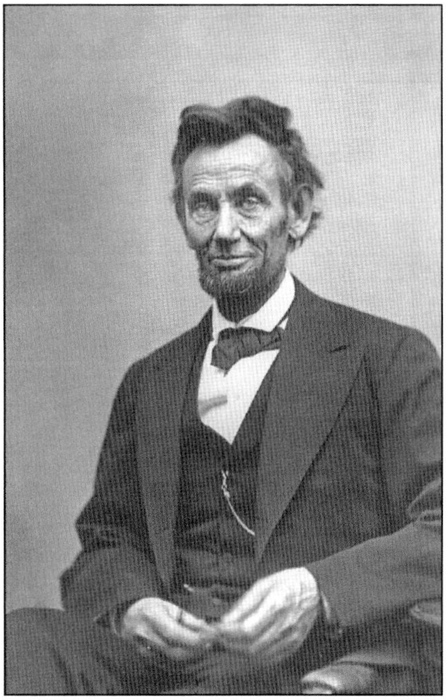

E.G. Munson of Waterford wrote the following in his diary on Saturday, April 15, 1865: "The nation mourns—deeply—the loss of our President—Abraham Lincoln—who was shot by a Human Fiend in Washington at about 9 1/2 o'clock last night—living until 22 minutes past this morning. Many a tear has fallen for him so suddenly and unexpectedly called away. Flags at half mast and buildings public and private draped in black. Vice President Andrew Johnson sworn into the Presidential office made so suddenly vacant at 11 a.m. today."

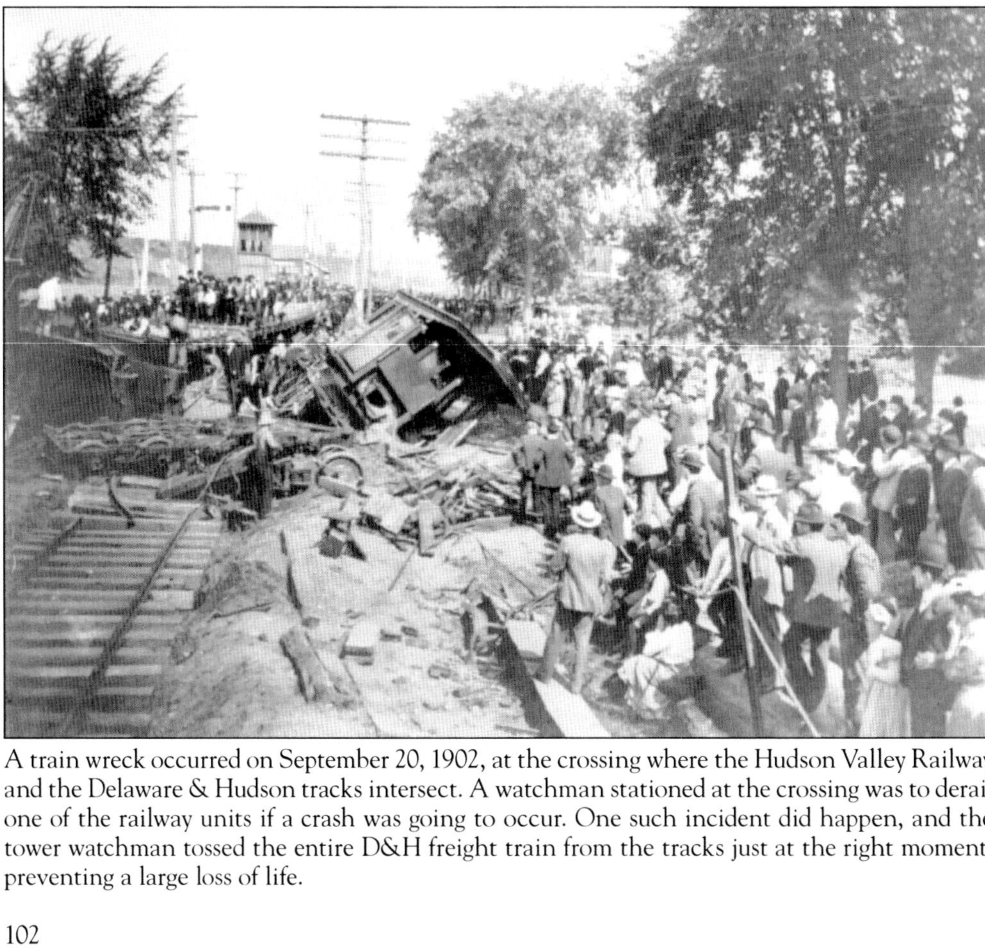

A train wreck occurred on September 20, 1902, at the crossing where the Hudson Valley Railway and the Delaware & Hudson tracks intersect. A watchman stationed at the crossing was to derail one of the railway units if a crash was going to occur. One such incident did happen, and the tower watchman tossed the entire D&H freight train from the tracks just at the right moment, preventing a large loss of life.

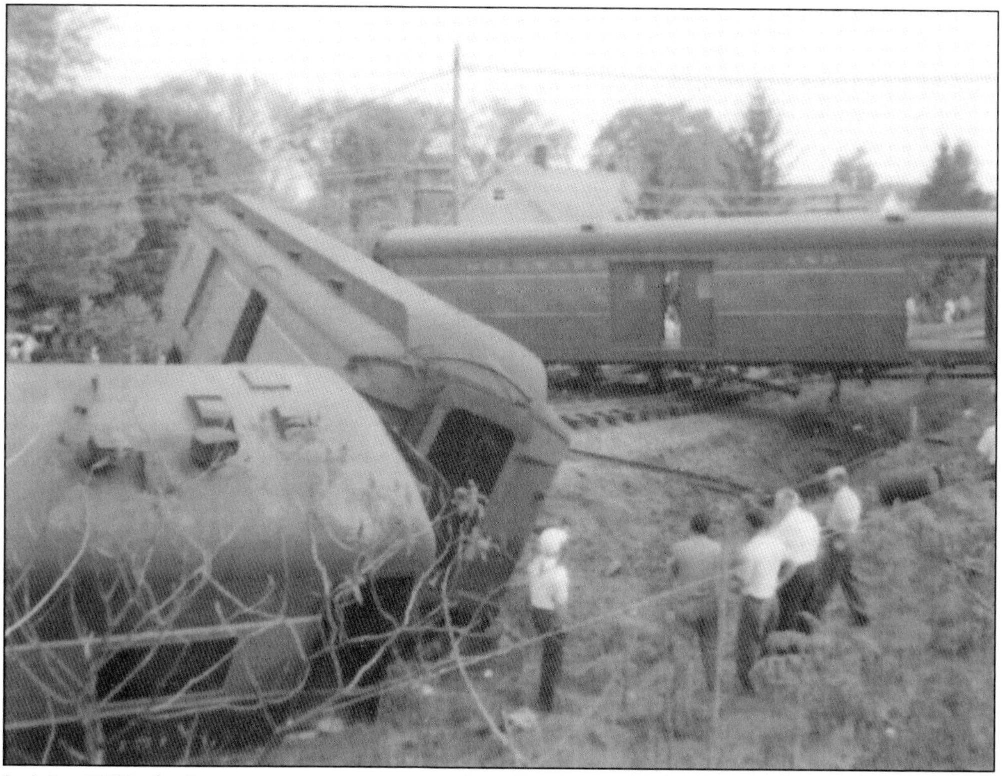

In May 1962, the Laurention train was traveling from Montreal, Canada, to Albany, New York, when it derailed next to the Waterford Rural Cemetery in Northside. The train cars ripped up hundreds of feet of track, coming to rest scattered all along the rail line. A crewman was fatally injured, and several other passengers had to be transported to a local hospital for medical treatment. (Courtesy of Michael D. Marchese.)

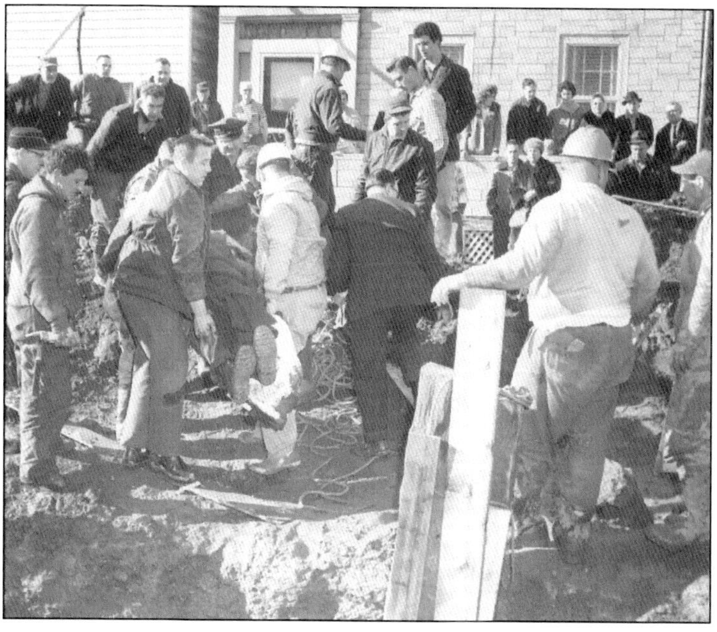

At right is the rescue of Herbert Wilson, a construction worker who was working on raising the D&H Railroad's Second Street Bridge in Waterford. On January 22, 1964, a retaining wall collapsed and pinned him under heavy concrete. A water main ruptured, and water was filling up the hole. After frantically working for two hours, the wall was pulled off by a crane and Wilson was rescued, escaping serious injury. (Courtesy of Dennis Rivage.)

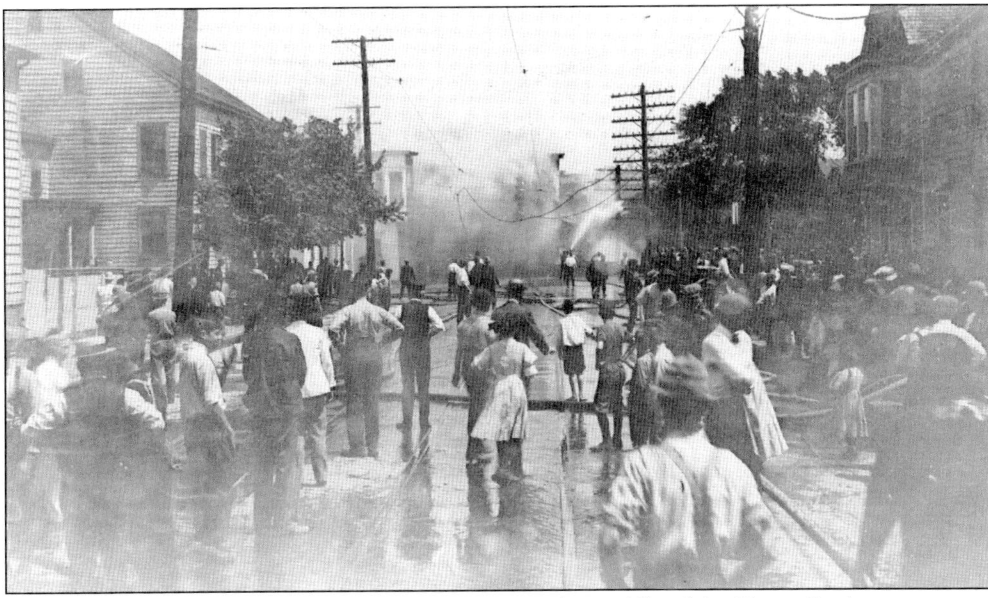

As the United Traction Company trolley was passing the middle of the Union Bridge, motorman Walter Wright looked downward and saw flames leaping from possible faulty insulation in the flooring. Written on the back of the postcard is the following: "This is just as the fire is breaking out at the Waterford end of the bridge, 12:55 PM, Saturday, July 10, 1909." (Courtesy of Gwen E. Terry Piacente.)

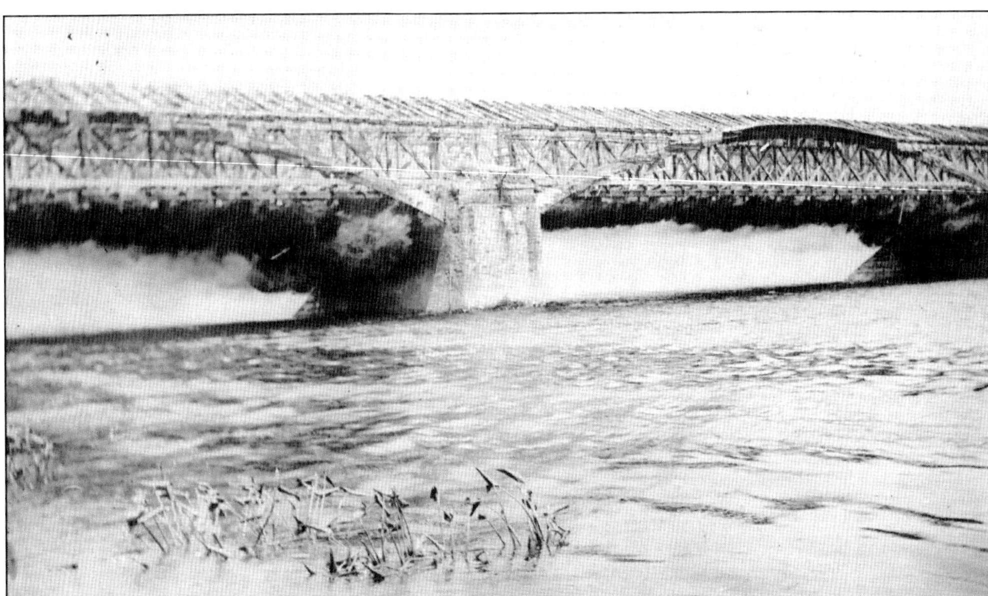

Opening to traffic on December 3, 1804, the 105-year-old Union Bridge is now fully engulfed in flames. A six-inch gas main pulled apart, causing a new inferno. In just 35 minutes, the destruction was complete. (Courtesy of Gwen E. Terry Piacente.)

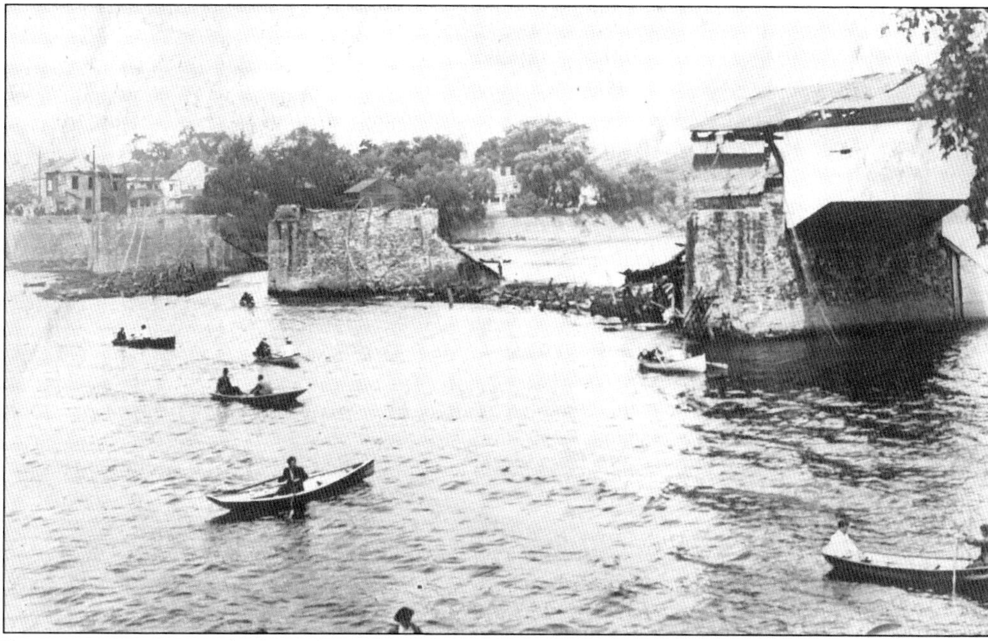

Boaters are getting a look at the 1909 Union Bridge fire. The fire, fanned by strong winds and exploding gas pipes, drove firefighters from the bridge. Six volunteers fell into the river and fortunately were rescued without serious injury. Along with normal foot, horse, and carriage traffic, the bridge served as a rail line for the Hudson Valley Railway. (Courtesy of Helen Grochmal Anderson.)

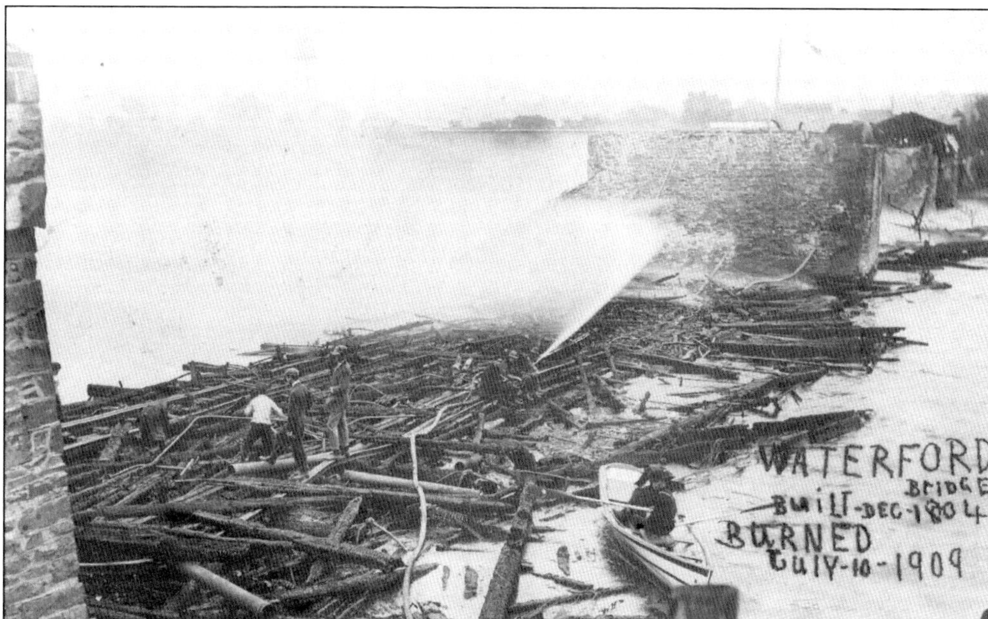

A note was written on the back of the postcard: "Dear Will—You will never again cross the Union Bridge, as this is all that is left of it. Not a timber is left on our end; only one span is left on the Lansingburgh side. This view looks towards the burgh. It burned at noon Saturday the 10th. The wind blew a gale at the time." (Courtesy of Mike Cicchinelli.)

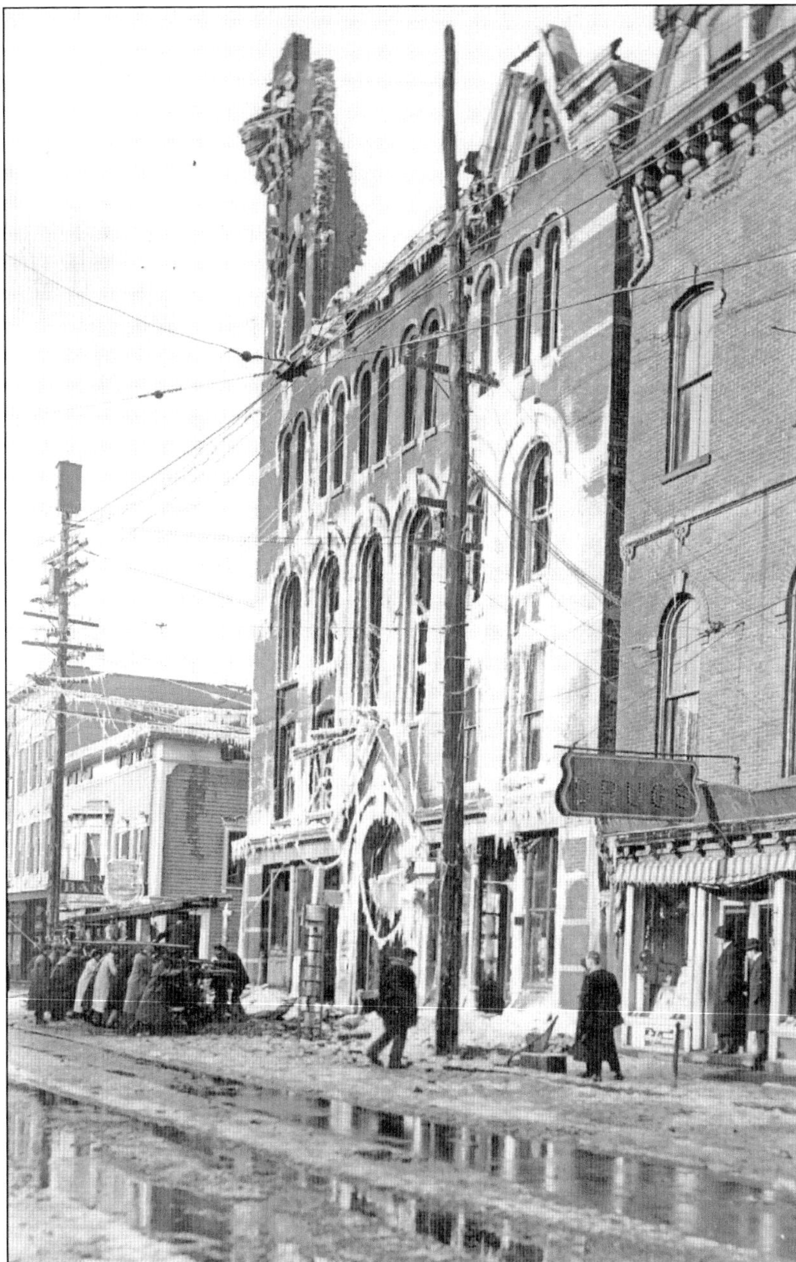

A fire broke out on July 11, 1841, that destroyed over half of the village, including the town hall. All the records of the town were lost in the fire. As a result, the people wanted to build a firebox to keep the records safe. After the cornerstone of the town hall was laid, the new civic structure was completed on September 16, 1843, and included a firebox. However, on January 6, 1914, another fire again destroyed the town hall. Many of the new records again were lost, as the fire box was too small. The Waterford Fire Department and their Button Steamer were assisted by the Murphy Company of Cohoes and the Twinning Company from Lansingburgh. This fire was contained to the town hall, which again was rebuilt and still stands today. (Courtesy of Fran Santspree Cullett.)

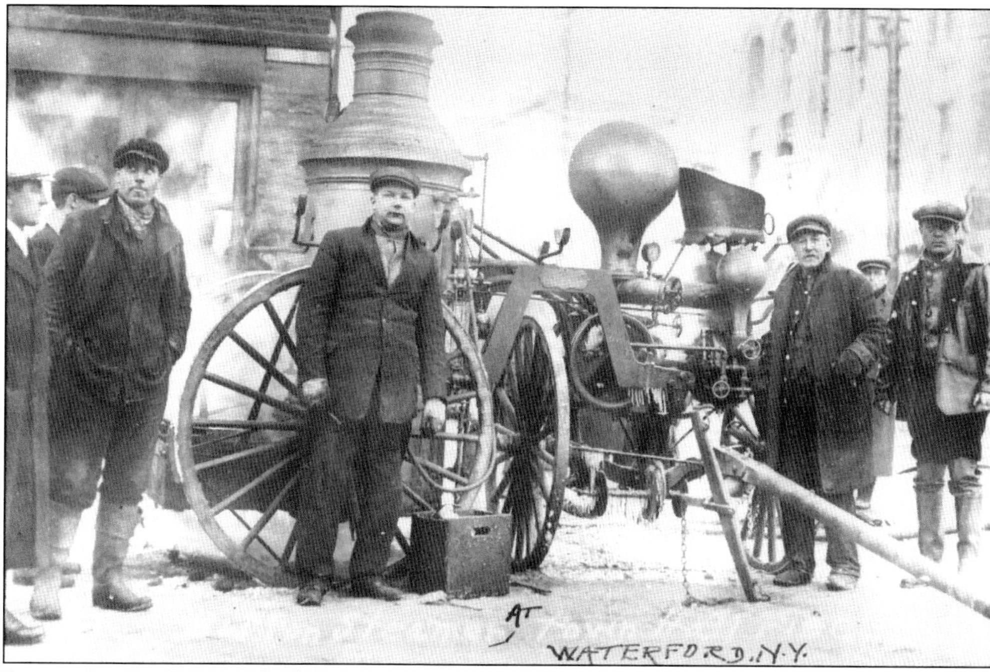

Responding to the town hall fire of 1914 are Al Batt (far right), engineer of the Knickerbocker Steamer Company, and Henry "Jersey" Gaunt (second from right), an expert machinist and specialist of fire engines. In front of the boiler is Russ Baker. (Courtesy of Dennis Rivage.)

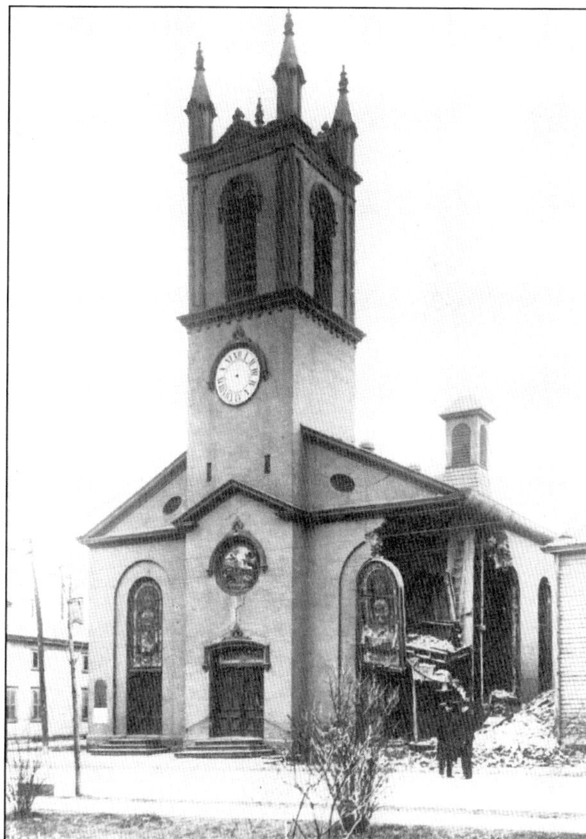

Pictured here is the damage to the Presbyterian church on the southeast corner of Third and Division Streets. This is a result of the flood of March 28, 1913; reportedly the rise of the Hudson and Mohawk Rivers was 28 feet above flood stage. The structure and foundation were so badly damaged the church had to be demolished. (Courtesy of Mary Michon.)

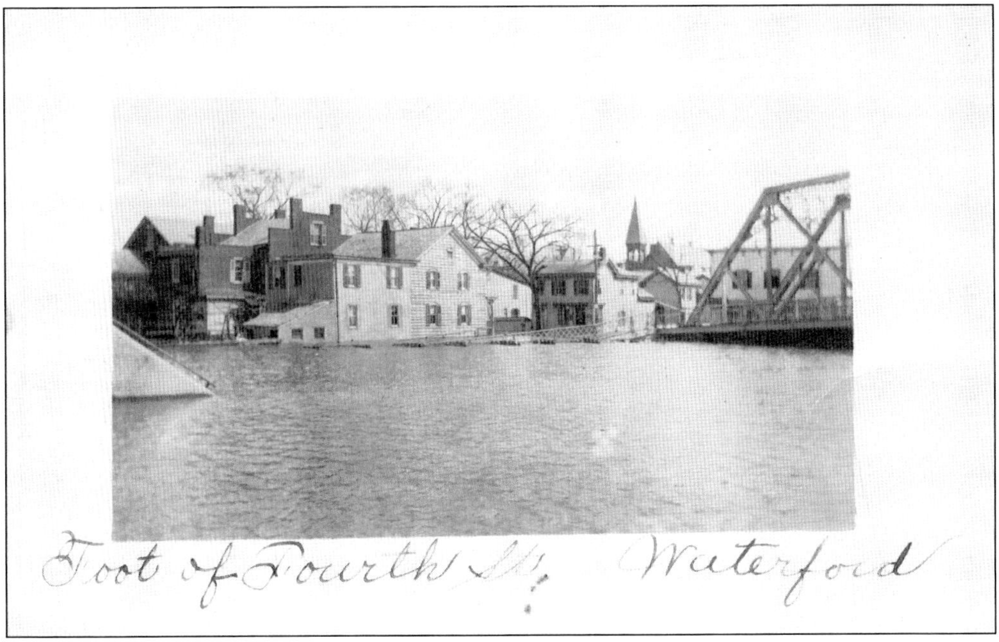

This scene was captured at the foot of Fourth Street, below Lock 2, of the flood of March 28, 1913. The note on the reverse reads, "You can see from this how the recent flood came up in Waterford. It was nearly wiped off the map. None of the water came in the house but nearly everyone around us got flooded out." (Courtesy of Kayla Keeler.)

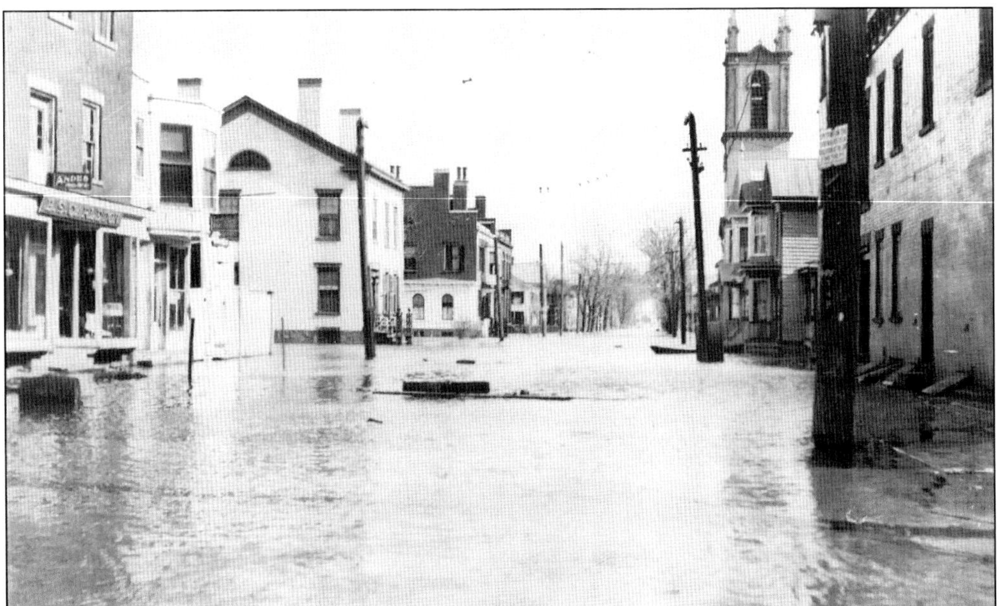

Waterford has had many disasters, one of which was the flood of 1913. That flood affected nearly the entire village. Pictured here is a view of the intersection of Broad Street and Third Street. It seems somewhat meaningless at the moment, but a sign on the pole reads, "Spitting on the sidewalk is a violation of the law—Fine $10.00." (Courtesy of Fran Santspree Cullett.)

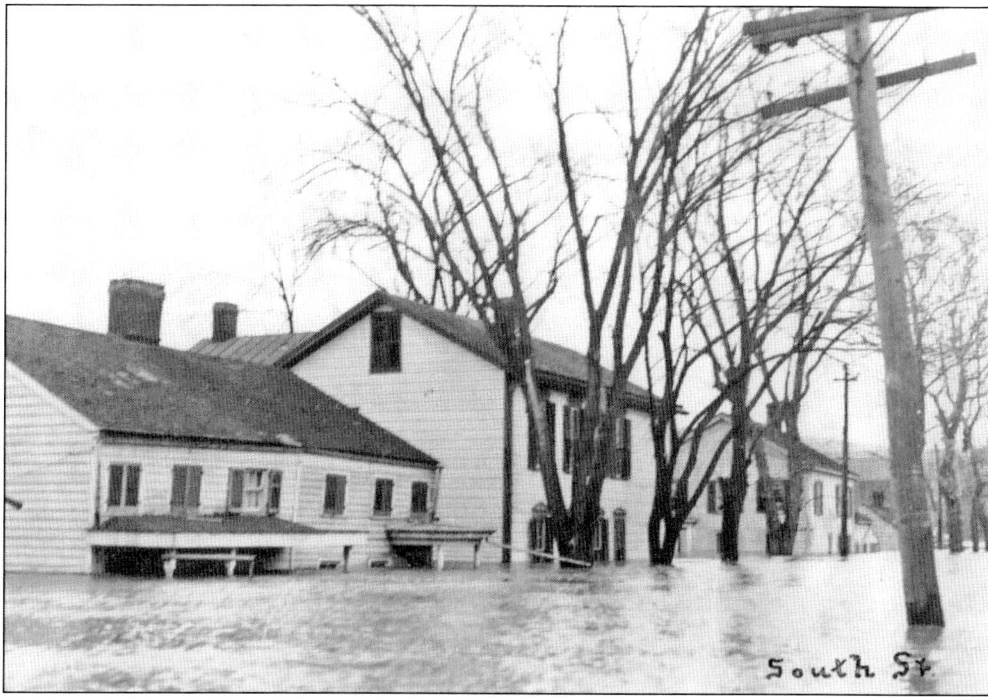

This is a scene from the flood of March 28, 1913, brought on by a three-day deluge of rain throughout the whole state. The raging Hudson and Mohawk Rivers met at the Battery. The homes along Front Street, South Street, and Dial City suffered the most damage, with waters rising as high as the second story of many of the homes. The newspapers described the ordeal as "Waterford's worse scare in history." (Courtesy of James T. Lefebvre, DC.)

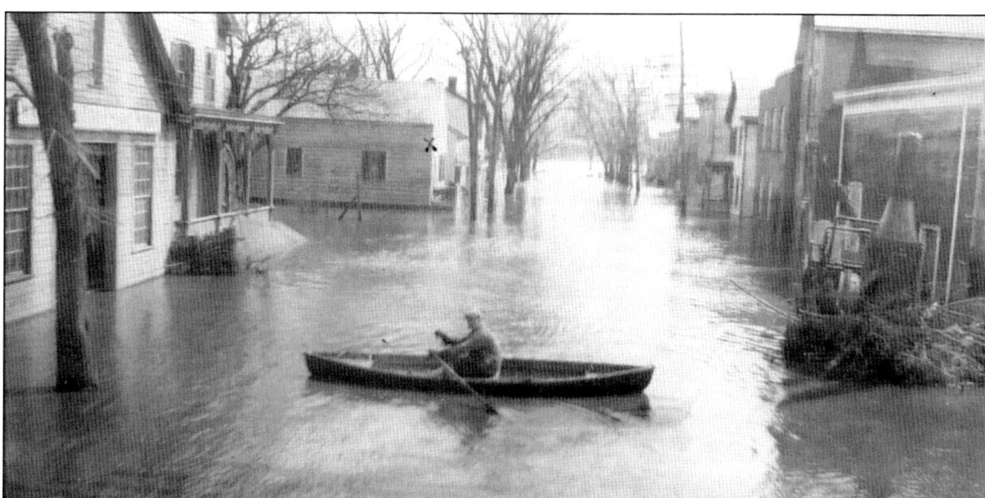

The water is receding rapidly, as evidenced by the current. In the foreground to the right, the residents have their furniture piled up in front of the house. They are beginning the clean-up of the mud and debris in their homes. The house in the background on the left, with the X and the waterline, provides more evidence of the floodwaters devastation. (Courtesy of J. Bert Mahoney.)

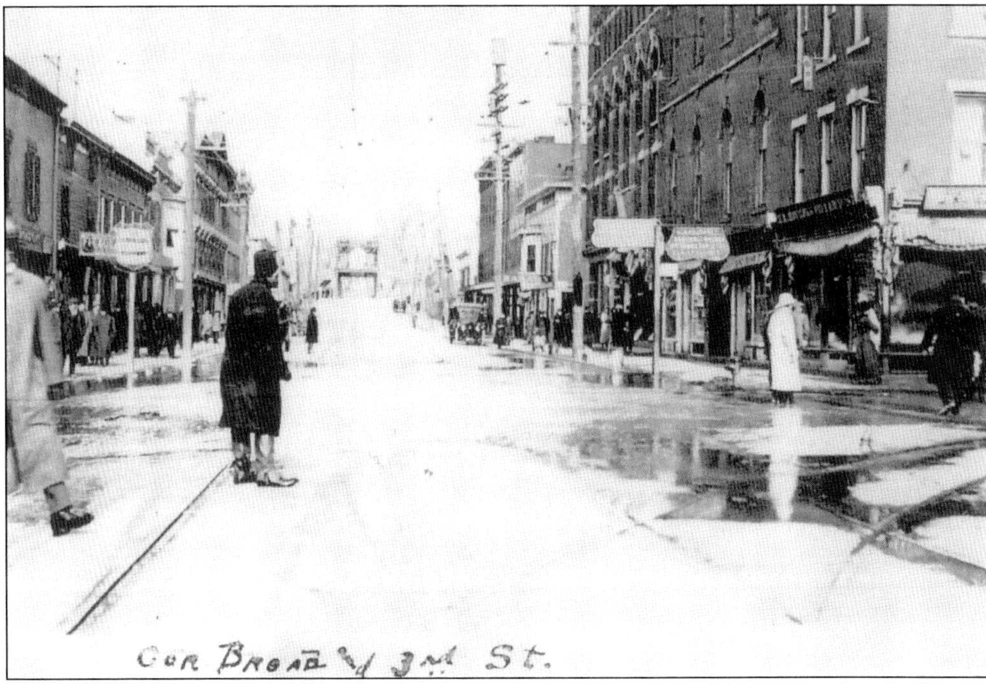

In the aftermath of the flood of 1913, the people gather to survey the damage The fire chief stands on the corner of Third Street and Broad Street to mark how high the water had risen. As in any disaster, people need to see the damage firsthand. (Courtesy of James T. Lefebvre, DC.)

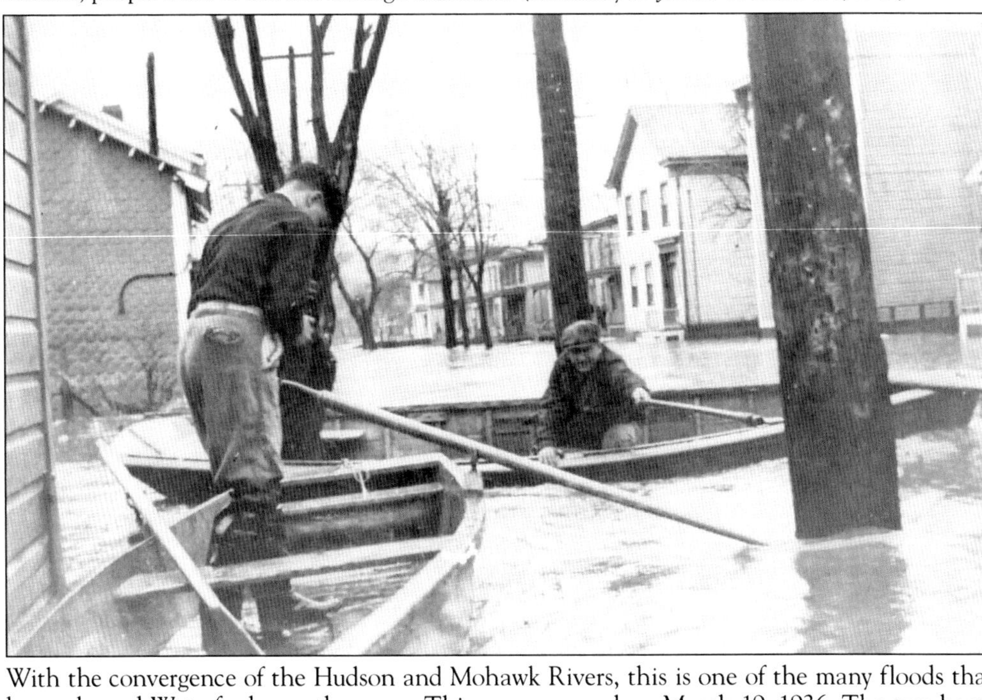

With the convergence of the Hudson and Mohawk Rivers, this is one of the many floods that have plagued Waterford over the years. This one occurred on March 19, 1936. The two boats are being held together, preventing them from drifting apart. The person in the left foreground appears to be pulling an unknown object from the water. (Courtesy of Mike Cicchinelli.)

Six

Police, Firemen, and Military

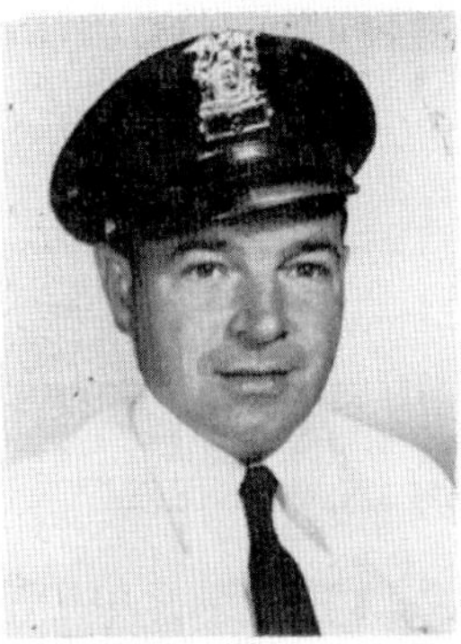

ADRIAN BECHARD

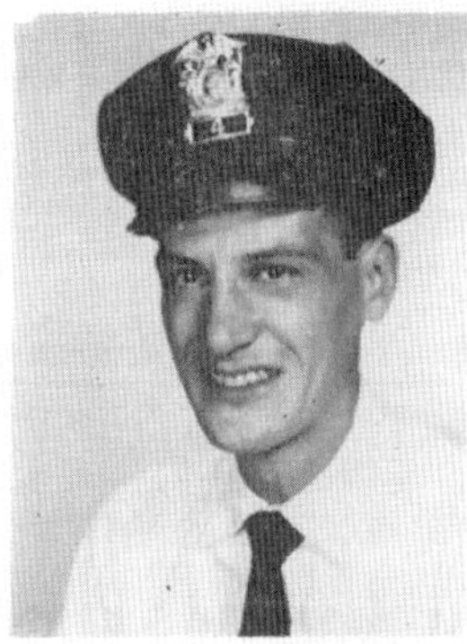

FRANCIS FALCONE

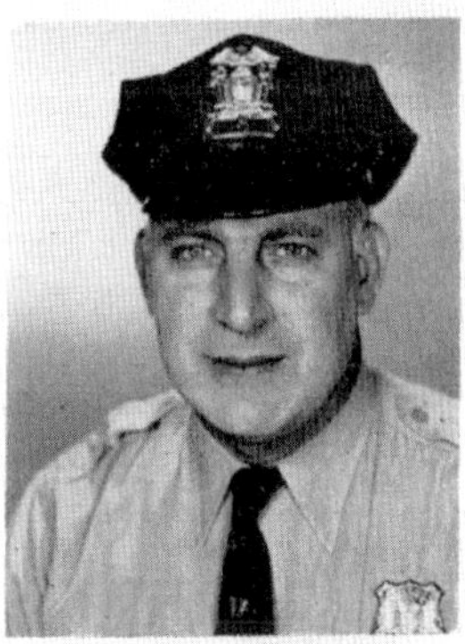

CHARLES FUSCO

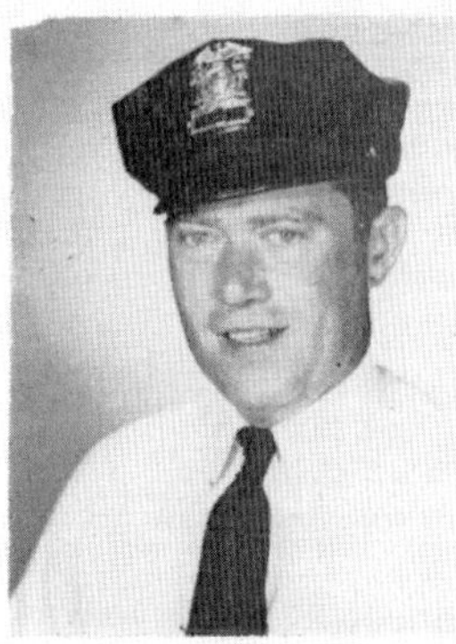

WILLIAM OLIN

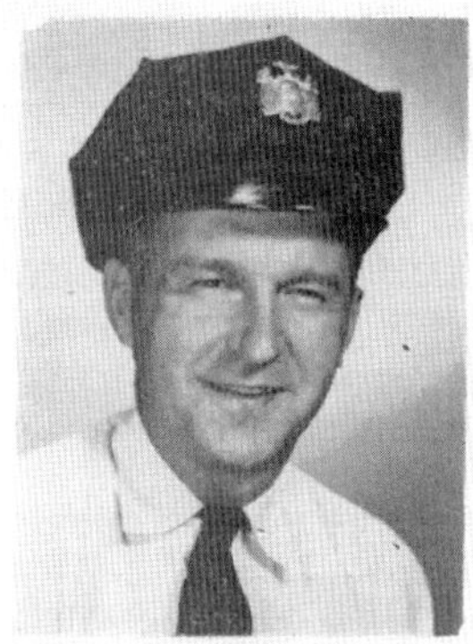

KEN VARLEY

The following is taken, in part, from an unidentified author: Because you don't see a cop in blue on the street corner or walking a beat as in many cities and towns don't think Waterford is lacking in police protection. May we remind you that a guardian of law and order in Waterford is not appointed as a police officer as in a city. He is sworn in as a Constable and furnish all personal equipment such as: uniform, gun, handcuffs, club and pay for the same himself. The Waterford policeman must work in industry or business to earn a living. He must have a great sense of love for his fellow citizen and to answer calls at all hours day and night and rush to protect the property and lives of his community. All members of the police are vested with the same authority and are of equal standing, that is, there are no chief or high ranking officers. Their orders come from the Town Board. The policeman turns in all reports to the Town Supervisor." (Courtesy of Dennis Rivage.)

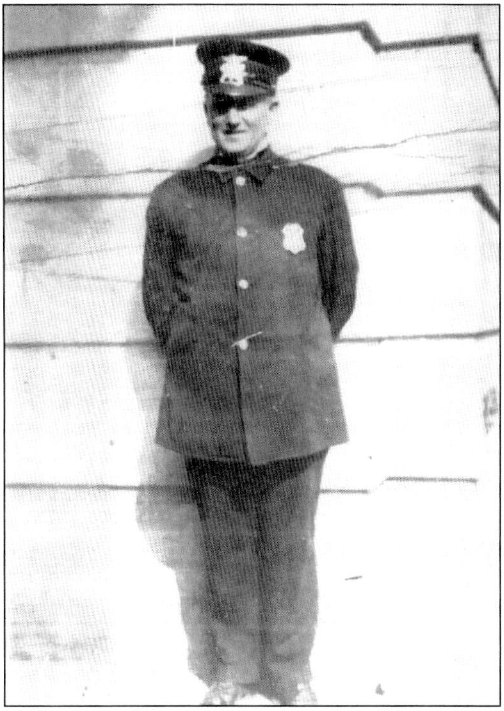

One of Waterford's most well-known and respected citizens, John A. Waldron was born in Waterford on February 17, 1867, the son of Daniel and Sarah Vanderwerken Waldron. On May 30, 1918, Waldron was appointed the first uniformed policeman in Waterford, with a salary of $88.33 a month. This appointment was met with great delight by the residents in Waterford, as Waldron was an extremely popular man. (Courtesy of Cheryl Sober Folkman.)

Posing in the door of his lunch wagon, believed to be the first restaurant in Waterford, is John A. Waldron. Waldron was a familiar fixture in Waterford, having started his horse-drawn lunch wagon named the Night Lunch in 1903, parking it at the corner of Third Street and Broad Street. Waldron was in the restaurant business for 38 years. (Courtesy of Cheryl Sober Folkman.)

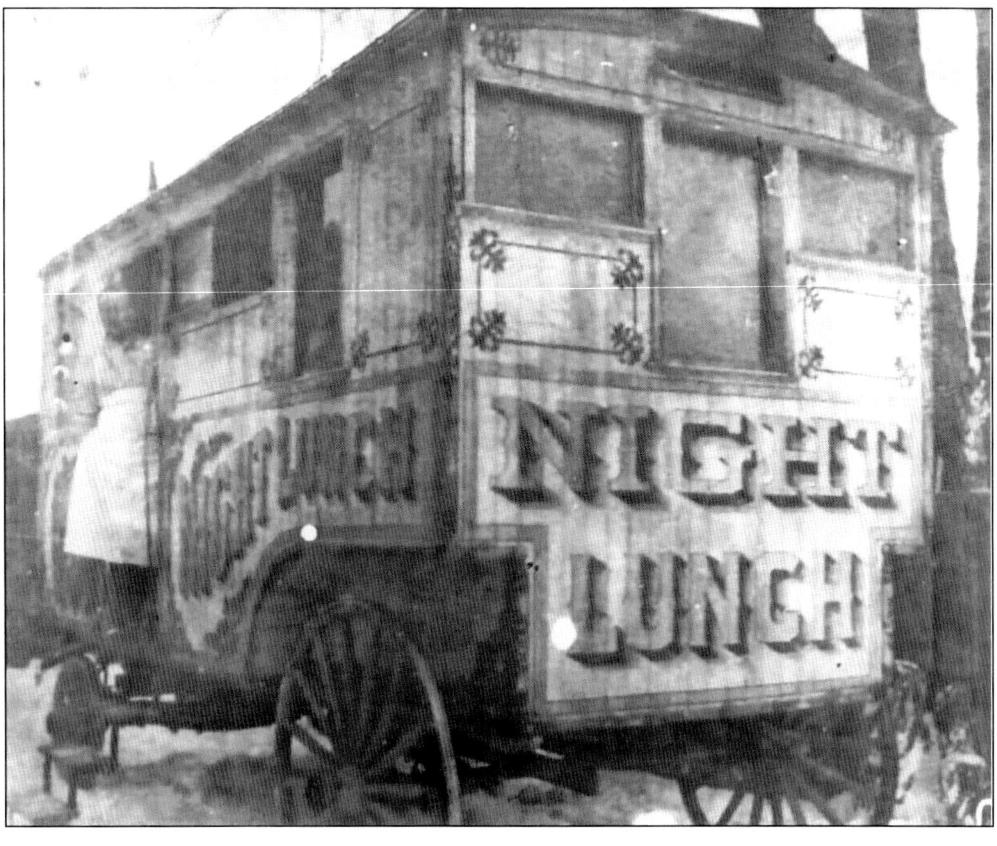

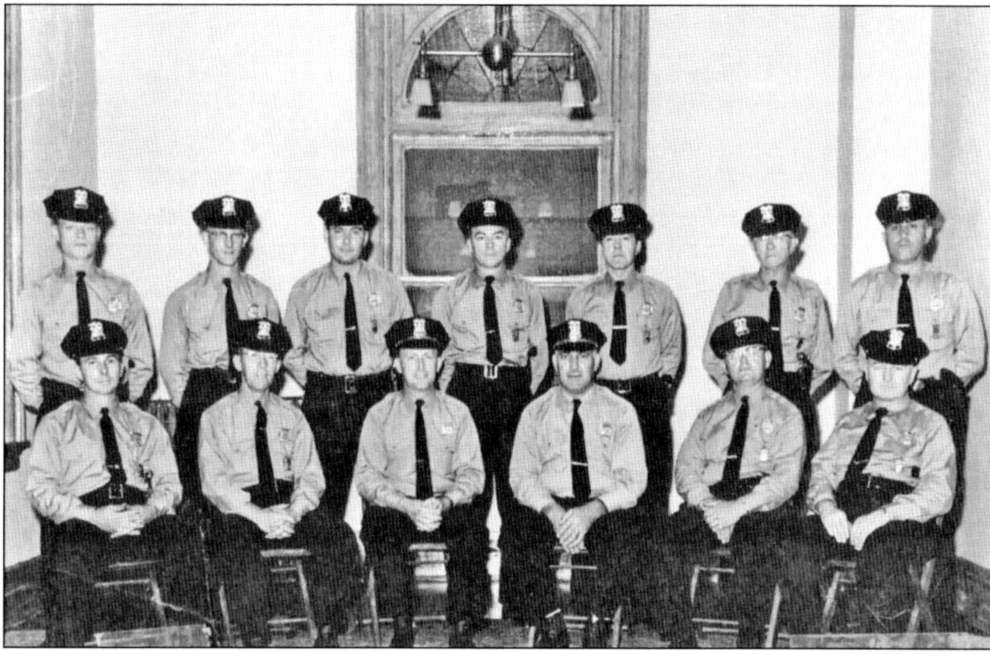

Pictured above is the Waterford Police Department of 1958. From left to right are (first row) George Trethway, Tom Dyer, Bill Cummings, Charles Fusco, Art Fredette, and Fred Leffler; (second row) Bill Plummer, John Willetts, A. Dale Hermans, Joe Bailey, Ray Stanley, Gene Osterhaut, and Liz Marchese. (Courtesy of Rob VanBramer, WPD.)

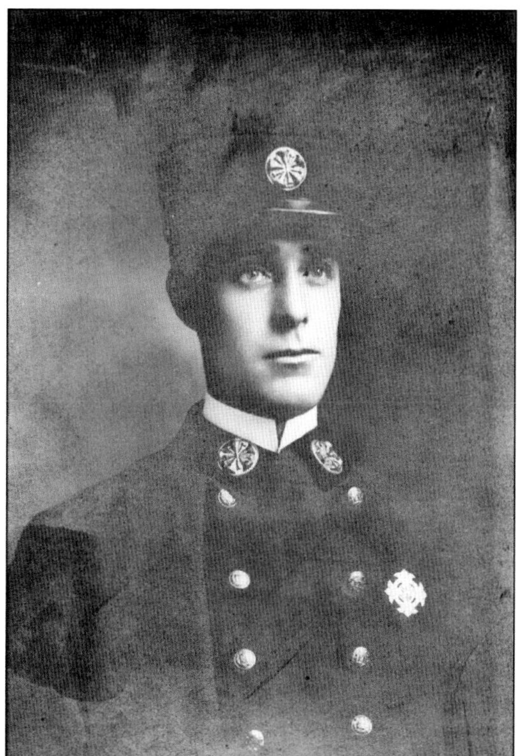

Serving in the 19th century, Frank Conroy was the longest-tenured Waterford fire chief in the history of the fire department. For many years, from 1812 and until 1886, the Knickerbocker Steamer Engine and Hose Company No 1 was the only fire company in Waterford. Joe Hartnett was the longest-tenured fire chief of the new era. Until after World War II, all fire chiefs came from the Knickerbocker Steamer Company No. 1. (Courtesy of Russ Van Dervoort.)

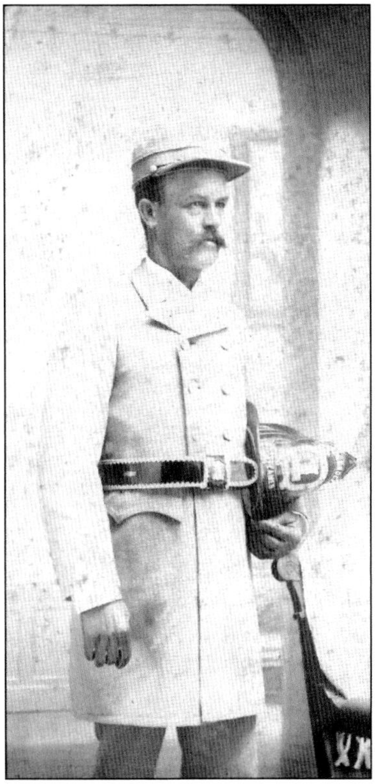

This is a very early photograph of a fireman in dress uniform. The insignia on his helmet reads "Knickerbocker Steamer." His belt buckle and emblem appear to have the number one, which dates the fireman to anytime after 1847, when the Knickerbocker Steamer Company No. 1 was formed after replacing the old Protection Engine Company No. 1.

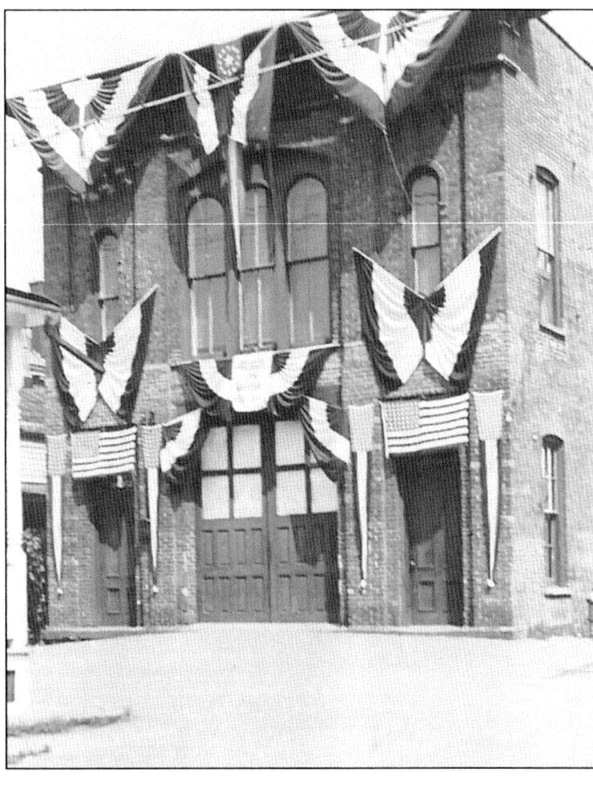

The Knickerbocker Steamer Company firehouse is located on Pearl Street. Organized in 1812, the name was originally the Protection Engine Company, changed in 1847 to the Knickerbocker Steamer Company. This building dates from 1867 and still houses the fire company. (Courtesy of Monroe VanValkenburgh.)

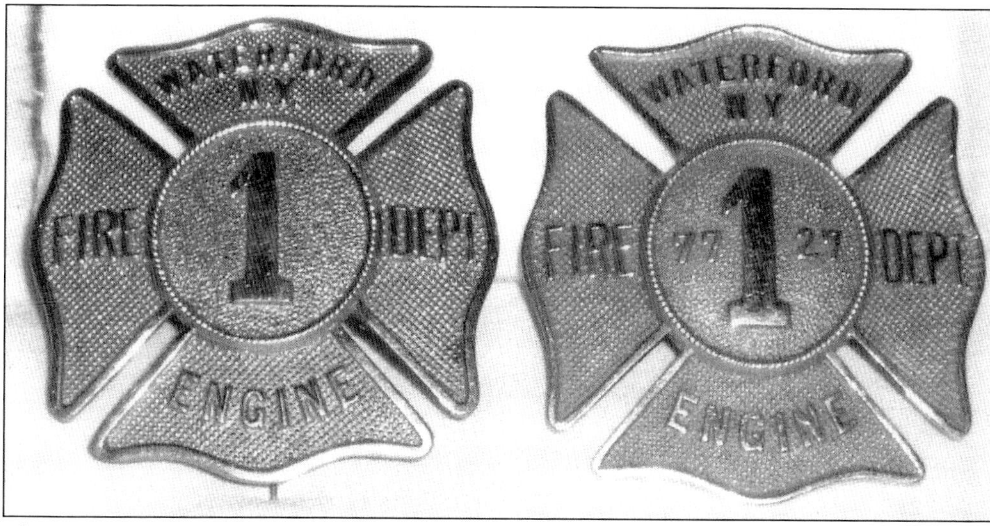

This is a standard-issue Waterford badge and a 14-karat-gold badge for 50 years of service with the Knickerbocker Steamer Company. This badge was presented to George Taylor, who served in the fire department from 1877 to 1927. Engraved on the reverse of the badge is this legend: "Presented by the Co. to George Taylor for Fifty Years Active Service." Taylor was reported to be the oldest active fireman in New York state.

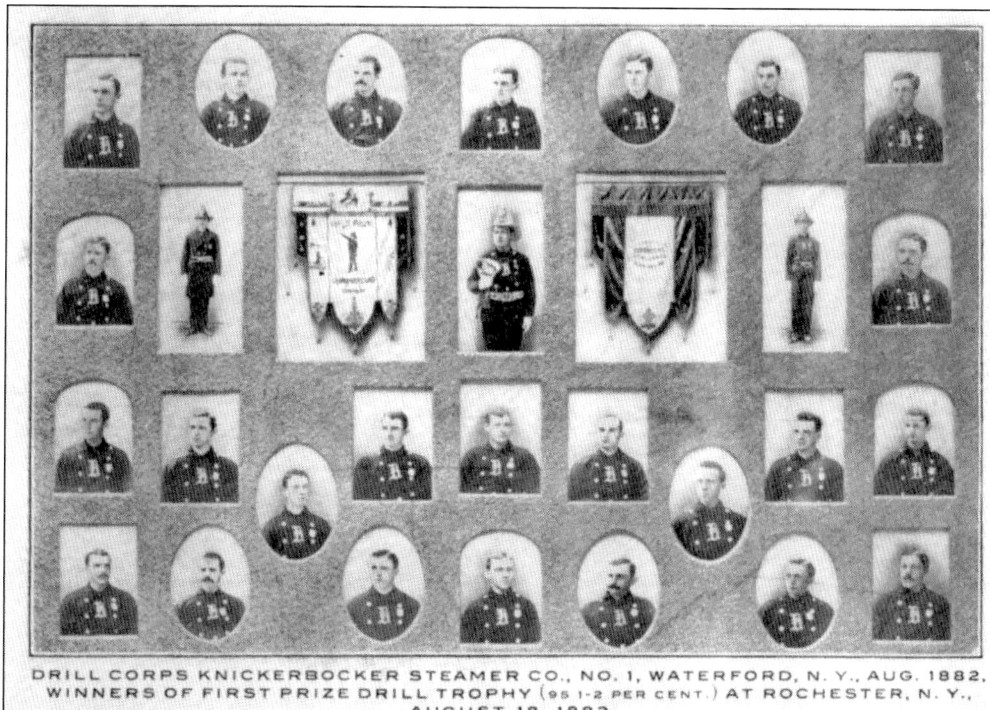

The Knickerbocker Steamer Company formed a marching drill team of Knickerbocker firemen and represented themselves and Waterford well in contests throughout New York state. Prizes would be awarded for the top three teams. At Rochester, they became state champions; rumors were started and accusations were made that these were not firemen, they were West Point cadets. (Courtesy of Russ Van Dervoort.)

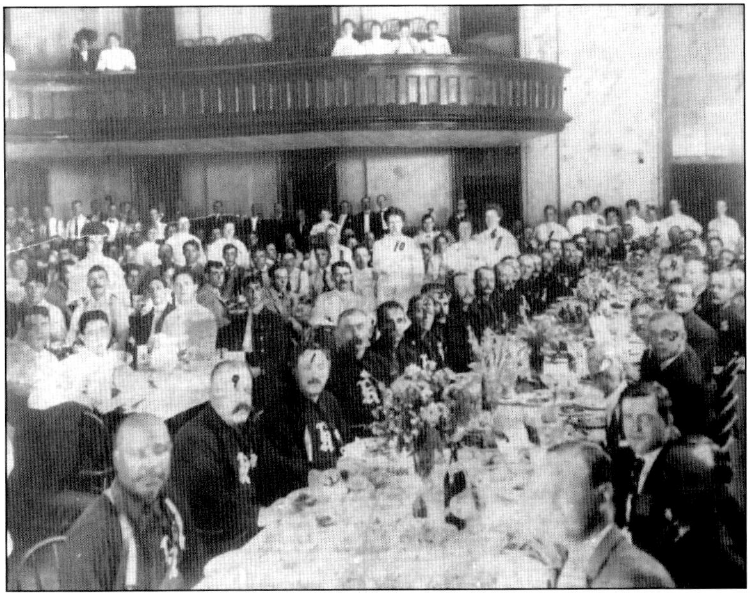

The Knickerbocker Steamer Engine and Hose Company No. 1, pictured here around 1888, is at a function on the upper level of the original town hall. The occasion is a dinner to celebrate the Knickerbockers having won the state championship at Rochester, in a marching drill contest. (Courtesy of Russ Van Dervoort.)

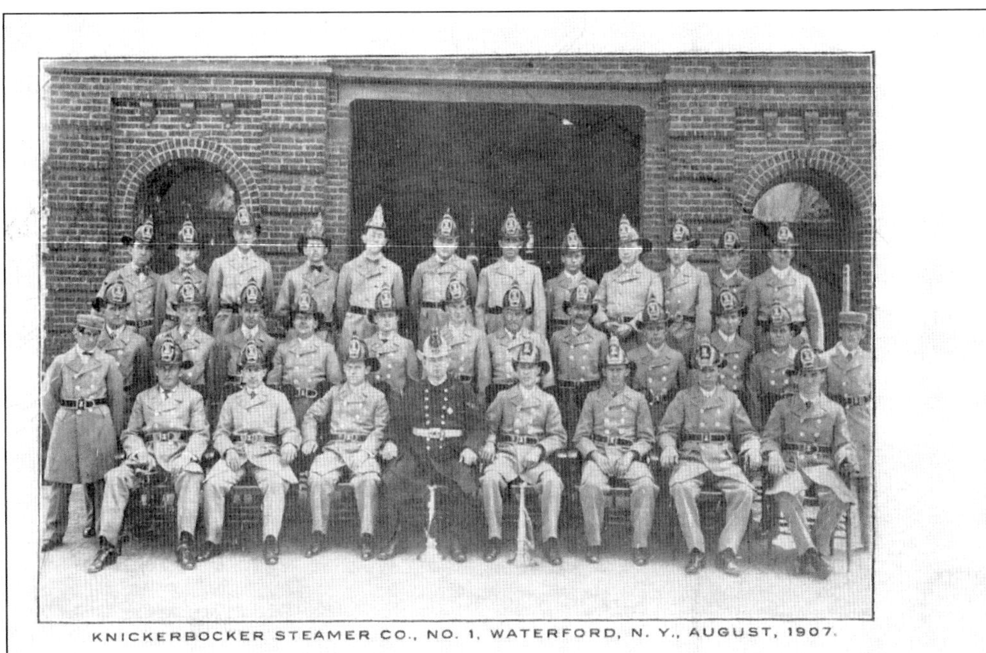

The Knickerbocker Steamer Company No. 1 is pictured here in full dress uniform. They succeeded the Protection Engine Company No. 1, which was organized in 1812 and existed until 1841. On August 2, 1847, the company adopted the name of Knickerbocker. The proud members of the vaunted company are pictured here in 1915, and the tradition lives on today. (Courtesy of Dennis Rivage.)

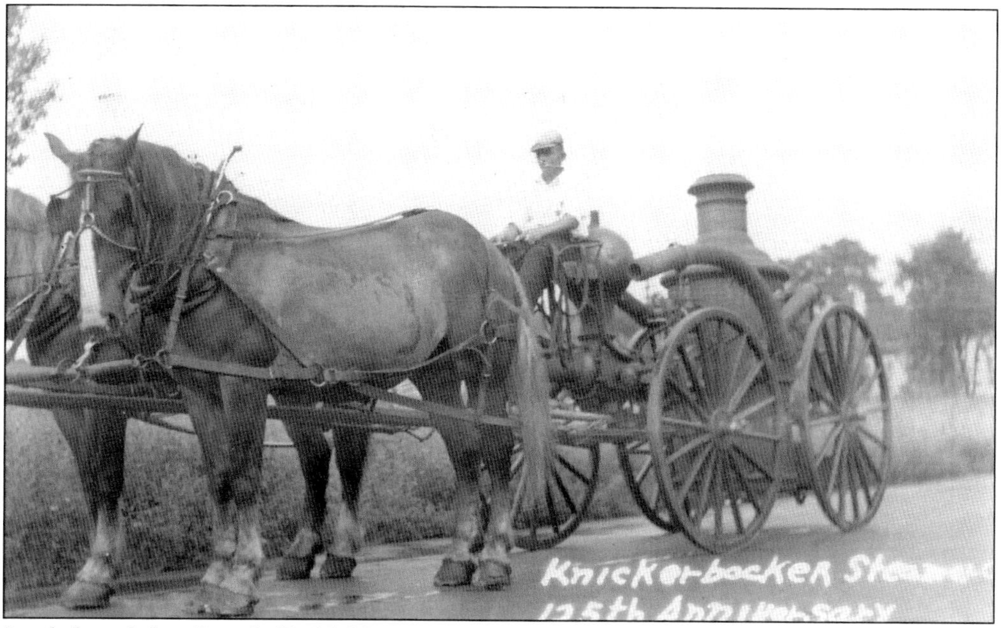

It is believed that Patrick "Paddy" Burney is at the reins of Knickerbocker's last steamer, shown during the 125th anniversary of their founding in 1847. The village had on hand a team of horses for the fire department and for garbage collection; Burney was usually the chauffeur.

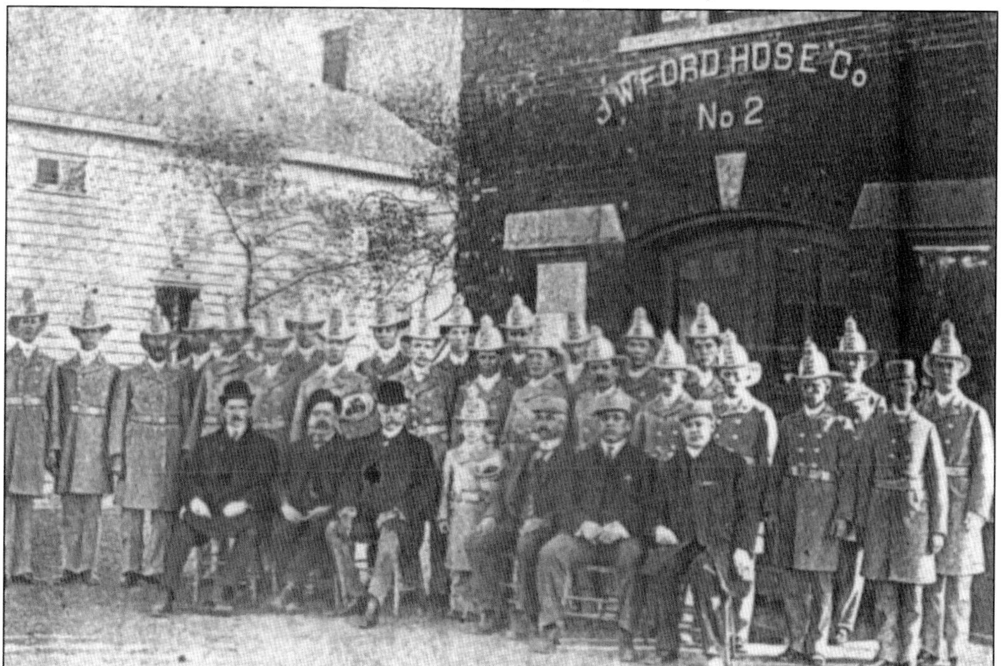

J.W. Ford Hose Company No. 2 was formed in 1899. Their initial headquarters was Father Curran's barn at St. Mary's Church on Division Street; by 1900, they had moved to a barn on Pine Street and established their own building on Division Street the following year. The gentlemen seated third from left is John Wheeler Ford, the company's founder, a mill owner, water commission member, and member of the school board. (Courtesy of Russ Van Dervoort.)

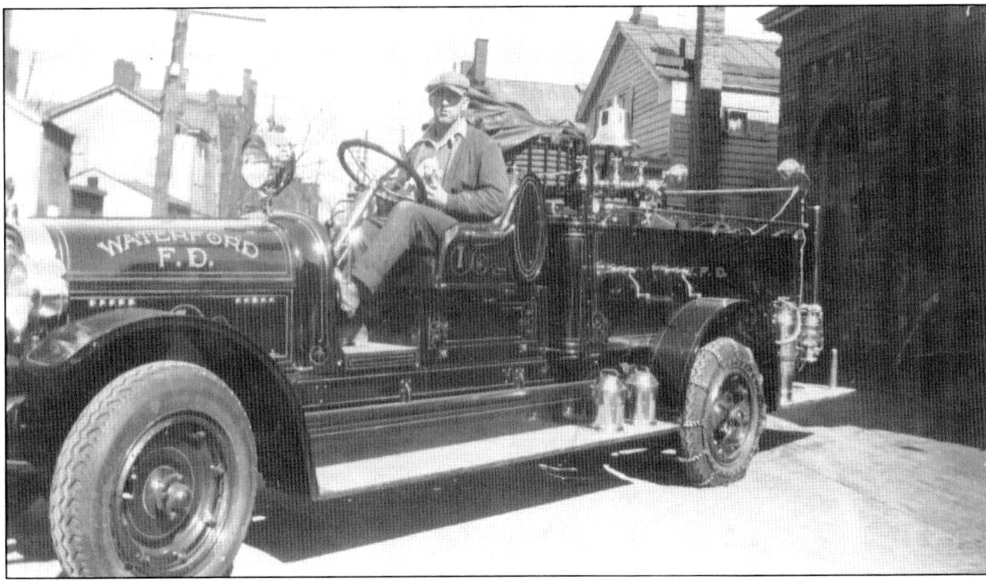

A fireman backs up a fire truck of the day into the Knickerbocker Steamer Firehouse. As time marched on, the latest available equipment was made available to the local volunteer firemen in the villages and towns. These small municipalities had no professional firefighters and totally relied on volunteerism to cover the ever-present danger of fires and other emergencies. (Courtesy of Russ Van Dervoort.)

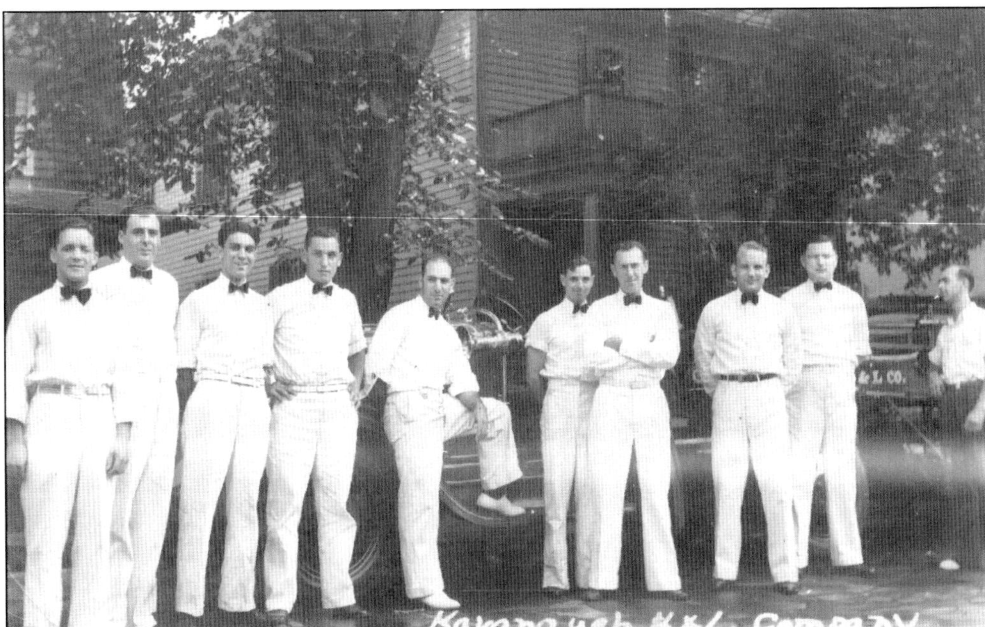

These firemen, pictured here in 1937, were part of the Kavanaugh Fire Company, organized in 1900. The firehouse was located on Fourth Street, next to the Waterford School and in front of Burgess Printing. The first apparatus was a hand-drawn truck. Later, it was adapted to a gasoline-powered tractor. (Courtesy of J. Bert Mahoney.)

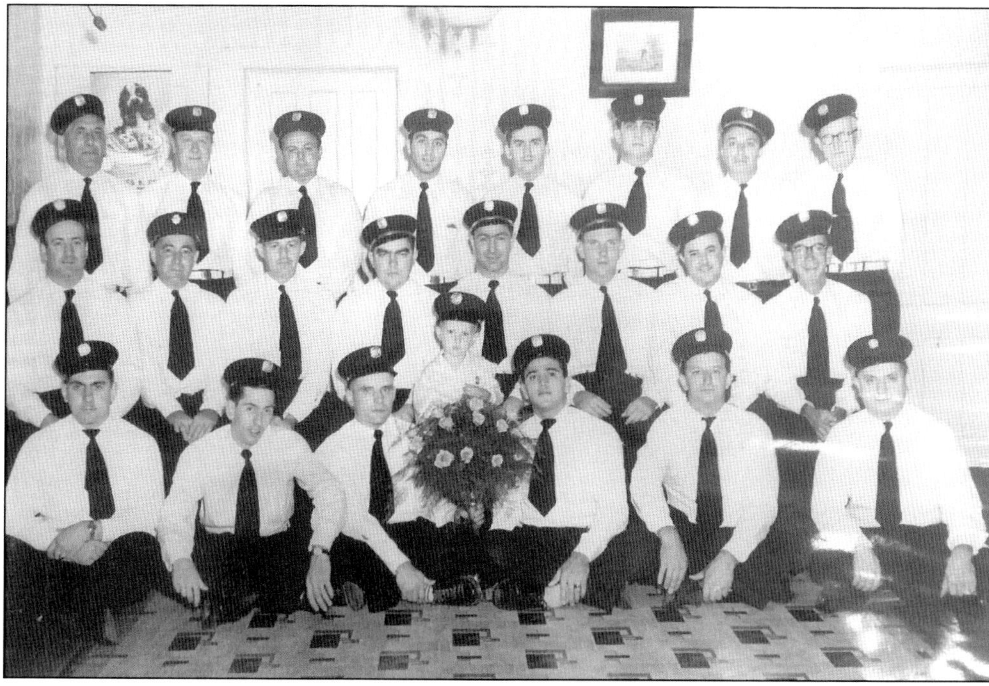

Kavanaugh Hook and Ladder Company members are pictured here during their 50-year celebration. From left to right are, (first row) Guido Pallozzi, Bill O'Connor, Harold Baker, Tom Doin (mascot), Dave Catallo, Modesto Cicchinelli, and Phil Pallozzi; (second row) Rufus Ferrara, unidentified guest, Harvey Clark, James Doud, John "Pep" Scarchilli, Fred Bessette, Armando DiPalma, and unidentified guest; (third row) Dick Cornetti, Lauren Brown, Frank Mot, Anthony Scarchilli, Walt Sorenson, Bob Kerr, Milt Whaley, and Pierre Hayes. (Courtesy of J. Bert Mahoney.)

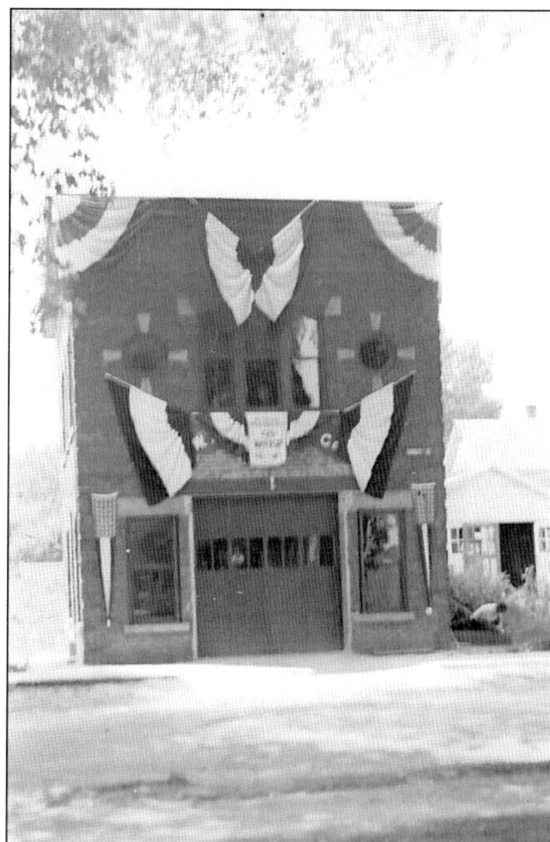

Pictured here is the Northside Hose Company, established in October 1886 by people who wanted to provide protection in the Northside community. Originally, there was a two-wheeled and then a four-wheeled hose cart, pulled by volunteers. This firehouse later moved to Saratoga Avenue. The original building located on Hill Street is now a private residence. (Courtesy of Ceil VanValkenburgh Maloney.)

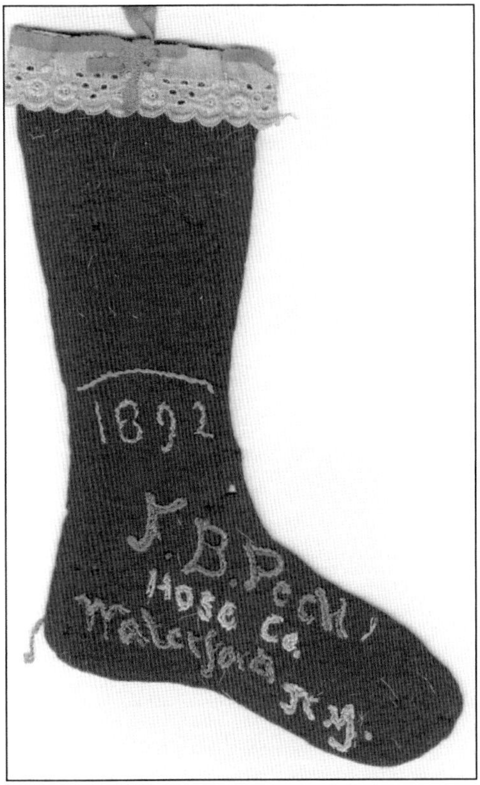

It was common for the firehouse to be the gathering place for neighborhoods on special occasions and holidays. Some fraternal organizations opened their doors as well for these festivities. One can only imagine what the handmade Christmas stocking was a part of, but it certainly could have been filled with fruit and candy for the neighborhood children.

The Northside Hose Company was given land on Hill Street, and the name was changed to the F.B. Peck Hose Company No. 1 in honor of local businessman Francis Bayard Peck, on the left in the suit and bowler hat. In 1964, an old school building on Saratoga Avenue was purchased from School District No. 2 and used until 1996, when a new structure was erected. (Courtesy of the F.B. Peck Hose Company.)

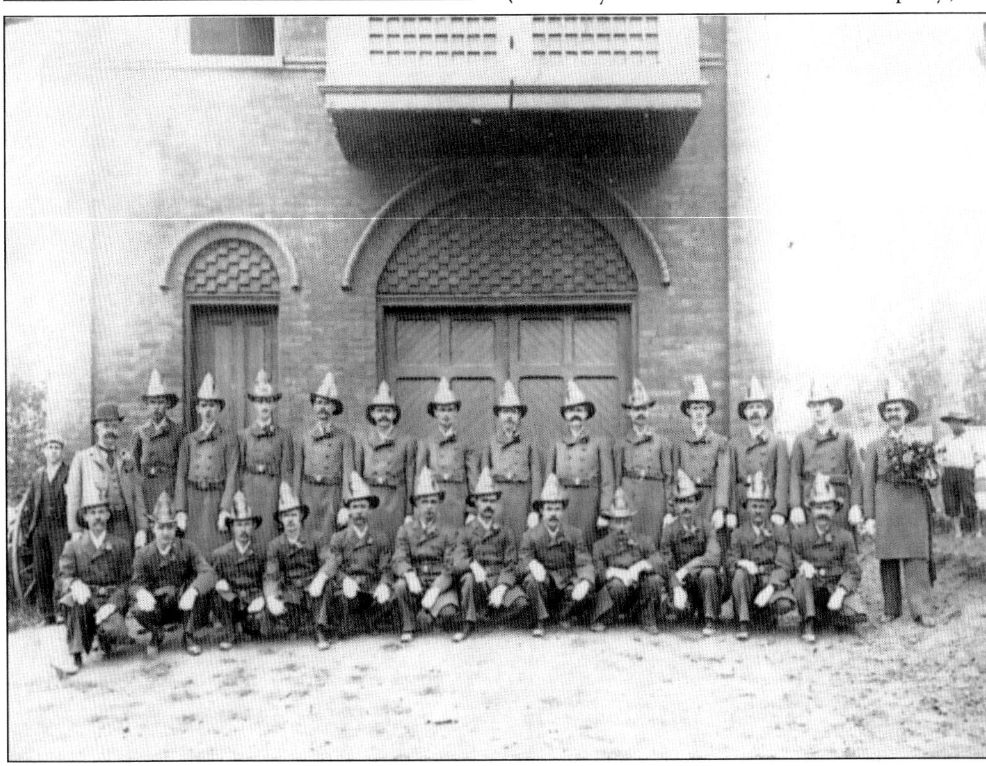

Firemen Joseph Lajanesse (left) and Merrick Dufrense (right) are pictured here in dress uniforms in June 1894. Both were members of the Peck Hose Company. Many firemen have asked what became of all the traditional and seemingly signature uniforms worn from the 1880s to the 1920s. It seems strange that no fire company had even one old uniform. It appears, through WHMCC research, that in most cases the uniforms were rented and returned. (Courtesy of WHMCC.)

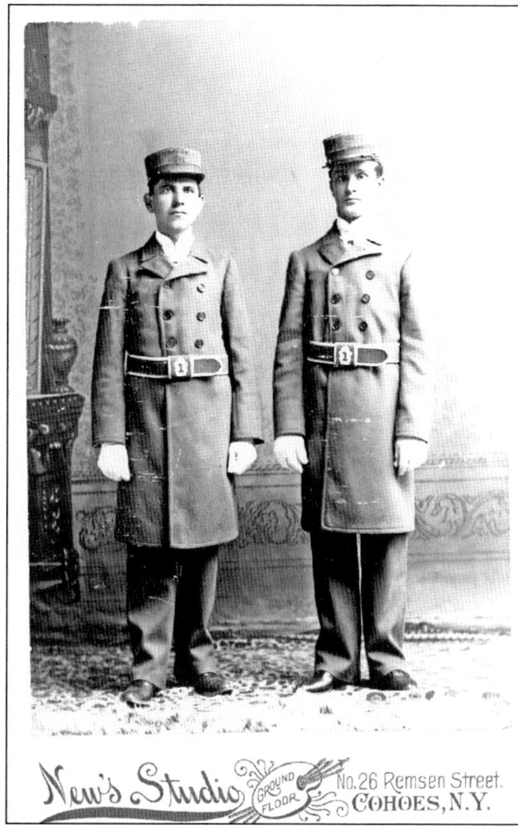

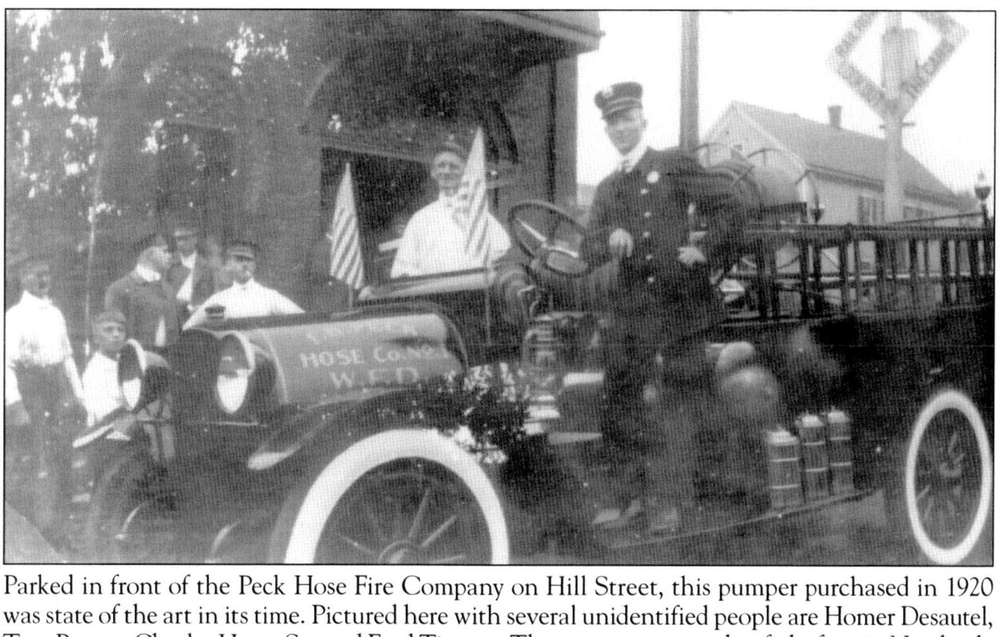

Parked in front of the Peck Hose Fire Company on Hill Street, this pumper purchased in 1920 was state of the art in its time. Pictured here with several unidentified people are Homer Desautel, Tom Patten, Charles Hayes Sr., and Fred Tierney. The pumper was used to fight fires in Northside and most likely used in other areas of the town and village when needed. (Courtesy of the F.B. Peck Hose Company.)

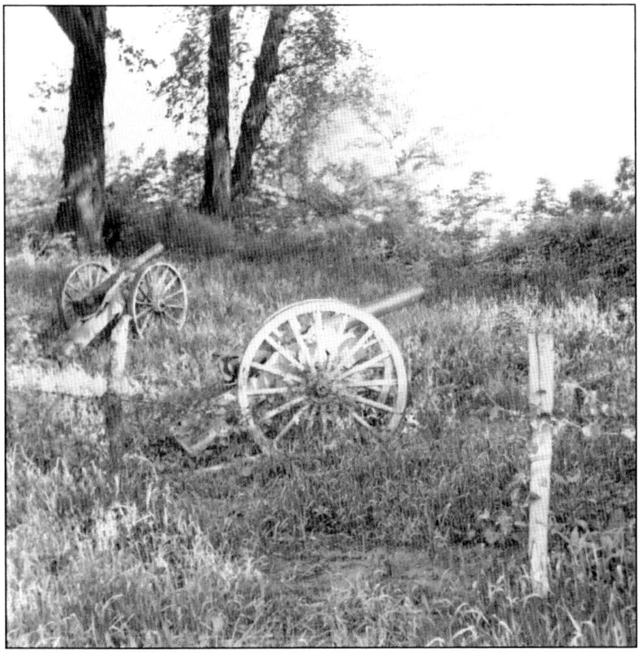

After the defeat at Fort Ticonderoga in 1777, General Schuyler's army retreated to the junction of the Mohawk and Hudson Rivers to Haver (Peebles) Island. There Col. Thaddeus Kosciusko erected three cannon fortifications, with troop entrenchments to stop General Burgoyne's advancement to Albany. Fortunately, the battle never occurred, as the British were stopped and defeated in the Battle of Saratoga. The cannons remained on Peebles Island until the 1960s. (Courtesy of WHMCC.)

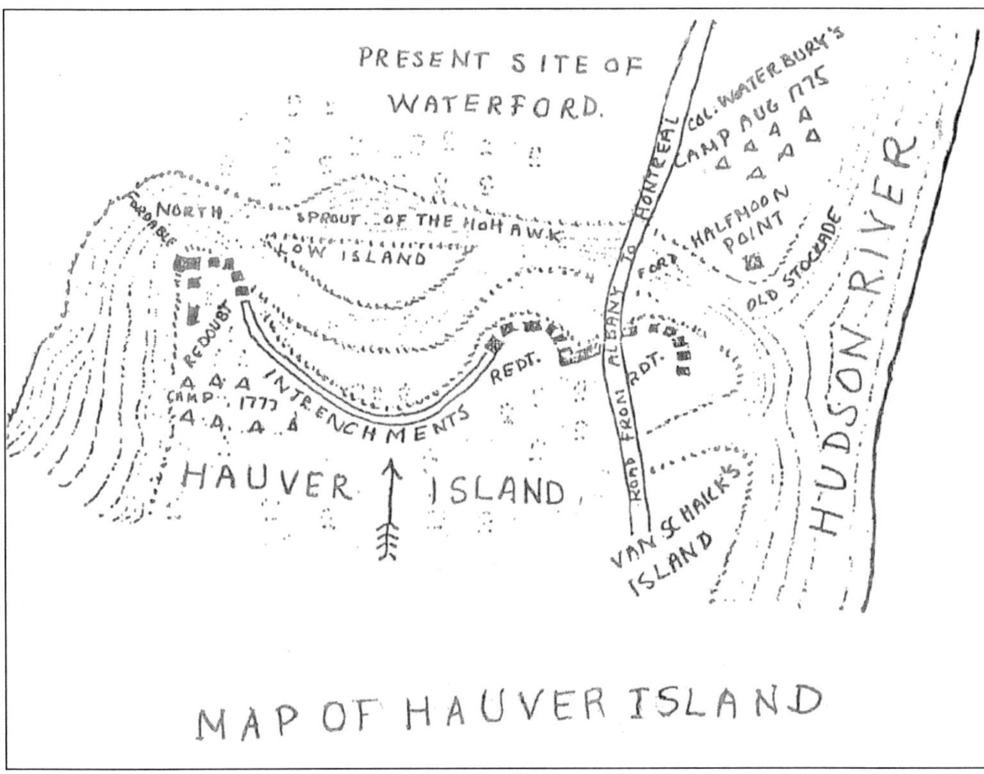

Haver Island, now Peebles Island, may have been used as a campground as early as 1709. Haver Island was again used as a camp and supply depot in 1777. Three earthwork batteries, possibly with blockhouses, were constructed by Thaddeus Kosciusko in August 1777. The site was occupied until 1782. (Courtesy of the Saratoga County Historian's Office.)

A letter written in part to Lt. Col. Van Schoonhoven on August 28, 1815, reads, "Sir, you are hereby commanded to order out the regt. under your command for review & Inspection on the eighteenth day of October next at William Neff's at nine o'clock in the forenoon completely armed & equipped. You will also order the comdts. of companies to appear with complete muster rolls & at the inspection to note every deficiency of arms & accoutrements. Be punctual in making your regimental returns. In haste By order etc. Alpheus Goodrich."

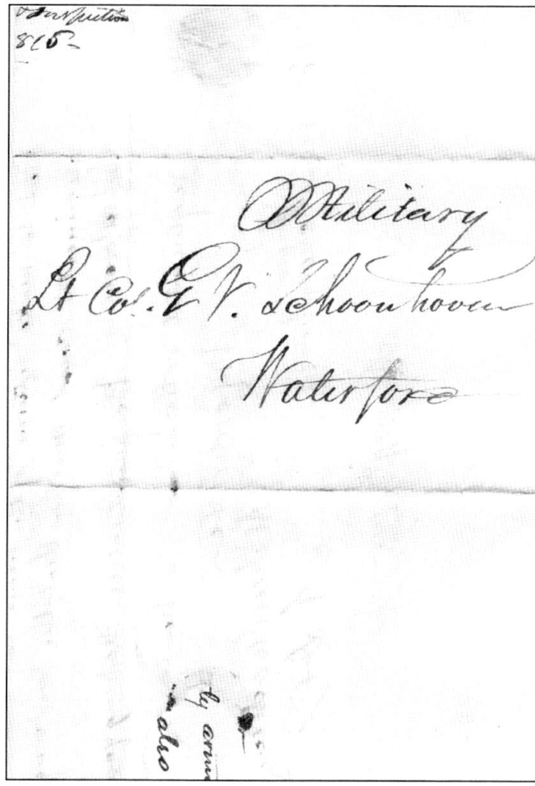

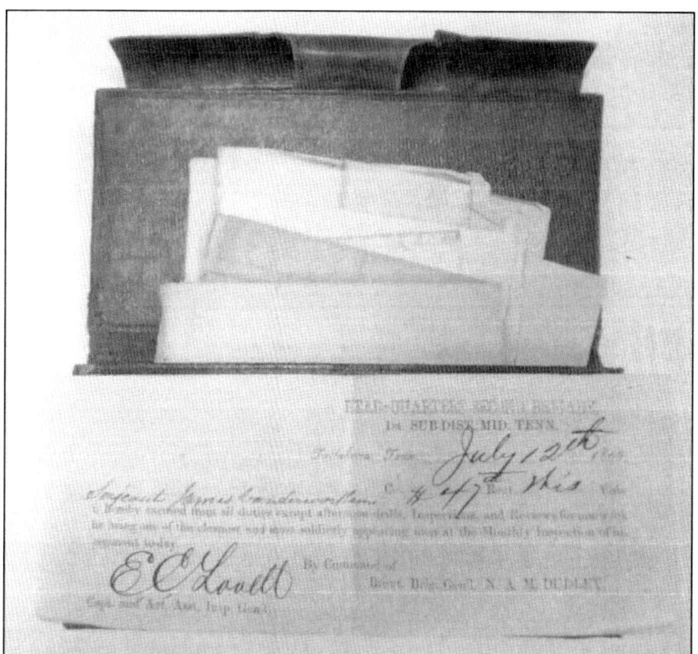

Pictured at left is the wallet of Lawrence Vanderwerken, whose son James was part of Company 47 of Regimental Volunteers. In part, the memo from July 12, 1865, reads, "Serjeant James Vanderwerken is hereby excused from all duties except afternoon drills, Inspections, and Reviews for one week he being one of the cleanest and most soldierly appearing men at the Monthly Inspection of his regiment to-day." (Courtesy of Helen Grochmal Anderson.)

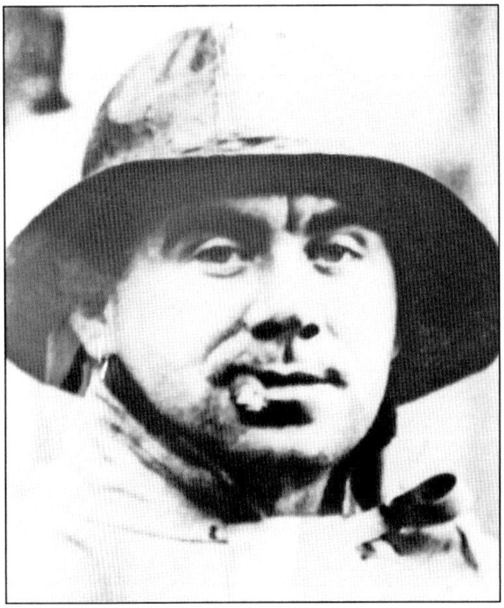

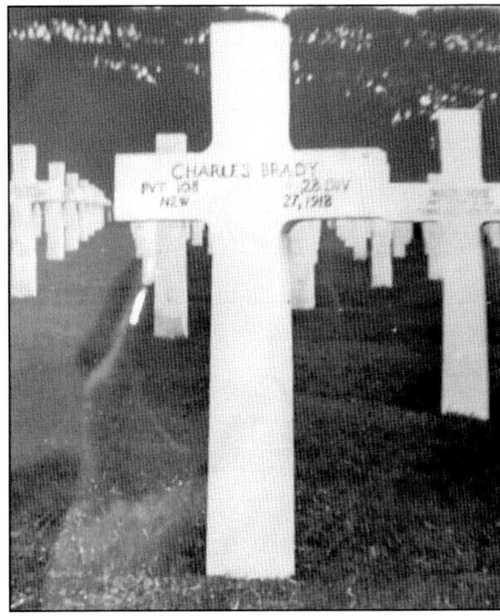

Pvt. Charles J. Brady was buried in the military cemetery at Romagne, France. The following letter was written in part by 1st Lt. Herbert B. Redrick of Company C, 108th Machine Gun Battalion, to Brady's mother, Catherine. "Private Brady was one of a number of brave men of my command killed in action—I feel honored in being able to assure you that he died as only a soldier can, courageously, at his post." The American Legion Charles J. Brady Post 235 was named in Private Brady's honor. (Courtesy of J. Bert Mahoney.)

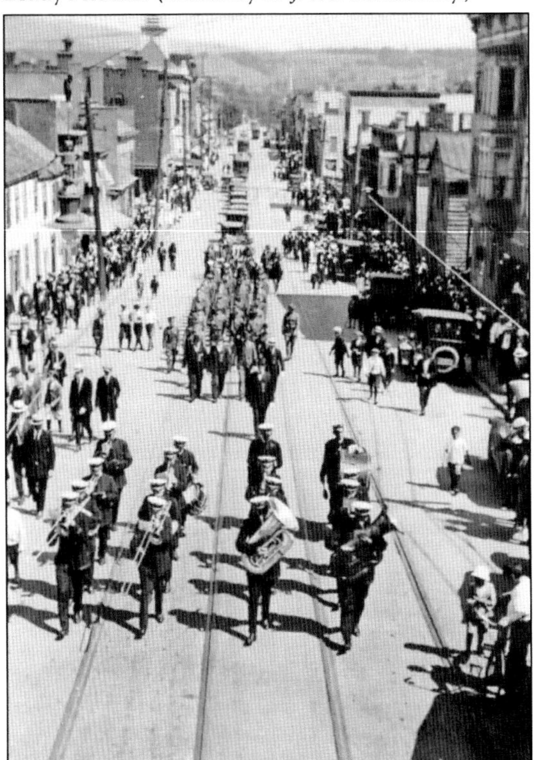

Pictured here is the funeral procession of John McGaffin. McGaffin served in the Spanish-American War, obtaining the rank of lieutenant colonel and later reenlisting in World War I. John McGaffin was the organizer and the first commander of the American Legion Charles J. Brady Post in Waterford. This is probably the largest funeral procession in the history of Waterford. Most of the viewers are following the procession to the Waterford Rural Cemetery, where he was buried. (Courtesy of Hugh Holton.)

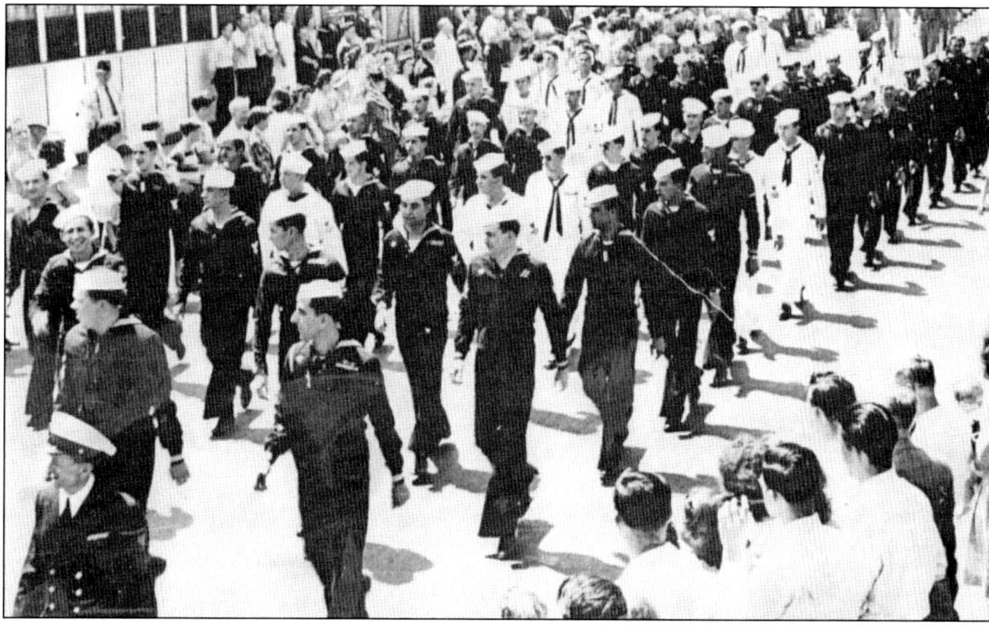

Waterford loves a parade, and on Sunday June 23, 1946, an estimated 4,000 residents lined the route to welcome home World War II veterans. By far, the feature of the parade was the final section headed by Col. Gerald W. O'Connor, grand marshal, leading almost 600 of the returned servicemen. Behind Colonel O'Connor and the color guard were about 30 Marines, 150 sailors, and over 400 soldiers. (Courtesy of J. Bert Mahoney.)

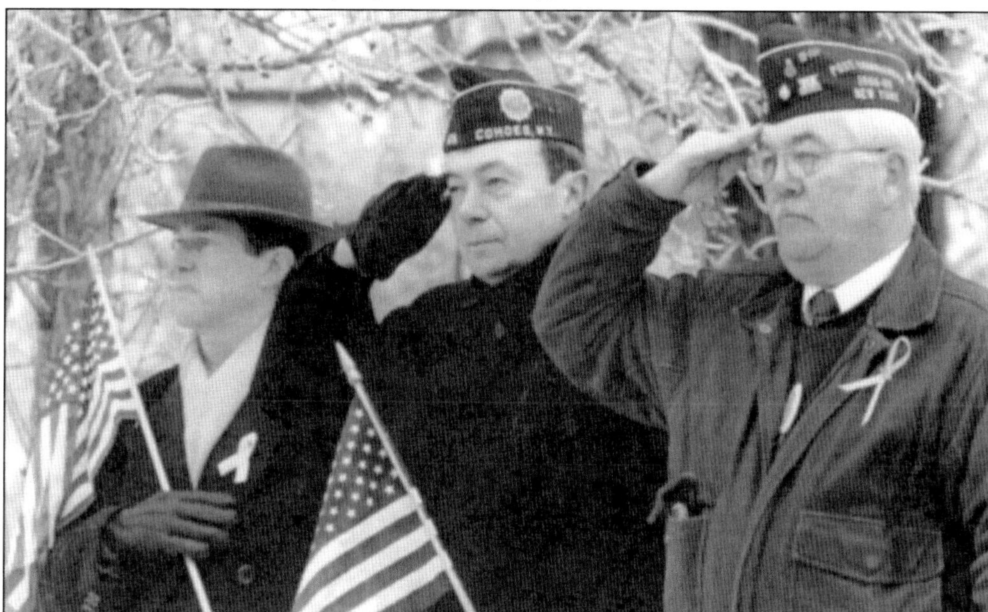

At a rally to support the troops on Saturday April 5, 2003, from left to right, US congressman Michael R. McNulty, assemblyman Ronald Canestrari, and Waterford mayor J. Bert Mahoney salute. McNulty lost a brother, William F. McNulty, during the Vietnam War; Canestrari is a Vietnam-era veteran; and Mahoney served aboard the aircraft carrier USS *Oriskany* for three combat cruises during that conflict. (Courtesy of J. Bert Mahoney.)

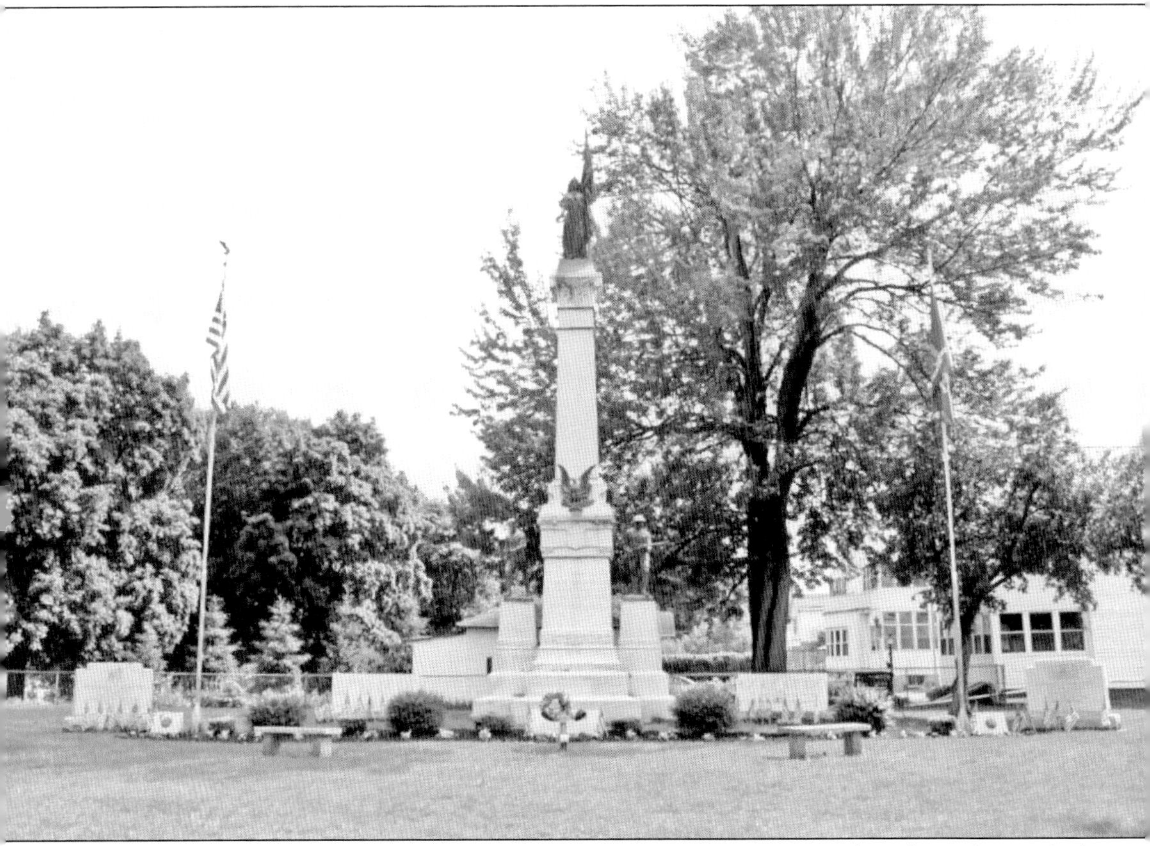

Soldiers and Sailors Memorial Park is located at First and Broad Streets in the village of Waterford. Chapter 214 of the laws of the State of New York 1922 note the following: "Act to authorize the Town of Waterford in the County of Saratoga to acquire, complete and maintain a park and monument in memory of Soldiers and Sailors, and to provide for the payment there for by issue of bonds laws 1922 chapter 214 in effect March 23, 1922." In 1922, Charles H. Kavanaugh donated the magnificent *Soldiers and Sailors Monument* to his hometown. In 1989, the Waterford Veterans Memorial committee added two monuments listing the names of all the known Waterfordians that made the ultimate sacrifice. The inscription on the Soldiers and Sailors Monument reads, "To the glory of God and in grateful remembrance of our heroes who served in all wars for the triumph of right and freedom." (Courtesy of Kayla Keeler.)

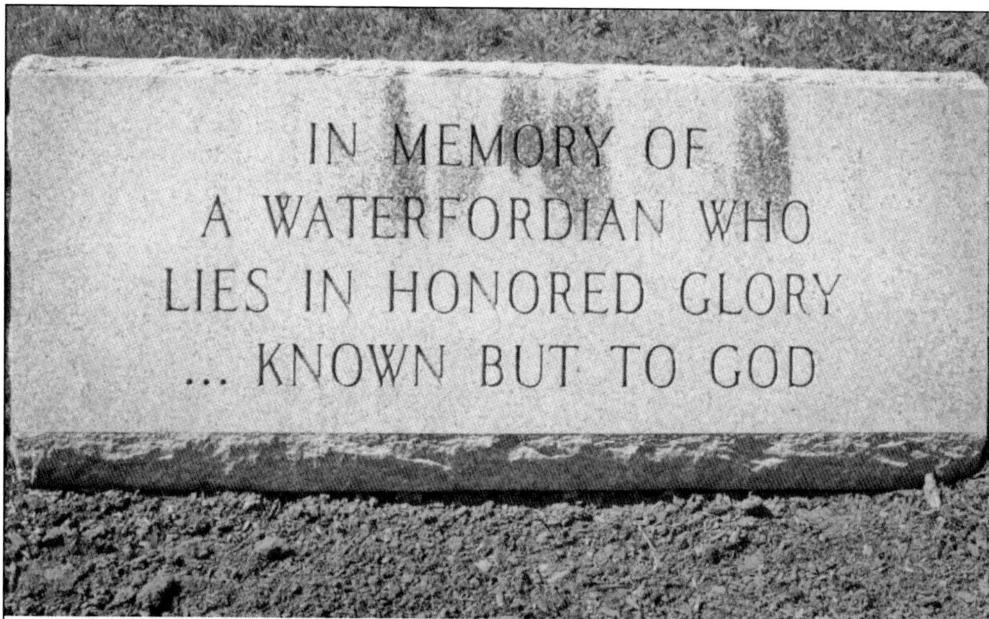

WE REMEMBER AND HONOR THOSE
WATERFORD SERIVCEMEN WHO GAVE THEIR
LIVES IN WARTIME

CIVIL WAR

Michael Rodn	John Murray	Aluring B. Usher	James I. House
Hirum Clute	Samuel Peters	John Wright	Jeremiah Welch
William Henry	Duane Shepard	Charles W. Shepard	James H. Gittings
George Black	J. G. Porter	Timothy B. Vanderkar	Lawrence B. Wells
Sylvester E. Black	Joseph Black	John E. Henry	John H Vanderwerken
Edward L. Indson	Patrick Conway	Charles Moat	Oliver Shaw
Leornard Vanderwerken	Benjamin Bace	Lawrence Higgins	

WORLD WAR I

Charles J. Brady	Frank Curtin	George B. Lambert	William J. Rocheleau
Ralph Spinks	Clarence G. Coons	John W. Briggs	Vincent Lanahan

WORLD WAR II

Maurice Baillafgeon	Donald J. Cramer	Eugene DiTommaso	Joseph M. Verchereau
Charles I. Bernardo	John S. Orloff	Eugene Chouiniere	Robert R. Brisson
Dominick T. Cassella	Victor H. DeVoe	Robert Hicks	Leland E. Hazzard
Albert C. Parker	Eugene Lessard	Robert J. Kidwell	Edmund F. Gould
Edward J. Sorensen	Milton Bryk	Joseph Scarchilli	Charles H. Malpass

KOREA	VIET NAM
George F. Hamilton	Frank J. Hutchins
William F. Hill	William W. Dziarcak
Roy F. Gamache	Louis V. Daigle
	Thomas F. Jourdanais

Shown here are the names of the fallen heroes who are listed on the monuments in Soldiers and Sailors Memorial Park. These brave men who made the ultimate sacrifice marched off to war never to return. They are forever linked to the history listed in these pages and the living memory of the community.